CW00665947

Over the Battlefield
OPERATION GOODWOOD

First published in Great Britain in 2005
and reprinted in 2013 by
PEN & SWORD MILITARY
An imprint of
Pen & Sword Books Ltd
47 Church Street
Barnsley, South Yorkshire
S70 2AS

ISBN 978 1 84415 153 0

A CIP catalogue record for this book is
available from the British Library

Printed and bound in England
By CPI Group (UK) Ltd, Croydon, CR0 4YY

Pen & Sword Books Ltd incorporates the Imprints of Aviation,
Family History, Fiction, Maritime, Military, Discovery, Politics, History,
Archaeology, Select, Military Classics, Atlas, Wharncliffe Local History,
Wharncliffe True Crime, Wharncliffe Transport, Leo Cooper, The Praetorian Press,
Remember When, Seaforth Publishing and Frontline Publishing

For a complete list of Pen & Sword titles please contact
PEN & SWORD BOOKS LIMITED
47 Church Street, Barnsley, South Yorkshire, S70 2AS, England
E-mail: enquiries@pen-and-sword.co.uk
Website: www.pen-and-sword.co.uk

OVER THE BATTLEFIELD

OPERATION GOODWOOD

IAN DAGLISH

Pen & Sword
MILITARY

To my father , Tony Daglish: 1922 – 2005

CONTENTS

ACKNOWLEDGEMENTS

The author remains deeply indebted to the many historians and old soldiers who have made the lengthy process of researching this book such a rewarding experience.

Thanks are extended to the custodians of the primary material so valuable to researchers: David Fletcher, Historian at The Tank Museum, Bovington; Allan Williams, Air Photo Archive Manager at The Aerial Reconnaissance Archive (TARA) at Keele University; David Porter at the Tactical Doctrine Retrieval Cell (TDRC); Peter Elliott at the RAF Museum, Hendon; and Stephen Walton, Archivist at the Imperial War Museum, Duxford. Though sadly stripped of its time-honoured title of 'Public Record Office', the 'National Archives' at Kew remains despite its drab and utilitarian new name a vital asset: its staff as helpful as ever and its treasures no less valuable. Alderley Edge Library has consistently triumphed in locating rare and out-of-print works needed by the author. Personal insights have come from several former soldiers on both sides of the action: Bill Close and Jim Caswell of 3rd Royal Tank Regiment; Richard Freiherr von Rosen and Alfred Rubbel of *503. schwere Panzer-Abteilung*; Patrick Delaforce and Denis Handford of 13th Royal Horse Artillery. Further help has come from the growing body of keen historians striving to solve the remaining puzzles of the Normandy campaign: Alain Verwicht, Didier Lodieu, Bernard Paiche, and Jean-Claude Perrigault. Charles Markuss has freely shared his comprehensive knowledge of the German Army; both he and Friedrich Tichy have assisted with German nomenclature and translations. Very special thanks are extended to Kevin Baverstock, cartographer and Normandy historian, for his continued encouragement and image processing expertise.

Philippe Wirton graciously granted access to his collection of battlefield photographs taken shortly after GOODWOOD. Simon Trew, Christopher Dunphie, and Bob Eburne contributed GOODWOOD maps. Norman Godfrey of 16 Squadron permitted the photograph reproduced on page 268. The author is grateful to Her Majesty's Stationery Office for permission to use Crown Copyright material. Photographs on pages 93, 95, and 96 are reproduced by permission of The Tank Museum. Aerial images based on photographs taken as the battle was fought below are © Crown Copyright 1944/MOD, reproduced with the permission of the Controller of Her Majesty's Stationery Office.

Lastly, particular thanks go to two individuals whose recollections and wisdom have helped to shape this book: Jimmy Taylor of 16 Squadron, Royal Air Force; and Geoffrey Stone, of 11th Armoured Division APIS (Air Photo Interpretation Section).

FOREWORD

An old soldier recently wrote that *'In writing about a military campaign it is certainly an advantage to have taken part.'*[1] With the greatest respect to the writer of those words, this author does not entirely agree. Six decades on from the Normandy campaign, the historian is better served with available source material than has ever been the case before. True, the reliable material is sometimes hard to find amidst a morass of ill-informed writing (and scantily researched film). But a very great quantity of source material is now available to those willing to conduct a diligent search. In the case of Operation GOODWOOD, at midday on 18 July no single participant had a very clear picture of the overall battle. Many first-hand accounts of the battle are imprecise with regard to the timing or even the location of key events, and many that purport to precision are discovered to be wrong. Unit histories can be found on both sides which even give incorrect dates for this major battle. Unit loyalties influence the records: a history of Regiment 'A' may state that a position was taken and then handed over to Regiment 'B'; while Regiment 'B' stoutly maintains that the position was taken by them after 'A' failed in the attempt.

Among the available sources, oral history has an important place. But it has to be viewed in perspective. Most soldiers of the Second World War had a fairly limited view of the campaigns in which they fought: as a general rule, the closer to the action, the narrower the perspective. Not at all exceptional was the infantry company commander who *'considered that 7, 8, and 9 Platoons should damned well know enough to enable them to do what they were told to do, and that regaling them with overmuch Big Picture was probably a waste of time.'*[2] Difficulties arise when soldiers 'flesh out' their stories, filling the gaps in their personal experience with information from other sources. These might be popular myths of the time, originating from battlefield fable or official propaganda. Inaccurate anecdotes find their way into general histories and poorly-researched television documentaries, to be absorbed and re-told by old soldiers, creating a 'feedback loop' of misinformation. Many a war story, widely repeated and acquiring in the repetition the status of 'historical fact', is found to stem from a single unsupported anecdote.

This is not to decry the great value of personal reminiscences, which often are found to contain nuggets of information lost in 'broad-brush' accounts of campaigns. And much Second World War history is 'broad-brush': recounting events on a global and theatre level; describing battles at the level of armies, corps, and divisions. On this scale, the detail of combat can easily be lost. The advance of an armoured division is considerably harder to visualize than, say, the image of a squadron of nineteen tanks, or a platoon of thirty infantrymen. This work will attempt to focus on the detail, the author believing that the story of smaller units' actions may often convey a better understanding of the battle as a whole. When the general histories occasionally descend to this level of detail (to add 'flavour') many neglect to get the detail right, whether by omission, ignorance, or by casual acceptance of anecdote. Of the very many studies of Operation GOODWOOD consulted by this author, publications ranging from 1947 to 2004, not one has been free of such errors. Quite often the best-known and most oft-quoted anecdotes have turned out to be the least defensible.

To complete the opening quotation: *'In writing about a military campaign it is certainly an advantage to have taken part. At least you know what the weather was like.'* What an indictment! But there exists today a body of Second World War historians prepared to question past assumptions and return to primary sources in search of answers. So, at sixty years remove, we progress closer to the truth. This author did not take part in the battle. He has nevertheless endeavoured to present a story as accurate as possible in its detail. Including *'what the weather was like.'*

This is the story of a battle. Rather than burden the story with too much technical material, a quantity of background information is presented in separate appendices, organized by topic, which the reader may consult as required. In these, specific subjects such as the mechanics of tank combat, the lie of the land, or examples of unit organization are covered without interrupting the narrative flow. Similarly, in cases where this work challenges the 'accepted wisdom', supporting evidence is presented in chapter-end notes rather than in the main text.

It would be foolhardy to hope that no errors have crept into this book. This will not be the last word on GOODWOOD. But, where this work appears to contradict earlier accounts, the author respectfully asks readers to consider that no single earlier study has enjoyed access to all the information contained herein.

Ian Daglish
Alderley Edge
2005

References

(1) 'Assault Division', Norman Scarfe, ISBN 1-86227-256-5. A very lucid story of 3rd Division including a useful account of actions on the eastern flank of GOODWOOD, sadly beyond the scope of this work. Quote from the Preface to the 2004 edition.

(2) 'Lion Rampant', Robert Woollcombe, 1955, p 42. This account of the 6th King's Own Scottish Borderers is one of the best stories of the life of a British infantry regiment, so lightly fictionalized that the real personalities behind the fictional names are easily recognised.

NOTES ON TERMINOLOGY

1. Wherever possible, direct quotations are presented verbatim, with original spelling, punctuation, and abbreviation. In the case of military terminology, the author hopes that the reader will be able to decipher (for example) such standard forms as 'rly' for railway, 'coy' for company, or 'tk' for tank from the context in which they appear. In a similar vein, units of measurement are generally reported in terms appropriate to the nationality. The British referred to guns by weight of shell (6 pounder, 25 pounder) and calibre in millimetres (75mm, 'eighty-eight'); whereas the German nomenclature favoured centimetres (7.5cm, 8.8cm; note however that the point is used rather than the German comma for decimals). Both imperial and metric measures of distance are used, as appropriate. For example, if a British unit advanced on a front estimated as *'two hundred yards'*, it would be misleading to record the measure as 200m, yet otiose to give it as 182.88m.

2. The spelling of French place names is often found to vary, even in French-language publications. For consistency (apart from verbatim quotations – see above), place names will be presented exactly as they appear - including hyphenation – on modern maps of the French *Institut Géographique National* (IGN).

3. English-language history has hitherto tended to anglicize German terms. As a general rule, names of German units, ranks, weapons systems, etc. will herein be presented in German form (again, verbatim quotes excepted). There are several reasons for this. Recent years have seen a 'creeping' of German terms (*Panzer, Schwerpunkt, Panzerfaust,* and even *Auftragstaktik*) into English-language texts. Adopted piecemeal, this can result in grammatical absurdities (e.g., 'panzers' or 'panzerfausts' in place of the correct plural forms *Panzer* and *Panzerfäuste*). It can mislead, since some German military terms such as ranks are not precisely equivalent to their literal English translations. Worse, in 'translating' into English some accounts have perpetrated gross inaccuracies (some of the worst offences commonly being found in photo captions). At a time when increasing use is being made of German sources, by historians of various nationalities writing in various languages, it seems all the more inappropriate to translate original terminology into a confusing muddle of pidgin-German terms. Longer quotes from German sources are of course translated. The author hopes that the reader will feel flattered rather than inconvenienced by these attempts at precision.

4. If the author occasionally refers to the Allied forces involved at GOODWOOD as 'British', this is by no means to disparage the part played by the Canadians (and other Commonwealth forces) in the Normandy campaign. From 13 July, 1944, the British Second Army became formally recognized as the 'British Liberation Army', with II Canadian Corps under its command throughout GOODWOOD. Only after GOODWOOD was Canadian First Army activated as a separate entity. A great many of the Canadians involved, while taking a pride in the Maple Leaf and owing a primary loyalty to their regiment, would have recognised themselves nevertheless to be an essential part of the British Army.

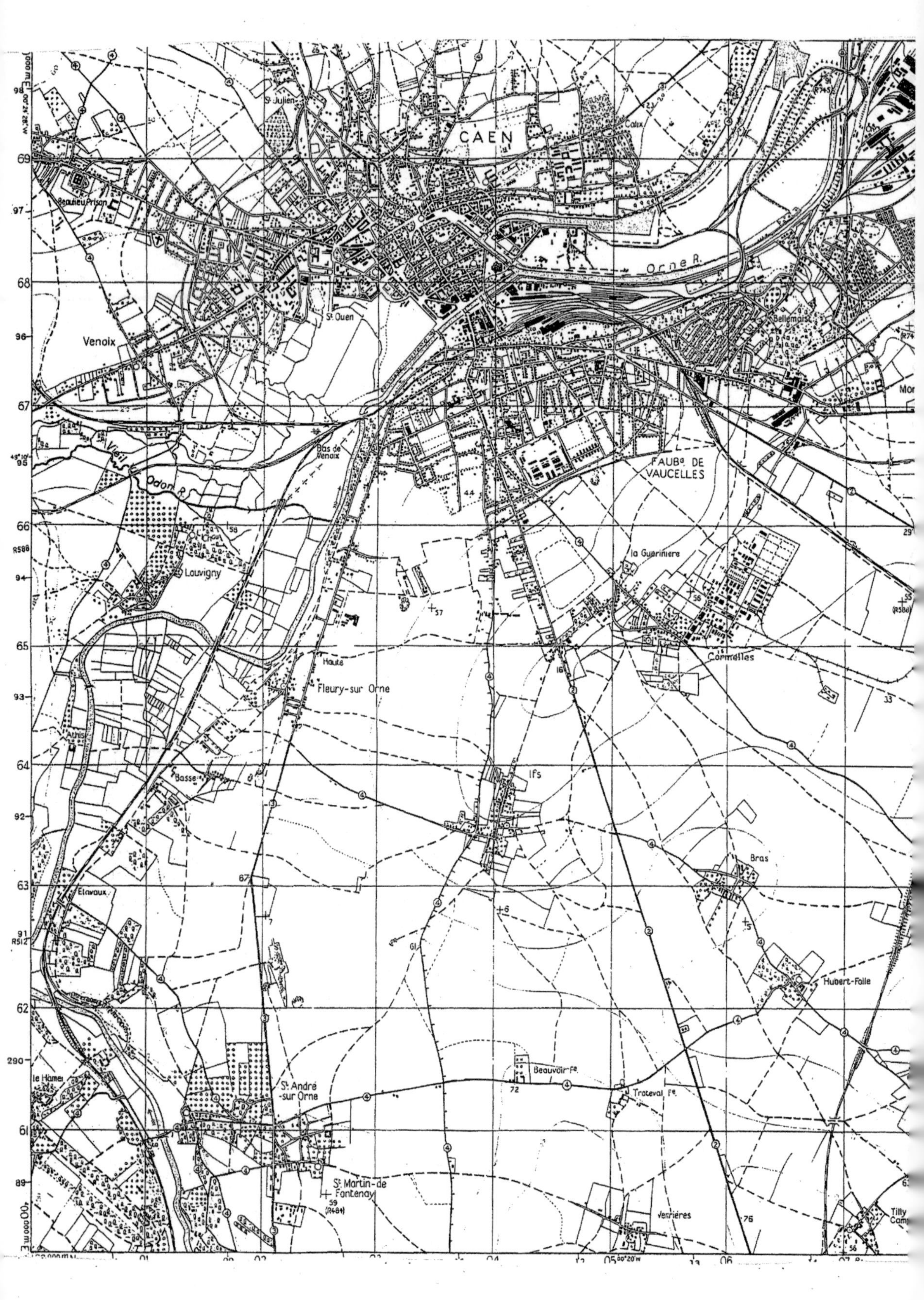

CAEN
St Julien
Calix
Beaulieu Prison
Orne R.
Venoix
St Ouen
Bellemaist
FAUBG. DE
VAUCELLES
Bas de
Venoix
Vieil
Odon R.
Louvigny
la Guerinière
Cormelles
Fleury-sur Orne
Haute
Athis
Basse
Ifs
Bras
Etavaux
Hubert-Folie
le Hamel
Beauvoir Fe.
Troteval Fe.
St André
-sur Orne
St Martin-de
Fontenay
Verrières
Tilly

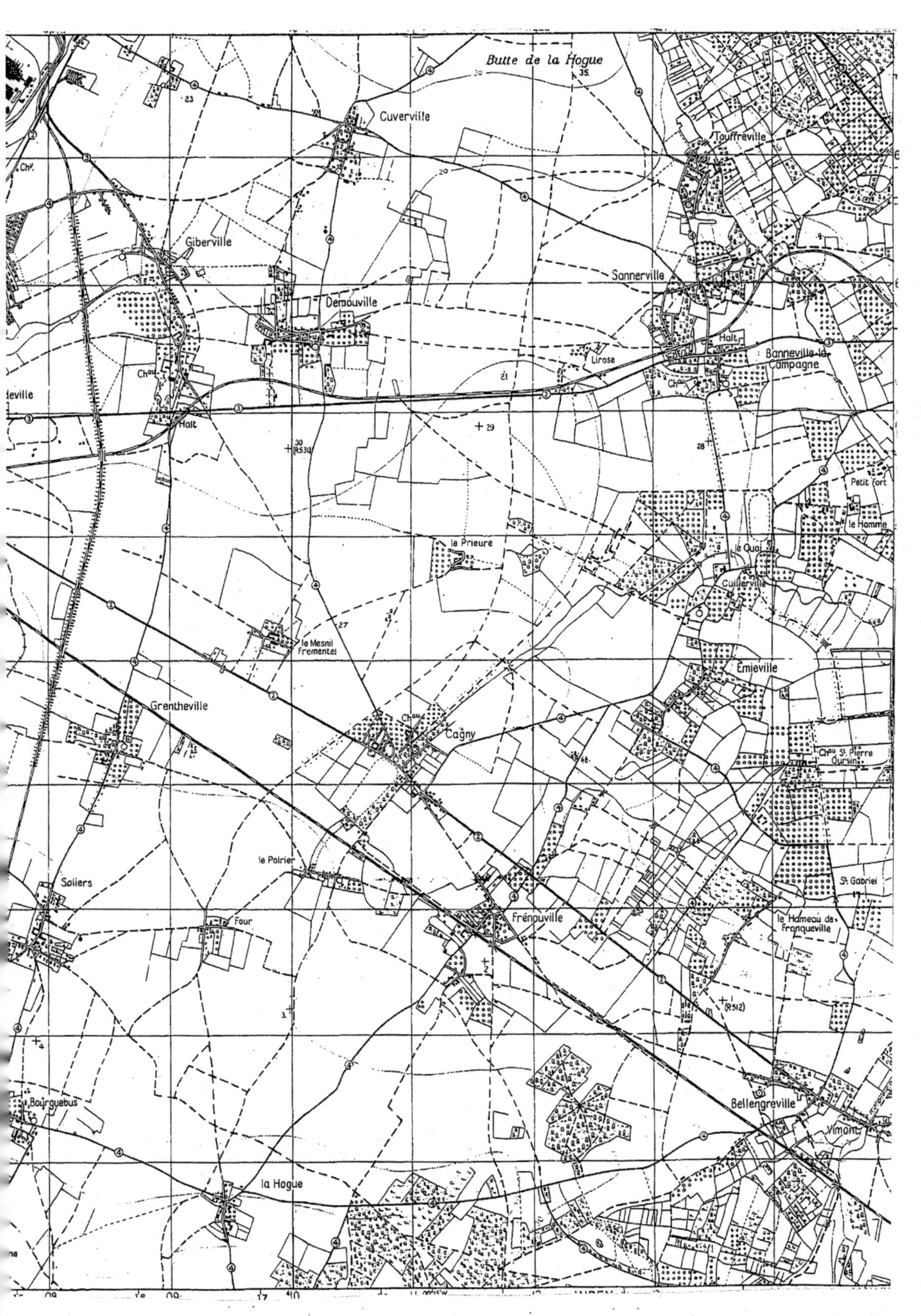
Butte de la Hogue
Cuverville
Touffréville
Giberville
Démouville
Sannerville
Lirose
Banneville-la-Campagne
Halt
Petit Fort
le Homme
le Prieuré
le Quai
Cuillerville
le Mesnil Frementel
Emiéville
Grentheville
Cagny
Chau St. Pierre Oursin
le Poirier
Soliers
Four
Frénouville
St. Gabriel
le Hameau de Franqueville
Bourguébus
Bellengreville
Vimont
la Hogue

Chapter 1

JULY, 1944: THE OPPONENTS

A month after the Normandy invasion, progress inland lagged far behind schedule. In the second half of July, Montgomery's British Second Army launched two major attacks at opposite ends of the British front line in Normandy. The second of these was Operation BLUECOAT, in an area of difficult terrain where an assault was totally unexpected. The first, Operation GOODWOOD, also involved logistical challenges. And here the assault came as no surprise at all.

BRITISH STRATEGY

The Allied invasion plan did not envisage becoming bogged down in Normandy. But by the end of June, a combination of dense terrain and

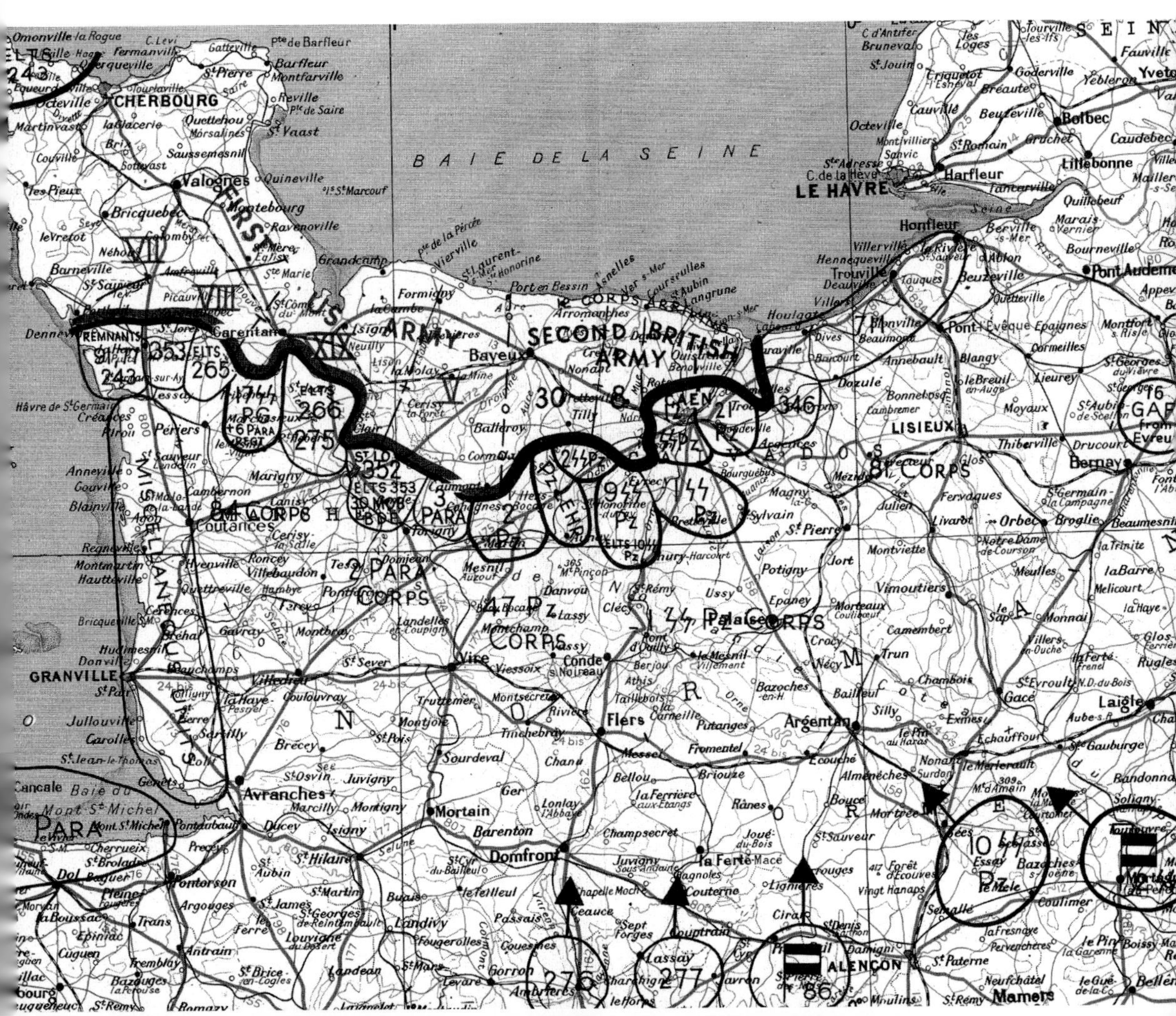

unexpectedly tenacious defenders threatened a return to First World War-style static warfare.[1] The huge cost to the defenders in manpower and matériel was not readily apparent to the Allied high command; the cost in British and American lives was all too evident, with little visible gain. A deadlocked battle was militarily and politically unacceptable. The over-arching need was breakout: a dramatic rupture of the German lines which would restore mobility to the Allied armies.

In military terms, the campaign can be likened to a 'meeting engagement'. From the day of the invasion, both sides began a race to reinforce the battle for Normandy. The Allies won the race. Up to the beginning of July, newly arriving German armoured formations were thrown straight into the line of battle. Meanwhile, growing Allied strength enabled British armoured divisions to be withdrawn into operational reserve (while much American armour was held in parks behind the congested battlefield). However, the longer the Normandy deadlock continued, the more time there was for German infantry divisions to complete their march up to the invasion front. These newly-arriving infantry formations threatened to replace the Panzer divisions in the line and permit the defenders to assemble their own strategic strike force in reserve. And if this were to happen, Montgomery was determined to hold any German strike force in the eastern, British sector, permitting the Americans in the west to erupt out of the Normandy bocage into the relatively open country of Brittany, opening the door to central France, the Seine, and Paris.

The principal goal of GOODWOOD was to make disengagement of the Panzer divisions from that sector unfeasible. That clarity of that simple goal has been clouded by debate as to whether GOODWOOD itself was a breakout attempt. Whatever his true intent, Montgomery certainly allowed his superiors (and many of his troops) to believe that a breakout was being attempted. But Montgomery's true intents are, as ever, hard to divine: in his accounts of the campaign, he consistently maintained that whatever happened was exactly what he had intended from the outset.[2]

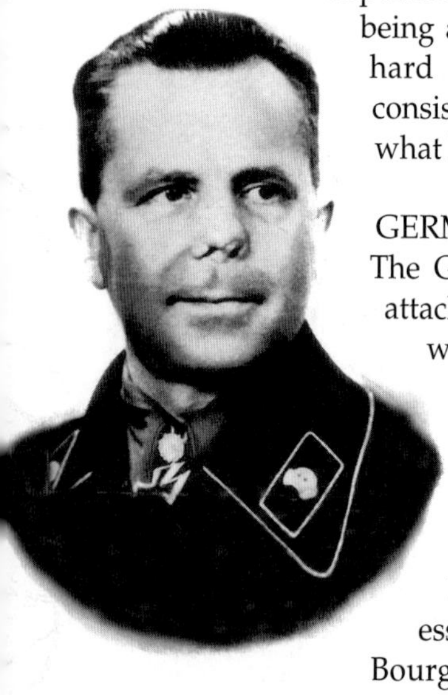

GERMAN STRATEGY

The German forces in front of Caen had no doubt that an attack was coming their way. The only questions were: from where; and exactly when? *I. SS-Panzerkorps* commander 'Sepp' Dietrich had turned a blind eye to the unauthorized (though entirely sensible) withdrawal of the last elements of *12. SS-Panzerdivision*, the 'Hitler Youth', from the rubble of Caen. With all defenders now on the eastern banks of the Orne river, Dietrich felt that he could at last 'concentrate on essentials'. The river was the front line. In front of the Bourguébus ridge was his Main Line of Resistance, a checkerboard of small villages and farm complexes turned

Eberbach.

into fortified outposts. Whichever way the inevitable attack was delivered was almost immaterial. Whether over Hill 112 to the west, through Caen itself in the centre, or from the British airborne bridgehead to the north, the same defensive plan held true.

With this strategy, *Panzer Group West* commander Eberbach and Army Group commander Rommel were broadly in agreement. They had little alternative. The German armour had been committed as it arrived in Normandy, piecemeal; its attacks had been reactive rather than strategic. The offensive 'edge' of the *Panzer* formations was daily being dulled. Montgomery harboured fears of a classic German counterstrike, a daring gamble risking all against the prize of inflicting a serious blow on the invaders. But even the will was now lacking. Hanging over all was Hitler's 8 July edict that any strategic offensive in Normandy should be avoided until 'sufficient' forces could be accumulated. Given that daily losses of men and materials outweighed new arrivals, this was never going to happen. Yet neither were local commanders free to adopt a logical defence: Hitler explicitly forbade any phased retreat to the Seine. So were strategic options closed off.

GERMAN DISPOSITIONS

The German front east of the Orne was covered by two corps. Changes of organization within each immediately prior to GOODWOOD had gone unnoticed, or at least incorrectly evaluated, by the British. South of Caen was SS-*Obergruppenführer* 'Sepp' Dietrich's *I. SS-Panzerkorps*, up to mid-July home to the powerful first and twelfth *SS Panzer* divisions: the '*Leibstandarte Adolf*

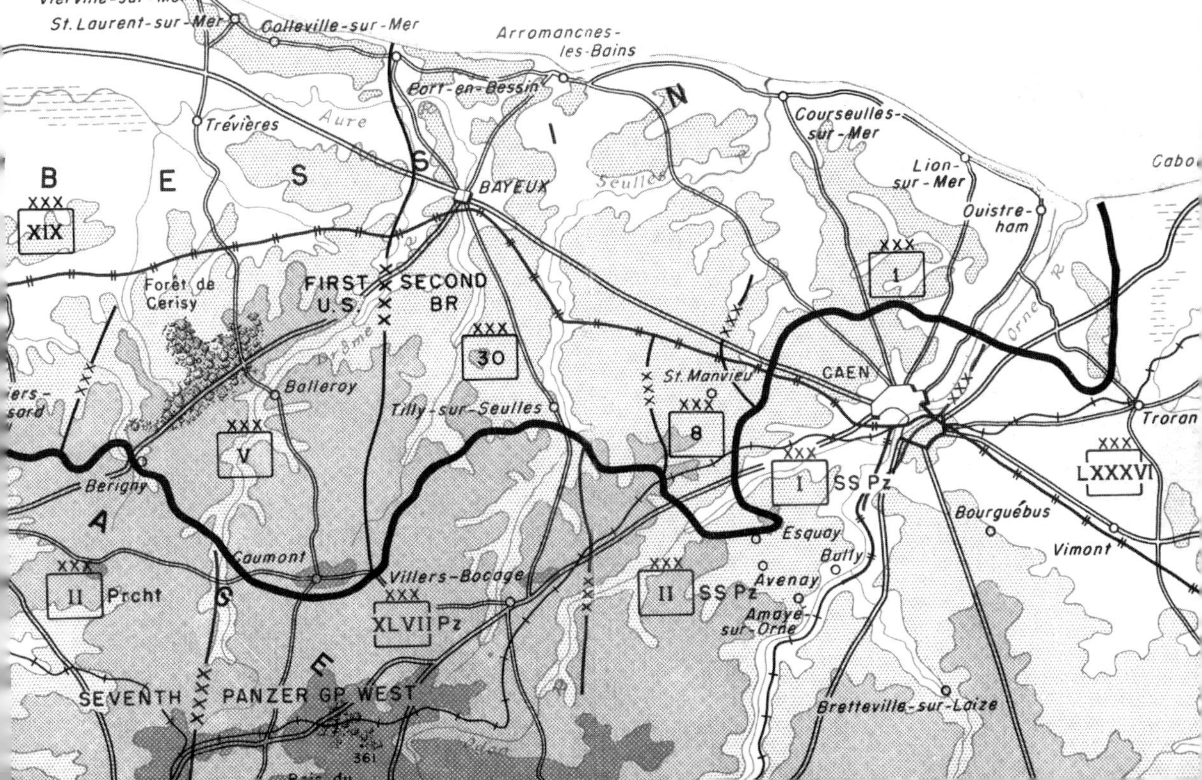

Hitler' and the *'Hitlerjugend'*. The latter had ended the long defence of Caen city on the night of 8-9 July, its last elements pulling back across the Orne for a long overdue period of rest and refitting. On the eve of GOODWOOD, the tired but still potent *Hitlerjugend* was in receipt of orders to move north to defend against the further invasion which Hitler was convinced was coming between the mouths of the Seine and the Somme rivers.[3] Meanwhile, on the night of 13-14 July, the first elements of *Generalleutnant* Schaek's *272. Infanteriedivision* completed the long journey from the Mediterranean coast. By 14 July, three of its infantry battalions were in the front line, beginning the relief of the LAH. The British observed the withdrawal of the armour, but by 18 July had failed to identify the newly-arrived infantry division. So, quite fortuitously, the disengagement of Dietrich's *1. SS 'Leibstandarte'* and *12. SS 'Hitlerjugend'* divisions from the front line was recognised by British intelligence, but in fact the German defences had been reinforced, and the continued presence of the SS Panzer divisions in the vicinity increased the depth and resilience of those defences in the face of the coming British hammer blow.

SS-*Obergruppenführer* 'Sepp' Dietrich a pace behind *Generalfeldmarschall* Erwin Rommel.

The boundary with *General* von Obstfelder's *LXXXVI Armee Korps* ran roughly along the line of the Chemin de Fer Minier (see Appendix 1). Obstfelder fielded three infantry divisions. *711. ID* (*Generalleutnant* Reichert) covered the front from the mouth of the Seine west to Franceville, just east of the mouth of the Orne. *346. ID* (*Generalleutnant* Diestel) held the front from the coast south along the high ground as far as Touffréville. And across the gap between Touffréville and Colombelles, directly in the intended path of VIII Corps' tanks, stood the unfortunate *16. Luftwaffenfelddivision* (*Generalleutnant* Sievert). British intelligence noted the disengagement of *21. Panzer Division* from the front line. It seemed logical that a division which had been continuously engaged since 6 June should be rested. But the deduction was wrong. The *16. LFD* was ill-trained, ill-equipped, still reeling from heavy losses suffered since 8 July, and in no state to hold the front alone. It was in reality no more than a 'veil' (*'Infanterieschleier'*), screening the armour. Far from disengaging, *21. Panzerdivision* remained vital to the defence of the sector.

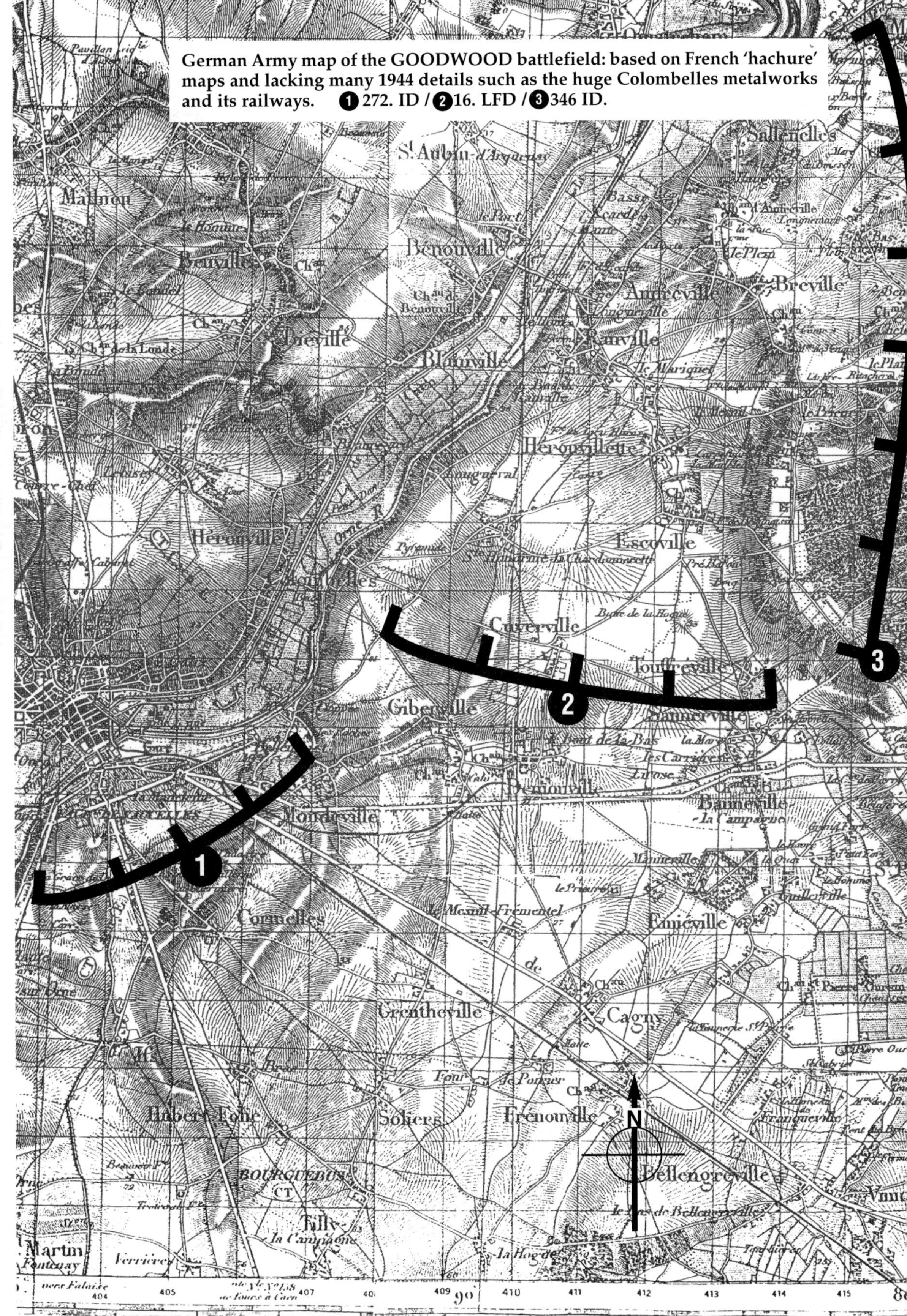

German Army map of the GOODWOOD battlefield: based on French 'hachure' maps and lacking many 1944 details such as the huge Colombelles metalworks and its railways. ❶ 272. ID / ❷ 16. LFD / ❸ 346 ID.

Tactically, there endured the disagreements inevitable in a force so riven by faction and influence. As will be seen, Rommel personally intervened across lines of command to order the placement of certain armoured reserves further forward than standard doctrine would have considered prudent. Also at lower levels of the organization, expediency was the order of the day. Within *LXXXVI Korps*, the true role of the weak *16. Luftwaffenfelddivision* was recognised by its nominal subordination to *Generalmajor* Feuchtinger; in practice the *laisser-faire* general left his subordinates to work out the details. So it was that Major von Luck exercised loose command, within his *ad hoc Kampfgruppe*, over elements of *16. LFD*; and Major Becker claimed to have tactical authority over batteries of *16. LFD* artillery[4].

THE PLAN OF ATTACK

British Second Army commander Lieutenant-General Miles Dempsey was an enthusiast for a British breakout attempt, and had championed the idea of risking the logistical difficulties of a major push around the east of Caen. On 13 July, Dempsey arrived at VIII Corps headquarters to present the GOODWOOD plan, including a new corps structure, to VIII Corps commander Lieutenant-General Richard O'Connor. By 15 July, the VIII Corps plan was complete. Only recently escaped from imprisonment in Italy, O'Connor had come to Normandy with something to prove. While he languished in a prisoner of war camp, the desert war had continued, new lessons being learned and new faces promoted. Presented with a plan of attack for his corps, O'Connor's role was reduced to its tactical implementation. The complex logistics of GOODWOOD left simply no room for manoeuvre. So it was that O'Connor's divisional commanders felt themselves 'micro managed' by a general keen to demonstrate his competence.

Lieutenant-General Richard O'Connor.

General Sir Miles Dempsey.

Faced with a virtual fait accompli, the three divisional commanders had different reactions. Second in line, Allan Adair's Guards Armoured Division was facing its first battle, and the general was content to take his orders and enthuse his troops. With their 7th Armoured Division third on the roster and last in line, the desert veterans General Erskine and Brigadier Hinde kept their counsel and accepted the orders as given. General Roberts of 11th Armoured had other ideas.

General Allan Adair

ROBERTS AND HIS ORDERS

There was some history in the relationship between Roberts and O'Connor. By 1944 Pip Roberts was a highly experienced armour leader. Commissioned on leaving Sandhurst in 1926, his immediate goal was the job of adjutant: 'a very important one' in which 'if you played your cards right you could have a very great influence in a regiment.'[5] Plainly, a man with ambition. Though it took him thirteen years to achieve that seemingly modest achievement, the period was an invaluable apprenticeship in the armoured arm. In the desert war, he advanced more rapidly. As Brigade Major, then as divisional staff officer, he rubbed shoulders with leading exponents of tank warfare. As commanding officer of a regiment (3rd Royal Tanks), as a brigadier (with 22nd and later 26th Armoured Brigade) and briefly of a division (7th Armoured, for a single week) he became an experienced and highly capable armour leader. By 1944, he was not only the youngest general officer in the British Army (at thirty seven), but had spent longer in the turret of a tank than anyone of similar rank.

General Pip Roberts.

With experience came a characteristic self confidence. Roberts had gained early experience of working alongside senior officers, and his own memoirs make clear his ability to form rapid judgements of his superiors. In his first brigade conference as acting brigade commander, 'I was slightly nervous;' however, 'I need not have worried; it went off all right, though the Divisional Commander made one or two comments which seemed to me rather irrelevant and I therefore made a rather non-committal reply.'[6] Later, attached to the American 1st Armoured Division after the disaster at Kasserine, he quickly assessed the divisional commander as, 'to my youngish mind, rather elderly... a very pleasant man but not, I thought, very forceful.' Outgoing corps commander Omar Bradley 'did not look much like a soldier, more like a college science master,' though, Roberts conceded, 'very sound and sensible'. The incoming George Patton however 'was too brash for me; obviously very forceful but making a lot of noise about it.'[7] Youthful self confidence won the approval of newly-arrived General Montgomery and of visiting Prime Minister Churchill; it was not diminished as Roberts returned to England with a second bar to his DSO and the prospect of commanding an armoured division.

Monty

Roberts' first experience of leading 11th Armoured Division into combat was largely successful, though hampered by the corps commander's interference in divisional operations. By mid July, Roberts' frustration with O'Connor was evident. During Operation EPSOM, Roberts' highly trained division had been split up. Separated from its own infantry brigade at O'Connor's behest, the division's tank regiments had been expected to fight alongside the infantry of 15th Scottish Division, with unfortunate results. Particularly hurtful was O'Connor's remarkably tactless aside in his letter of 8 July to Roberts, summing up that operation. It is hardly a coincidence that Roberts included the letter in full as an appendix to his memoirs, with its closing comment that 'you may find that for a period you may be forced to do the work more properly allotted to an Armoured Brigade.' To a confident divisional commander, this slight rankled. To an armour leader with advanced ideas about cooperation between infantry and tanks, the corps commander's tactics appeared unsound. Nor did Roberts hold British 2nd Army commander Dempsey in high regard. Denied permission to sack his infantry brigade commander after EPSOM, Roberts did not hesitate to go over the heads of both O'Connor and Dempsey to seek Montgomery's approval for the change. Monty concurred (he liked youthful initiative, within limits).

O'Connor's GOODWOOD plan again separated the brigades of 11th Armoured Division. As well as charging its tank regiments with driving a wedge through the German lines, he also gave the division the task of securing the west-flank villages and woods of Cuverville and Démouville and the east-flank town of Cagny. This would preoccupy Roberts' entire infantry brigade. 'So, right at the outset, I was going to be minus almost half the division… a severe handicap to my further operations. As it were, one hand behind my back.'[8] He protested. 'Feeling rather strongly about it, I put it all on paper and sent it to the corps commander. I got a reply that the present plans could not be changed and if I felt they were unsound, then he would get one of the other divisions to lead.' In such a battle of wills, Roberts did well to achieve even a partial concession from his superior, and the concession reflected well on O'Connor's sense of fair play. Still, Roberts knew his judgement was right and felt no reason to be grateful. 'He would only ask me to "mask" Cagny, not to take it. I really had no alternative but to accept… but still think it was a stupid arrangement.'[9] Seeds of resentment were sown which would bear bitter fruit once the battle got under way.

References

(1) Though total British Army casualties in the Second World War were far fewer than those suffered in the First, nevertheless daily casualty rates suffered by the Allies in the Normandy campaign equalled and exceeded the worst days of 1914-1918. This is well covered in 'Raising Churchill's Army', David French, 2000, ISBN 0-19-924630-0, p 147.
(2) The origins of the GOODWOOD plan are considered in detail in 'Operation GOODWOOD: The Great Tank Charge', Ian Daglish, 2004, ISBN 1 84415 030 5.
(3) Daglish, 'GOODWOOD', p 62
(4) See Appendix 7 for personalities and units. The relationship between von Luck and the tank battalions of 21. Panzerdivision is unclear: von Luck's claims of seniority were later disputed by surviving armour commanders. As will be seen, the operations of 22. Panzerregiment and 503. schwere Panzerabteilung were severely disrupted by the 18 July bombardment; on the day, their coordination with the Panzergrenadiere appears to have been minimal. In his turn, Alfred Becker even states in his own diary that from the arrival of 16. LFD, its commander Generalleutnant Sievert subordinated his own artillery to Becker, the general even moving into Becker's artillery headquarters in order to benefit from its superior wireless and telephone equipment.
(5) 'From the Desert to the Baltic', G P B Roberts, 1987, ISBN 0-7183-0639-2, Roberts, p 11.
(6) Roberts, p 92
(7) Roberts, p 134
(8) G P B Roberts, interview at Staff College, Camberley, 1979
(9) Roberts p 171

The 'Pont Tournant' over the Orne River
Lone glider near the Orne River bridge
'London' Bridge (First Bailey bridge erected in Europe)
Major Howard's three gliders
'Pegasus' Bridge over the Caen canal

Chapter 2

MID-JULY: THE APPROACH TO BATTLE

It is well to remember that many great battles of history occurred not in isolation but as the culmination of campaigns. Nor did the combatants very often turn up rested and fresh, full of enthusiasm for the day ahead. On the morning of 18 July, 1944, most of the troops preparing for battle had been in action for weeks. Even those who had not previously seen combat had endured a gruelling approach to the coming battle.

CROSSING THE ORNE

In the early minutes of 6 June, the only crossing over the Caen Canal and the Orne River between Caen and the sea was seized in one of the outstanding airborne operations of military history. Major John Howard's 2nd Oxf and Bucks glider-borne light infantry secured the defended bridge at Bénouville and held the crossing until the main force of 6th Airborne Divison arrived. Howard's task was not only to deny the crossings to the Germans for counterattacks against the invasion's eastern flank, but also to preserve the

Major Howard's glider landed just forty-seven yards short of the objective.

Colombelles bridge.

The Calix bridge eventually broken and blocked by sunken boat.

Vaucelles bridges and the great Citroen factory.

bridges intact for future use. From early in the OVERLORD planning, it was felt that the only way to secure the flanks to the eastern landing beaches was to place an airborne division east of the twin waterways. So the bridges would be needed to sustain 6th Airborne Division after its drop to the east. This was done. The bridges were preserved; German attempts to break through were prevented.

By 6 June, only two serviceable crossings remained available to the Germans in the Caen sector: the railway crossing between Calix and Mondeville (half way between the metal works and the main railway station, just beside the massive present day viaduct of the Autoroute de Normandie); and the single surviving road bridge between Vaucelles and Caen, battered but still just passable.[1] Late in the morning of 6 June, *Oberst* Hermann von Oppeln-Bronnikowski received orders from the dynamic *LXXXIV Armeekorps* commander General Marcks. Impatient with the slow response to the invasion, Marcks redirected Oppeln's *22. Panzerregiment* away from the Bénouville bridgehead. Instead, his armoured regiment was to lead an armoured thrust through Caen towards the invasion breaches. Around midday his leading elements attempted to cross at the Vaucelles bridge. As they pushed through the rubble-strewn boulevards of Vaucelles, they were caught bunched around the crossing by an air bombardment which caused further damage to the bridge and considerable disruption to the advance. Thereafter, the Panzer battalions passed Caen only by lengthy detours: *I. Bataillon* looping wide around the west of the city while *II. Bataillon* went east, crossing the railway bridge situated two kilometres down the river, by the Mondeville abbatoir, to struggle forward around the eastern side of the city. The consequence of the confusion and delay was that the only German

***Vorpostenboot* sunk in the Caen Canal.**

armoured force to reach the landing beaches on D Day arrived late on the scene. Only one small detachment of six tanks reached Sword Beach about 20.00 hours, too few to influence events or even to dwell long in so exposed a position.

Soon after D Day it became clear that sustaining the Orne bridgehead would require more than the lone pair of bridges at Bénouville. Between 8 and 9 June, 71 Field Company, Royal Engineers completed a second crossing, codenamed LONDON. A pontoon bridge was thrown across the Caen Canal about 600 metres south of the Pegasus Bridge at Bénouville, another almost alongside the 'pont tournant' (formerly a swing bridge) over the Orne River at Ranville. Between the two was a third, linking bridge over the intervening small watercourse. These were memorable constructions: they represented the first of 1,500 Bailey Bridges to be completed in the course of the campaign for northwest Europe.[2]

ROADS AND BRIDGES

Preparatory to GOODWOOD further crossings were constructed, and still more were planned. The original Pegasus Bridge crossing (now codenamed EUSTON) was planked over and reinforced to Class 40 standard. A thousand metres to the north, a new pair of Bailey Bridges was constructed, these codenamed YORK. YORK 1 crossed the canal at le Camp Romain and YORK 2 the river at la Haute Écard. Like the Bénouville bridges, these too were capable of bearing tanks, making a total of three Class 40 crossings each served by separate lanes for wheeled and tracked vehicles. These lanes, intended solely for VIII Corps traffic, were constructed differently for wheeled or tracked use. The construction of these six parallel roadways leading to the bridges was a huge engineering enterprise, completed between 13 July and last light on 16 July. The engineering resources of 2nd Army, VIII Corps, and even some divisional Royal Engineers were called upon. The

Constructing LONDON Bridge, the first Bailey bridge in France.

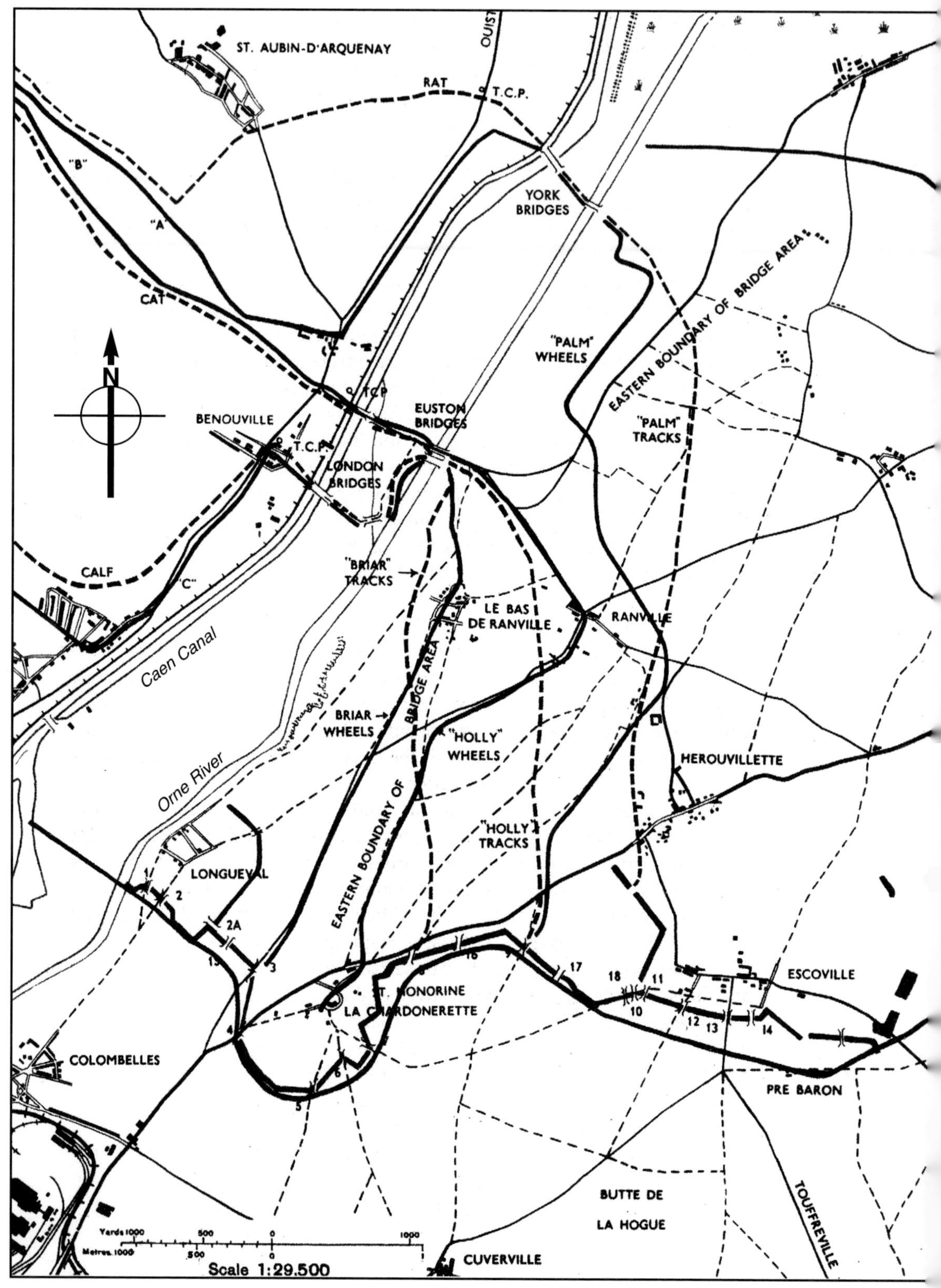
ST. AUBIN-D'ARQUENAY
RAT
T.C.P.
"B"
"A"
YORK BRIDGES
CAT
EASTERN BOUNDARY OF BRIDGE AREA
"PALM" WHEELS
N
TCP
BENOUVILLE
EUSTON BRIDGES
T.C.P.
"PALM" TRACKS
LONDON BRIDGES
CALF
"C"
"BRIAR" TRACKS
LE BAS DE RANVILLE
RANVILLE
Caen Canal
BRIAR WHEELS
BRIDGE AREA
"HOLLY" WHEELS
Orne River
HEROUVILLETTE
EASTERN BOUNDARY OF
"HOLLY" TRACKS
LONGUEVAL
1
2
2A
15
3
16
17
18
11
ESCOVILLE
ST. HONORINE
LA CHARDONERETTE
10
12
13
14
4
COLOMBELLES
6
5
PRE BARON
BUTTE DE LA HOGUE
TOUFFREVILLE
Yards 1000
500
0
1000
Metres 1000
500
0
CUVERVILLE
Scale 1:29.500

tracks east of the river were built by I Corps. Forward of the start line, individual divisions would be responsible for engineering their own thoroughfares. Likely routes, especially those in use by German wheeled vehicles, were identified from aerial photographs, although the effect of the planned bombing was an unknown factor giving some cause for concern.

To the west of the Caen Canal, the six parallel approaches were codenamed, north to south: RAT, CAT, and CALF for tracks; A, B, and C for wheels. East of the Orne, the equivalent routes were: PALM tracks and PALM wheels; HOLLY tracks and HOLLY wheels; and BRIAR tracks and BRIAR wheels.[3]

Even three Class 40 crossings were manifestly not going to be enough. I Corps, who held responsibility for the construction and maintenance of the crossings, planned to construct a further two crossings between the start of the battle and the end of the first day. The northern pair of bridges (TOWER 1 and 2) would cross the Caen Canal north of the Ouistreham lighthouse, and the Orne near la Basse Écarde. The southern pair (TAY 1 and 2) were to cross the canal south of Blainville-sur-Orne, and the river between Longueval and St-Léonard. Still further south, engineers of II Canadian Corps would repair or rebuild bridges over the river between Caen and Vaucelles, 'as soon as the situation permits'. But so long as this stretch of the Orne remained under enemy fire, any Canadians seeking to cross the river dry-shod would have to take their turn over the British bridges to the north.

ACROSS COUNTRY

By mid July, the three armoured divisions composing VIII Corps were dispersed within the Normandy bridgehead. On receipt of orders, all three began hasty preparations to be ready for action east of the Orne on 18 July. Units were to reach their starting positions 'without being detected by the enemy and without interfering with the operations and maintenance of the rest of the Army.' This was a tall order.

Any repositioning of divisional-scale units within the narrow confines of the crowded Normandy bridgehead presented major problems. Relocating a 1944 British armoured division with around 15,000 men and 3,500 vehicles was never an easy task. In this case, although the distances appeared small on the map – barely fifteen miles – the difficulties involved would be greater than ever. Roads or even useful tracks running from west to east were few. Caen itself was still an almost impenetrable mass of rubble, only recently abandoned by the Germans, while much of the area between Caen and the sea had recently been a hotly contested battleground. The passage between the north side of Caen and the sea crossed numerous troop concentrations: rest and holding camps, supply depots, airfields and their construction units, artillery emplacements. The route ran across supply lines: by early July the substantial damage caused to the Arromanches 'MULBERRY' harbour in the June storms was being offset by the fortunate capability of numerous small ports to receive unexpected volumes of seaborne supplies. Consequently, numerous coastal villages along the 'Côte de Nacre' (Normandy's 'pearly' coastline) became sources of vital supplies which had to be transported south. The three armoured divisions would have to pass at right angles across the supply lines of two front-line corps: II Canadian and I British.

11th Armoured would lead. From encampments midway between Caen and Bayeux, the respective headquarters of the division and of 29th Armoured Brigade plus the whole of 159th (Infantry) Brigade were to set off on the night of 16-17 July. Using the two southerly pairs of bridges, they would establish themselves in the bridgehead. 29th Brigade's Motor Infantry Battalion and three armoured regiments would follow, ending the night concealed about 7,000 yards west of the crossings. Their night drive proved difficult.

Major Bill Close of 3rd Royal Tank Regiment recalls the first leg of the journey on the night of 16-17 July.

As anticipated, our night move proved to be horrendous, moving nose to tail along dusty winding tracks, tank commanders peering with bleary eyes out of their turrets, trying to maintain station on the tank in front.

Close warned his tank commanders of the 'dire consequences' of dozing off; but most managed to arrive at the holding points around 01.00 hours without undue incident.[4] Finally arriving in the assembly area, it seemed to Bill Close 'that 3rd RTR reached its concentration area as much by luck as judgement'. In a little wood between Périers-sur-le-Dan and Beuville (still there today, on the western side of the D222) they 'camouflaged ourselves... We were told to stay out of sight and get as much rest as possible'.[5]

A 23rd Hussars officer recalls similar experiences on the night of 16 July, after 1 Troop, C Squadron received orders to move at last light, about 23.30.

At about eleven, the engines started rousing into life, and after what seemed an interminable delay, the whole Regiment was on the move, bound eastwards. The roads were thick with dust and within a few seconds the tank in front was merely the dim outline of the Commander's head floating on a cloud of fine grey dust. One of our Commanders caught his head on a branch as we left harbour and fractured his skull, but I think he lived. This was to be a nightmare drive, there was no vestige of moonlight and by midnight it was just a pitch black, cold, dusty hell.[6]

The 2nd Fife and Forfar Yeomanry fared no better. An officer recalls,

We set off in a light rain that mingled with the fine dust. Everything was coated with a film of sticky mud, making goggles useless and life miserable. We came to a marsh bridged by a causeway of faggots and stones, weakened by the two regiments ahead of us. A Halftrack stopped with engine trouble, so I pushed it out of the way, but as we drove past it the causeway gave way, and my tank was stuck at an angle of 45 degrees. The tank behind tried to pass to the left, but slithered the other way. The road was completely blocked, so the following squadron found a by-pass, while our two tanks were slowly sinking in the bog. A couple of Armoured Recovery Vehicles, ARVs, appeared and after two hours' hard work we were on our way again. It was a race against daylight, and we only just got to our concentration area as morning came.[7]

The following night, they too would cross, while the Armoured Reconnaissance Regiment would travel all the way from Bayeux to the Orne. Joined by Royal Artillery, Engineers, and supporting armour, they would complete the divisional assembly east of the bridges just before H Hour.

Two miles to the east of Bayeux, Guards Armoured Division received the call on 14 July.

A warning order was that the division was to take part in a major attack East of Caen; rather unkindly, as we thought, it was to be called "Operation Goodwood".

The Guards were not even to set off until the evening of 17 July. There was time for a briefing, recorded by the divisional historians.

On Sunday, July 16th, a perfect summer morning, all officers assembled at Divisional Headquarters to be addressed by General Adair on the impending battle. Beside talking about the Operation in detail he stressed that it was the first in which the division as a whole was to take part and spoke so much from his heart that all who heard him were deeply moved and impressed…[8]

An officer of the Coldstream Guards was similarly impressed.

On Sunday [16 July] *all officers in the division went to listen to the divisional commander, Major-General Alan Adair. We learnt of the wonderful tank country beyond Caen, flat and open cornfields; and that we had 700 tanks to be let loose on the enemy's possible 30. He was impressive and cheering… "Good straight cool shooting", he bawled out.*[9]

Come Monday 17 July, the Guards division rolled in four great columns as far as the western boundary of the Bridge Traffic Control Area, between Hermanville-sur-Mer and Beuville, the line of the modern D60, about four kilometres west of the canal. Boscawen later recalled,

It was an awful approach march, cross country on a very dark night with only tail lamps, and, worst of all, a thick cloud of dust everywhere. The dust was appalling. I had made my co-drivers drive as I thought it would rest the first drivers, but this turned out to be a mistake. The visibility was so bad that it needed the best possible driving to keep going without running into everything. Because of this I lost one of my tanks, which went into a ditch and was not seen again until after the battle.' Another tank, the Troop Sergeant's Firefly, 'also broke down due to dust in the petrol filter. This disappointed me a lot. My own tank, being driven by the co-driver, hit something, but no damage was done. Eventually we arrived at about one in the morning drawn up in a long column in a field west of the bridge over the Orne... We filled up with petrol, shook the dust off and got down under a blanket for a few hours' sleep.[10]

Though last in the line, 7th Armoured Division had set off earlier, from positions to the north of Tilly-sur-Seulles, to pass the night of 16-17 July in a Forward Assembly Area north of the Bayeux – Caen road (today's N 13) about twelve miles east of the Bridge Area. In theory, the tracked vehicles of the

division's 22nd Armoured Brigade would follow a Canadian brigade onto CALF track, cross LONDON bridges at H+60 (i.e., 60 minutes after H Hour), then follow BRIAR track to the battlefield.

Passing three armoured divisions over three bridges was not the only challenge. Until more Canadian bridges could be built, the crossing and provisioning of two Canadian infantry brigades would also have to take place over the original three pairs of bridges, Canadian movements being carefully fitted in between those of VIII Corps. And a further infantry brigade and two Royal Artillery Field Regiments were to be passed over the bridges by I Corps during the night of 16-17 July. Traffic Control and Bridge Area organization were to be necessary elements of the GOODWOOD plan.

PROBLEMS

For all the difficulties of traffic management in the Bridge Area, still greater problems awaited at journey's end beyond the bridges. Just west of the area where VIII Corps would form up for the coming battle lay the parallel waterways of the Canal de Caen and the Orne River. And beyond these obstacles, the bridgehead east of the Orne held by 6th Airborne and 51st Highland Divisions was little larger than in mid-June. The 'Forming Up Place' for the coming VIII Corps offensive was not even big enough for a single division to deploy, let alone three. As the first of the divisions crossed the waterways, turned through ninety degrees to face south, and prepared for battle, the rest of VIII Corps would have to wait their turn to pass over a bottleneck of bridges before displacing forward to occupy Concentration Areas vacated by the division ahead.

David Stileman was an 8th Rifle Brigade officer commanding 11 Platoon, G Company.

> *It was about 1.00 am that we arrived in this sea of golden corn strewn with gliders from the D Day landings. And the corn was so high that not only did it cover a Bren Gun Carrier but the whole area was so congested that one had to ask the driver to move up a few feet in order to open the door of one's vehicle.*[11]

The problems imposed by the line of advance were not over. Moving out of the Concentration Areas and on out of the Forming Up Places east of the Orne, the attacking force faced substantial minefields. Though laid by friendly forces, these were still a problem. The open fields south of Ranville had seen six weeks of bitter fighting during which the Orne bridgehead had been defended with extensive entrenchment and mining. In the expectation of a major German armoured assault on the Orne bridgehead, maximum use of mines and wire had been authorized. Many of the mines laid went unrecorded. As July wore on, crops seeded before the mines were laid grew ever higher, hampering detection. And anyway, systematic clearing of all the

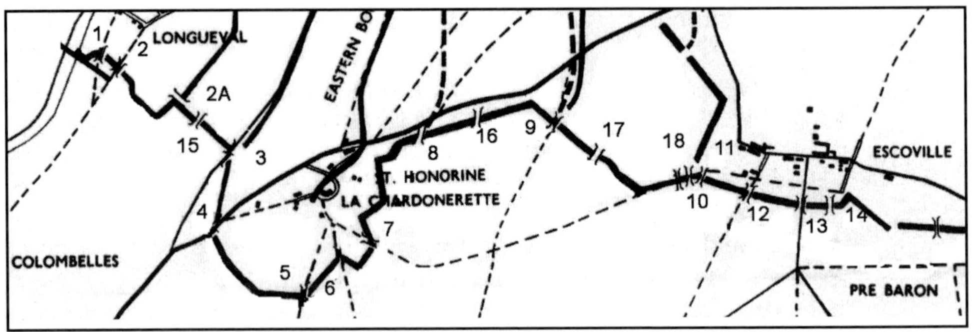

The eighteen minefield gaps constructed by 18 July.

minefields prior to the proposed attack was not even considered due to the desire to retain a shroud of secrecy over the plan. Looking down over the whole area were German observers atop the tall chimneys and water towers of the Colombelles metalworks.

Initially it was agreed that, with VIII Corps' own engineers being fully occupied with urgent road building, I Corps would undertake the mine clearing required for the GOODWOOD advance. This task was given to the Commander Royal Engineers of 51st (Highland) Division, reinforced by a Field Company, RE from 3rd Division. On the night of 15-16 July, the sappers set to work. They quickly ran into problems. Their records of British minefields were hopelessly inadequate for the task. Mines laid in haste had gone unmarked; others had been displaced by shellbursts and concealed by the crops. A change of plan was urgently agreed, and on the night of 16-17 July the sappers employed a different technique. Instead of working from patterns and records, they used the gapping drill appropriate to an enemy minefield. By daybreak, fourteen gaps had been cleared and wired off with cattle fences.

As 11th Armoured would be first to pass through the minefields, Pip Roberts had a particular interest in the work. He was not impressed.

> *As we were the leading division, we would be the first to go through the minefields; it was absolutely vital that we had a clear run… My CRE's main task was to see that there were enough gaps, that the gaps were wide enough and well signed. Initially 1 Corps' plans for this were quite inadequate.'* [12]

Roberts toured the front line on 17 July and was unimpressed. Via corps commander O'Connor, pressure was applied to Crocker's I Corps to improve the situation: as a minimum three additional gaps and a barrier marking the edge of the uncleared areas were needed. The pressure worked. After frantic efforts during the night of 17-18 July, four more gaps were opened, the surfaces of some of the gaps were regraded, the minefield and the 'funnels' leading into the gaps were wired, and the fencing was marked with white tape. Roberts conceded that, 'In the end, it was just all right, but only just.' Some of his officers were less dismissive of the sappers' efforts. About 01.00 hours on 18 July, two majors whose respective squadron of tanks and motor company of infantry would be operating in partnership in the assault walked forward to inspect the work. Bill Close, commanding A Squadron, 3rd RTR, recalls,

> *Noel Bell, commanding G Company 8RBs [8th Rifle Brigade] and I walked down to the minefield to recce the taped lanes which we hoped would be well signed. There seemed to be no problem – the entrances to the minefield were guarded by immaculately dressed Provost NCOs, all white belts and gaiters. I didn't think we would have any difficulties in getting through the minefield.*[13]

In fact, the dangerous work was still continuing unseen in the fields ahead. Only at 05.15 hours would it be completed, in the nick of time and mere minutes before the planned aerial bombardment. And later, after the battle lines had moved on, it would take three Field Companies, RE a full five days work to clear all the rest of the mines on the 51st (Highland) Division front.[14]

DECEPTIONS, DELUSIONS, DIVERSIONS

In hindsight, the concern to conceal preparations for Operation GOODWOOD seems futile. During the night of 11-12 July, 153rd Brigade of 51st (Highland) Division launched a major raid, supported by armour, whose objective was to place Royal Engineer sappers in close enough proximity to the Colombelles chimneys to achieve their destruction. The raid failed, and the German observers maintained their lookout through the long hours of summer daylight. Whether the chimneys' destruction would have altered the situation greatly is questionable. Even after the ground was taken by the Canadians (and the chimneys brought down by the retreating Germans)

German patrols guard the front, east of the great blast furnaces and chimneys of the Colombelles metalworks.

artillery observation from the hills of the Bois de Bavent continued to be effective.

The Germans regarded Caen as the 'hinge' of the defence of Normandy. Even with the city itself lost, they determined to hold an arc of defensible terrain from the English Channel to western banks of the Orne River. Whether the attack came from the west of Caen, between the city and Hill 112, or from the east, between Caen and the Bois de Bavent, was almost irrelevant. The heart of the defence in either case was the Bourguébus ridge astride the Falaise road. This low but tactically important ridge afforded a vista from Hill 112 in the west to the Bois de Bavent in the east. Before it stretched open country with stone farmsteads and villages transformed into strongpoints with interlocking fields of fire. And in front of them flowed the Orne River.

Had the German defenders been given full details of GOODWOOD, would their defensive strategy have been any different? Arguably, preparations to move *12. SS-Panzerdivision* (the *Hitlerjugend*) away north to the Pas de Calais area might have been postponed. Dietrich's *I. SS-Panzer-Korps* could have been edged closer to the impending action. Such moves might have made a difference. It has been argued that better British tactics on 18 July could perhaps to have succeeded in breaking through the meagre defences of certain parts of the German line, which foreknowledge might have led the defenders to strengthen. Perhaps. But this argument risks taking 'what if' speculation too far. On 18 July the 'fog of war' was a factor

Construction of the tracks went on in full view of the German observers.

influencing both sides' performances. Besides, it could equally be argued that a greater concentration of defenders on the ground on the morning of 18 July would simply have presented a richer target for the planned bombing. In the event, some powerful German units well forward on the 'shoulders' of the forthcoming British assault were to be virtually obliterated. And since the trench warfare of the First World War German defenders had learned the importance of 'thinning out' the front lines in expectation of bombardment, defending in great depth and holding back reserves with which to regain the tactical initiative.

On balance it is safe to conclude that the Germans were reasonably well prepared for the assault Second Army was planning. Their lookouts in Colombelles monitored the extensive engineering works on and around the proposed bridges; on the night of 16-17 July, Luftwaffe reconnaissance aircraft dropping flares took photographs which clearly revealed the one-way flow of traffic over the crossings. Nevertheless, Second Army stuck to its elaborate deception plan.

The transfer eastwards of the armoured divisions of VIII Corps was made substantially more difficult by the order that all movements be made at night and in total radio silence. Units were to 'lie up' under camouflage through the hours of daylight. The history of 23rd Hussars recalls the regiment's second successive night advance, no less difficult than the first.

The Eleventh Armoured Division moved across the Orne. It was all done with the greatest secrecy. Camouflage officers were attached to each unit and we were told that it was vital that we should all be in and camouflaged before first light. It would not be true to say that our march was without hitches. The night was dark, the dust was appalling and the route badly marked. The combination of those three things resulted in two-thirds of the Regiment going the wrong way within two miles of the start, and they eventually reached the harbour by a route that was highly original if nothing else, twice practically motoring into the sea.[15]

The British hoped to convince the Germans that the expected assault would indeed be projected through XII Corps, to the west of Caen. In support of this ambition, various diversionary operations were planned. On the night of 15-16 July the three infantry divisions of XII Corps commenced Operation GREENLINE. This is not the place for the detailed (and interesting) story of GREENLINE, which can be summed up by the words of an infantry colonel angered at the loss of seventy-one officers and men in an action abandoned half-way through and during which contact with the enemy was never made.

This operation was excused as a feint for ops EAST of the ORNE and CAEN. Even if this was the case there seems no reason for Operation GREENLINE to have been such a dreadful pointless muddle.[16]

Similarly, further still to the west XXX Corps was instructed to execute Operation POMEGRANATE, attempting on 16 July to secure the small town of Noyers-Bocage. Once again, the story of POMEGRANATE deserves separate telling. While the actions fought are of great interest, the results were inconclusive other than keeping the defenders busy (and drawing in important parts of the elite *9. SS-Panzerdivision, 'Hohenstaufen'*).[17]

THE CROSSING

The fact remained that, if 11th Armoured Division was to be squeezed into the bridgehead before the start of the operation, there simply was no room east of the Orne River for the other two armoured divisions. Only after the battle had started would Guards Armoured be able to cross over to the ground vacated by 11th Armoured, and only after the Guards advanced to battle would there be room for 7th Armoured to follow. Even with three crossings available, the sequential transfer of three armoured divisions, with yet further units belonging to different corps interspersed, was a huge traffic management challenge.

Lieutenant Robin Lemon of 3rd RTR recalled,

We lay hidden all day on the 17th, and that night the regiment crossed the river Orne into the concentration area in the bridgehead. Traffic control must have been a nightmare. There was dust and more dust, as our tanks rumbled through the night. Dawn broke bright and clear. As the light grew stronger, the shapes of the 6th Airborne gliders that had landed on D Day appeared all round us.

Later, the 23rd Hussars arrived on the scene.

As twilight gave place to darkness, the Regiment sprang to life, the tanks shook themselves free of their camouflage and began to move out of harbour. Vast palls of dust, like a thick fog, obscured the drivers' vision and hurt the eyes, but this time no mistake in the route could be made, for it was clearly marked. Eventually we crossed the river Orne by a Bailey Bridge, and by degrees we found and entered the concentration area. It was already crammed to bursting point with the leading regiments, with their tanks, attached guns and riflemen's vehicles, interspersed with enormous and weird-looking objects which loomed blackly all around us. They proved to be derelict gliders, for we were in the open space in which the Sixth Airborne Division had made their landing on D Day. We huddled up against the sides of the gliders, and, beating off continual mosquito assaults, we slept for what was left of the night.[18]

While the maintenance of the actual bridges was a I Corps responsibility, Traffic Control fell to VIII Corps. Units arriving at the western boundary of the Bridge Area would come under the control of the VIII Corps Traffic Office. All vehicles halted on this line and topped up with POL (petrol, oil, and lubricants) while awaiting the traffic officers' summons. From 21.00 hours on 16 July, only 'up' (eastbound) traffic would be allowed. 'Sidings' were provided west of the bridges to hold any traffic arriving out of turn and permit last-minute changes to the order of march. Similar sidings on the east bank of the Orne would hold any 'down', westbound traffic until the 'one way' order ended, some time on 19 July. (Until then, the plan ruthlessly asserted, even casualties would have to be held within the densely packed bridgehead east of the Orne crossings.)

The Guards followed 11th Armoured Division. At least some of their officers were appreciative of the efforts of the military police.

The 5th Guards Armoured Brigade led the way, the tanks moving across the fields along bulldozed tracks marked with white tape, so as to avoid the final ruination of the few still serviceable roads. The heat was intense, the dust and the dirt indescribable and the night inky black; apart from the discomfort thus caused and in spite of excellent signposting by the Divisional Provost Company, the finding of the tracks was an almost impossible task. [19]

An infantry officer with the Welsh Guards similarly recorded,

'It was after midnight and very dark. Long lines of vehicles were formed up near the entrance to the field with their engines ticking over and despatch riders sitting astride

Bull-dozed tracks reinforced with metal supplemented the country roads.

their machines opening and shutting their throttles. Somewhere the Regimental Sergeant-Major was shouting at someone; we might have been on any exercise in England. Then suddenly, we were on the move, bumping and swaying out of the field and into narrow lanes, with their tall enveloping hedges dimly moving past on either side. Every road junction we came to was beautifully sign-posted by the Provost Company with illuminated arrows and boards lit by electric torches with directions for 'tracks' and 'wheels' in black type… The hypnotic winking of the next vehicle's convoy-light soon sent one into a fitful doze; there is no room for excitement in the coma induced by a night drive in convoy. Sometimes at one of the many halts I would get out to stretch my legs, but without knowledge or curiosity as to where we were.' By the dawn, 'We came to a halt on what seemed to be a long ridge which sloped away gradually into the distance on the right. [The writer was facing north near the west bank of the Caen Canal, just south of Bénouville.] I got out and found myself on an artificially constructed track with chain netting laid over its bull-dozed surface. Twenty yards to the left was another which I knew from the signposting to be the tank track. [The writer was now looking at CALF from Track 'C'.] On either side of us were cornfields, their tall crops almost ripe. A thin ground mist lay over everything… It was going to be hot later on. One by one the vehicles shut off their engines.'[20]

18 July had dawned. The Guards infantry were going to be doing a lot more waiting as the day wore on.

FORMING UP

The initial avenue down which three successive armoured brigades were to advance was going to be barely wide enough for a single tank regiment at a time, and 3rd Royal Tank Regiment had been selected to lead. 3rd RTR and its supporting elements were to form a multi-arm regimental task force of mobile, armoured vehicles. During the afternoon of 16 July, Colonel Silvertop had been briefed on his regiment's part in GOODWOOD, and received under his command A Squadron, 22nd Dragoon Guards (Sherman flail tanks), H Battery, 13th Royal Horse Artillery (eight self-propelled 25 pounder Sextons), and G Company, 8thRifle Brigade. The following day the regimental group was further augmented by two troops 26 Assault Squadron, Royal Engineers, with ten Churchill AVRE.[21] The Sextons and the motor infantry were old friends, used to operating with 3rd RTR as an intimate part of the regimental group. The flails were less welcome. The General Officer Commanding, Pip Roberts, had denied the need for minesweeping tanks in the vanguard of his division, but had been overruled.[22] The flails and the AVREs were placed under command of 8th RB; the infantry company and artillery battery commanders took up their accustomed battle stations, in their respective vehicles at Silvertop's side.

3rd RTR moved out of their little wood at midnight, initially bound for a holding area east of the bridges, around Ranville. By 02.30 hours on 18 July, the regiment and its supporting elements were assembled at the final Concentration Area in the fields immediately west of the ruins of Amfréville, occupying an area which on 6 June had been 'DZ-LZ N' (Drop/Landing Zone November), and more recently had been a no man's land during the long duel between 6th Airborne and *346. Infanteriedivision*. Tanks, carriers, and half-

tracks parked-up alongside the battered remains of 6th Airborne's gliders. An 8th RB officer recalled, 'Along with our friends of A Squadron [3rd RTR] we had only two hours breather.'[23] There was little time to rest, but tired men took what sleep their duties permitted.

Reveille sounded at 04.30 hours. Officers were summoned to an O (orders) Group, the first at which the newly-joined A Squadron, Dragoon Guards flails were represented. At 05.30 arrived the Liaison Officer with confirmation from Brigade that H hour was indeed to be 07.45. By 06.10 the regiment was again on the move and shortly began to enter the newly-cleared minefield gaps. Bill

Close's A Squadron tanks and David Stileman's carriers followed the white-taped paths, nose to tail. In the half-light, one Rifle Brigade carrier strayed onto a mine, losing a track. But this was the exception, and as dawn broke the regimental group was emerging into its Forming Up Place.

References

(1) '21. Panzer-Division' J-C Perrigault, 2002, ISBN 2-84048-157-X, p 252-253; Alfred Becker diary

(2) 'Les Ponts Bailey', Philippe Bauduin 2002, ISBN 2-86743-471-8, 2002, p 23; Scarfe, 'Assault Division' p 39. 'Welsh Bridges to the Elbe' by J H Roberts, 2000, ISBN 1-898893-00-4 contains excellent detail of British Army bridging.

(3) BAOR Battlefield Tour notes, 1947, Section V p 15-17. Some accounts have maintained that each of the three armoured divisions used a different set of bridges. It is easy to see how this impression was created: 'Rat' apparently relating to 7th Armoured, the 'Desert Rats'; 'Calf' to 11th Armoured, the 'Black Bull' division; etc. But the appearance is deceptive. The code names had no relevance to the movement plan.

(4) 'A View From the Turret', Major W H Close, 2002, ISBN 0-9533359-1-7, p 115.

(5) W H Close, interview at Staff College, Camberley, 1979

(6) 'The Battle: A Tank Officer Remembers', G S C Bishop, p 42-43

(7) 'And Came Safe Home', unpublished W Steel Brownlie diary

(8) 'The Story of the Guards Armoured Division', Rosse & Hill, 1956, p 36-37

(9) 'Armoured Guardsman', R Boscawen, 2001, ISBN 0 85052 748 1, p 26

(10) Boscawen, p 27

(11) Stileman, interview at Staff College, Camberley, 1979

(12) Roberts, p 171

(13) Close, p 116

(14) BAOR BFT Section VI RE Plan, p20

(15) 'The Story of the 23rd Hussars', G S C Bishop, 1946, p68-69. This account mistakenly states that the regiment crossed the bridges on the night of 16 July. In both his published histories of the 23rd Hussars, Bishop occasionally mistakes key dates, which need always to be carefully cross-checked.

(16) Col. J W Tweedie unpublished report, Stirling Castle archive; see also 'History of the Argyll and Sutherland Highlanders 2nd Battalion, McElwee, 1949, p 46; and 'History of the 15th Scottish Division', H G Martin, 1948, p 65-76.

(17) 'Blue Flash: the Story of an Armoured Regiment', Alan Jolly, 1952 (144th RTR); BAOR BFT Section IV, p 8

(18) Bishop, 23rd Hussars, p 69

(19) Rosse & Hill, p 19

(20) 'Welsh Guards at War', L F Ellis, 1946, ISBN 0-948130-52-0, p 173-175

(21) See Appendix 6 for detailed unit structures.

(22) Roberts was overruled by his senior, the founding father of 11th Armoured, Major-General 'Hobo' Hobart: *'My dear boy, if there should turn out to be mines anywhere on your route, it will ruin the whole operation, and then you'll look pretty silly.'* Roberts was as unconvinced as he had been eighteen months earlier at El Alamein. There, his 22nd Brigade was allocated six of the first-generation flail tanks to clear the advance through deep minefields. Roberts was sceptical. *'The idea was fine, but here, in its infancy, it was very unreliable. Frankly, I had not got much faith in this concept… and I was thankful that we had the sappers… to pick up the mines by hand if the Scorpions failed.* (Roberts, p 113) The Scorpions did fail and Roberts' scepticism was reinforced.

(23) Stileman, interview at Staff College, Camberley, 1979

Chapter 3

18 JULY, DAWN: THE BOMBING

The major British and Commonwealth offensives in Normandy typically began with a simultaneous salvo from massed artillery batteries announcing the start of a sustained bombardment. GOODWOOD was to be different.

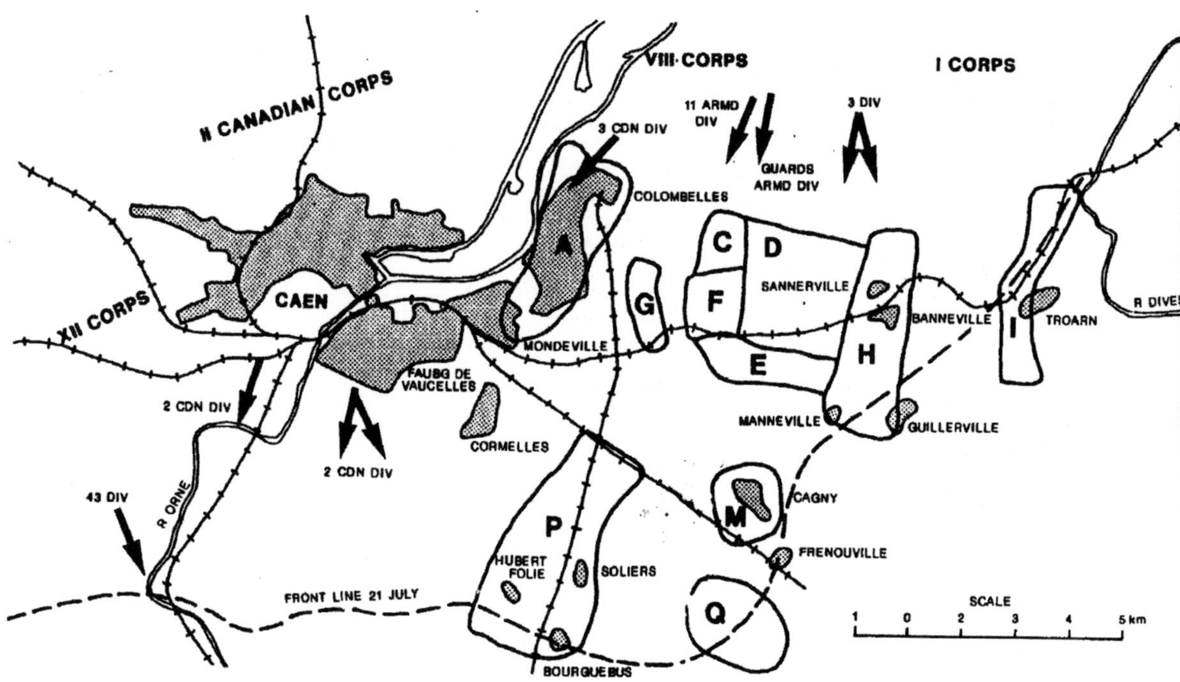

THE ARTILLERY SHORTFALL

In October, 1941, Churchill foresaw that 'Renown awaits the Commander who first, in this war, restores the artillery to its prime importance on the battlefield.'[1] By 1944, the British artillery arm had most certainly regained its 'prime importance' based on the experience, equipment, and sheer professionalism acquired in the war years. In raw numbers, the Royal Artillery outnumbered the British infantry arm: the two arms by then accounting respectively for 22% and 19% of Army manpower, followed by the Royal Engineers with 9% while the Royal Armoured Corps accounted for a mere 4%.[2] And in Montgomery, 21st Army Group indeed had a commander cognisant of the vital role of artillery.

The ubiquitous 25 pounder field gun.

Operation EPSOM had been delayed until the end of June mainly in order that shortages of artillery ammunition resulting from the great storm in the Channel could be made up.[3] When the great operation commenced, it was with the support of over seven hundred guns. The infantry and armour remained throughout the ensuing battle under the 'umbrella' of artillery support. The arrival in Normandy of *II. SS-Panzer Korps* with its two armoured divisions turned the EPSOM offensive into a dogged defence of ground taken. But before the élite German force could come to grips with the British, its ground forces had first to pass under that artillery umbrella. *9. SS-Panzerdivision* reported its assaults stopped by massed artillery described as being reminiscent of the First World War. (Although by the crude measure of guns-per-kilometre of front, the British artillery available for EPSOM was barely two-thirds that employed at the Somme, its close integration with the front line troops and responsiveness to their needs made it remarkably effective.) One SS officer's battle report ended quoting Dante: 'abandon hope all ye who enter here.' Another SS officer reported on the events of 30 June,

Futile attempts to get the attack moving again. Each attempt saw the enemy artillery fire rise to hurricane force and smash the squads and platoons… the 9th and 10th SS-Panzer Divisions simply could advance no farther.[4]

The battery was reduced to a single *Wespe*.

Against an enemy underpinned by this wall of fire, unit élan and individual heroism could not prevail. These were novel experiences even for units accustomed to harsh fighting on the Russian front. An artilleryman of *9. SS-Panzerdivision* recorded that on 1 July his battery of six *Wespe* self-propelled 10.5 cm guns was quickly reduced by counter-battery fire to his gun alone, which spent the day dodging incoming fire. Ammunition resupply was next to impossible. Communications were hampered since radio transmissions were rapidly detected, inviting enemy artillery concentrations, and telephone lines to the batteries from their remote radio emplacements were repeatedly cut by shells.[5]

The field telephone: undectable but its wires vulnerable to artillery fire.

By July, the Allies' Normandy bridgehead was packed tight with military units. When hundreds of guns might be called upon to support a single corps action, finding the space for so many guns and their provisioning became a problem. For Operation GOODWOOD, some logistical difficulties were insurmountable. When the three divisions of VIII Corps crossed the waterways east of Caen and turned south through the minefields, they would be moving ever further from the supporting artillery, left behind north and west of the city. On paper, the guns allocated to the GOODWOOD operation looked impressive. However, by the time the leading regiments emerged from the minefield passages to reach the Start Line for the operation, they would already be close to the extreme range of some of the supporting batteries. Later in the morning, as it led the way into enemy territory, 29th Armoured Brigade would have to rely mainly on the guns of its accompanying 13th Royal Horse Artillery, whose three eight-gun batteries of self-propelled 25 pounders were apportioned between the three armoured regiments. And even those batteries would have to divide their time between moving and firing. To make matters worse, 2nd Army was experiencing a shortage of field artillery ammunition.[6] For the field batteries within range, 500 rounds per gun could be spared, but overall the artillery support available fell short of the ideal.

The battlefield was still in range of naval artillery, and this would go some way to filling the gap. But still more was needed, and the army had turned to the strategic air forces.

WAITING AND WATCHING

In the small hours of 18 July, the forces arrayed to lead the morning's assault awaited the dawn. The last vehicles had reached their assigned places for what remained of the night and engines were switched off. With maintenance tasks complete, vehicle crews grabbed a last opportunity to sleep. An officer still awake noted that,

> *Apart from the distant drone of a motor cycle, diminishing as it passed away up the column, and the snoring and coughs of my men… complete stillness settled on us… It was unbelievably quiet.*[7]

A mist lay over the trampled crop in the fields serving as parking lots for a mass of vehicles. Then, as the first troops on the ground were being roused for 'stand to' in the pre-dawn hour, there came from the north a distant, droning buzz, which rapidly resolved itself into the sound of aircraft. Men emerged from vehicles and shelters to stare upwards as ghostly silhouettes passed in the dark sky and began to drop marker flares on target areas behind the enemy lines. A Guardsman recalled,

> *Possibly the only time in the history of the 2nd Battalion Grenadier Guards when all ranks were up before reveille was on July 18th, 1944, for at 05.00 hours a distant thunder in the air brought all the sleepy-eyed tank crews out of their blankets.*

The noise grew steadily: a deep, pulsing throb from four-engined heavy bombers. The RAF Bomber Command Lancasters started to appear overhead a little after 05.00 hours. Southbound in groups of three, scattered across the sky in no particular formation, the stream of bombers became increasingly dense: an awesome spectacle accompanied by an overwhelming roar of engines. They flew unusually low, at barely three thousand feet. As the sun rose the black undersides of the big night bombers were silhouetted against the lightening sky.

Then, when the throb of multiple Rolls-Royce Merlin engines appeared to have reached its climax, there came a different cacophony of sound as the artillery to the rear opened up. This was 'APPLE PIE 1', the first phase of the morning's complex artillery programme. While thousand pound bombs plunged from the night bombers onto distant enemy positions, and German antiaircraft guns opened up in reply, eight Royal Artillery Field Regiments backed up by one heavy and four medium regiments commenced counter-battery fire against known and suspected enemy Flak positions. This fire was to be maintained so long as heavy bombers were overhead, after which those

An unusual sight: Bomber Command bombing in daylight.

same regiments would from H–100 to H–10 (that is, from 06.05 hours to 07.35) progressively transfer their attentions from Flak positions to counter-battery fire against enemy field gun, howitzer, and rocket emplacements.

In less than an hour from their first appearance, over nine hundred[8] British heavy bombers (Halifaxes as well as Lancasters) had passed overhead, released their bombloads, and turned for home leaving huge pyres of dust and smoke over the German lines to the south. Their departure afforded the defenders little respite. As the counter-battery fire of the Army's artillery reached a crescendo, it was supplemented by big guns of the Royal Navy. Six-inch shells from cruisers HMS *Enterprise* (seven guns) and HMS *Mauritius* (twelve guns) and enormous fifteen-inch shells from the two guns of monitor HMS *Roberts* worked-over known and suspected German gun positions on the flanks of the proposed battlefield.

Around 07.00 hours, more and more vehicles of the leading British units were starting engines. By now, the sun was rising in a blue sky, quickly

Medium bombers over Colombelles.

dispelling the early mist of a summer morning. But away to the south, all that could be seen was an appalling cloud bank of smoke and dust, pulverized earth and debris thrown up by half-ton bombs and continually stirred by large-calibre shells. And now a different force appeared overhead. The medium bombers of the Ninth United States Army Air Force arrived: twin-engined bombers, B25 Mitchells and B26 Marauders, charged with raining 500 pound high explosive bombs on to the villages to the east of the corridor down which VIII Corps was shortly to advance: Cuverville, Giberville, and Démouville; and with laying a carpet of 260 pound fragmentation bombs over the corridor itself.

Soon after yet another Air Force made its appearance, this time the United States' Eighth. These were the American heavy bombers, today reassigned from daylight raids over the heartlands of Germany. Unlike the British bombers, they flew at their accustomed high altitude: precisely arranged 'boxes' of B17 Flying Fortresses and B24 Liberators making their stately entrance over the battlefield. A British officer recalled,

> *the whole northern sky was filled with them as far as one could see – wave upon wave, stepped up one above the other and spreading out east and west till it seemed there was no room for any more... The bombers flew in majestically and with a dreadful, unalterable dignity, unloaded and made for home... Everyone was out of their vehicles now, staring in awed wonder till the last wave dropped their bombs and turned away. Then the guns took up in a steadily increasing crescendo the work which the bombers had begun.'*[9]

While the task of the mediums of the Ninth was to shower the direct path of VIII Corps with fragmentation bombs, the heavies of the Eighth were to reach further back behind German lines. Their first targets were Troarn and the Dives valley to the east, from 07.00 hours. Successive waves visited the area south of the Caen to Paris railway with concentrations of 20 pound and 100 pound fragmentation bombs up until 09.30 hours.

THE BOMBING SHORTFALL

Unfortunately for the American mediums and their later wave of heavies, visibility around the VIII Corps objectives was poor. The corridor of the initial ground assault, roughly four miles long from Escoville to the Caen to Troarn railway and barely a mile across, was surrounded by the devastation of the earlier bombing. To the west the enormous metal works and to the east the foothills of the Bois de Bavent had been pummelled. Alongside the end of the corridor, the little town of Cagny had in the final ten minutes of the RAF assault received up to 650 tons of bombs. Delayed fusing of big 500 and 1,000 bombs meant substantial cratering,[10] with dry Norman soil blasted high into the air and carried southwards on the breeze in clouds of increasing density. Many of the newly-arrived American bombers could not find their targets in the murk and a good quarter of the American heavies carried their bomb loads back to Britain.

This was understandable. Private soldiers and generals alike had little experience of seeing modern heavy bombers operating over the battlefield. Barring the invasion itself, Bomber Command so far supported Montgomery's Normandy campaign on only three occasions: bombing German rear areas on the night of 14-15 June, Villers-Bocage on the afternoon and evening of 30 June, and Caen on the evening of 7 July. This last was the closest the heavy bombers had come to the troops on the ground. And an overriding concern of both soldiers and airmen was to avoid friendly casualties. To this end, on 7 July the bomb lines had been set far back from the front lines (actually, so far behind that little direct damage was inflicted on the main German defences). Harris insisted on a safety margin of six thousand yards. And even so, strenuous efforts were made to ensure that the bombing in progress did not 'creep' back towards friendly troops. As one bomber pilot recalled,

> *All the way from base right up to the target, we were working, as we put it, for the Government. But once the bombs were gone, then we were working for ourselves. So the final run-up time on "Government business" was critical, with everyone feeling: "If only we can get over the next three minutes, I stand a good chance of getting home." There was a tendency to bomb at the earliest possible moment.'* [11]

'Working for the Government.'

The devastated City of Caen: to the north castle hill; south of the Orne River is the flattened suburb of Vaucelles and the main railway station.

Frequently, the bomb line would creep back as premature releases were emulated by following aircrews. Striving to overcome this tendency was the Master Bomber. He supervised the bombing raid from high above, calling on his deputies when the red aiming marker flares became obscured to 'Back up the reds! Back up the reds!'

On the night of 7 July, the bombing was extremely accurate, and friendly casualties were averted. But they were averted at great cost. The following morning, the ground assault of Operation CHARNWOOD would run into a German line largely untouched by bombing which had fallen on empty rear areas and on the unfortunate inhabitants of Caen. And when after bitter fighting the city was finally reached, the rubble and devastation resulting from the bombing presented a serious obstacle to the would-be liberators. Similar means were adopted to achieve accuracy on 18 July. One German observed, 'thousands of bombers. Each wave dropped smoke signals after they had unloaded, to indicate to the next wave to start dropping more bombs.'[12] Not so far from the truth: these were the red flares designed to refresh the aiming points.

So, on seeing heavy bombers in direct support, the soldiers had a number of thoughts. One of these was concern that the bombs might fall short. On the morning of 18 July, some did.

> *Then came the Marauders, speedy and glistening white in the sun. A whistling scream and crash shook everyone's attention away from the sky to find that a jettisoned bomb had fallen beside Fourth Troop, 'B' Squadron, just as the Troop Leader was talking to his men. Lieut. Cochrane was badly wounded and two men were killed.*[13]

Against this, it should be noted that advancing close behind an artillery barrage carried the very real risk of being hit by 'short' rounds, as was to be seen later that morning. And once again, the caution of the air planners was to exact a price. The RAF had been asked to neutralize the three adjacent villages of Touffréville, Sannerville, and Banneville, using delay-fused High Explosive bombs since cratering was deemed acceptable in this area. As will be seen, the effect on the latter two villages was utterly devastating. But without informing the Army, Bomber Command had unilaterally decided that Touffréville, northernmost of the three, should not be made an aiming point for fear of hitting British troops. When they came to take Touffréville, British 3rd Division would pay a heavy price for being spared the possible risk of accidental damage.[14]

Set against soldiers' fears of 'shorts' from the aerial bombardment was the tremendous morale uplift of seeing such extravagant pounding of the enemy, 'Vastly impressive and encouraging to our own troops,' the 11th Armoured Division historian recorded.[15] Closest of all to the aerial bombardment was the 3rd RTR group. Already in their Forming Up Place, the vehicle crews had nothing to do but watch the show while enjoying a last cigarette in the open air. 'We heartily cheered. We thought nothing could survive such an onslaught.'[16] But then, amid all the excitement, there came to some of the men a further thought. To what extent had the enemy really been suppressed?

HEAVY BOMBERS OVER THE BATTLEFIELD

In 1944 the use of medium and heavy bombers on the battlefield was a science in its infancy. It was politically charged. Only by massive effort in the course of the First World War had the British air arm won its independence from Army and Navy. The proudest heritage of the fledgling RAF of the 1920s was the Independent Air Force of 1918, the little force that had extended its reach beyond the battlefield to strike at the industry and the morale of Germany.

(17) Through the lean years of the 1930s and the early days of the renewed war with Germany, the RAF had endured as junior partner of the three services: starved of resources pre-war, relegated to a support role with the Army in France, with the Senior Service in the defence of the coast and the Battle of the Atlantic. Now, sanctified by the memory of the Battle of Britain and enthused by the prospect of retaliation in the skies over Germany, the Royal Air Force was unwilling to play second fiddle to the Army. And despite its title, the United States Army Air Force felt likewise. Major General Carl Spaatz was no less determined than Air Marshall Sir Arthur Harris that the war should be won by strategic bombing. The two might disagree (violently!) on the tactics of the air war over Germany, but neither the United States' strategic bombing force nor RAF Bomber Command would lightly countenance the diversion of their heavy bombers in direct support of Army operations.

Politics (and war-winning strategies) apart, in 1944 the practical effectiveness of heavy bombers on the battlefield was little understood. In many quarters it was to remain so to the war's end and beyond. At its simplest: bombing the battlefield had great appeal. While the payload of an artillery shell is typically something under ten percent of its overall weight, that of an aircraft-delivered bomb is virtually its entirety. Aircraft could deliver explosives to the battlefield in a volume and density unapproached by conventional artillery. A modern adage has it that: 'cluster bombing from B-52s is very, very accurate: the bombs never miss the ground.' The point being

German front line: the west-east road from the Orne River, past the S.M.N., to Cuverville, and the proposed British 'Armoured Corridor'.

made is of course that strategic bombing has until recent years been a rather blunt instrument. But the irony would have been lost on many 1944 generals. Until experience and analysis proved otherwise, it was easy to be convinced that little on the ground could survive such a bombardment as was delivered on the morning of 18 July. The truth was sometimes different.

By 1944, the Allied strategic bombing forces' equipment, training, and – increasingly – experience were geared to the destruction of urban and industrial areas. Even in the most heavily bombed targets, human beings have historically proved surprisingly resilient to the effect of high explosive. While Hamburg eventually lost 47% of its housing, 3% of the populace died; Frankfurt lost 33% of its housing, yet 'only' 1% of its people.[18] Once targets moved from cities and towns to the countryside, the likely impact of bombs on military units was even less. The work of the British Operational Research Sections was later to reveal that the density of bombs required to make an area militarily impassible was inversely proportional to that area's level of development. That is, while a density of five bombs per acre (typically

Air Marshal Sir Arthur Harris.

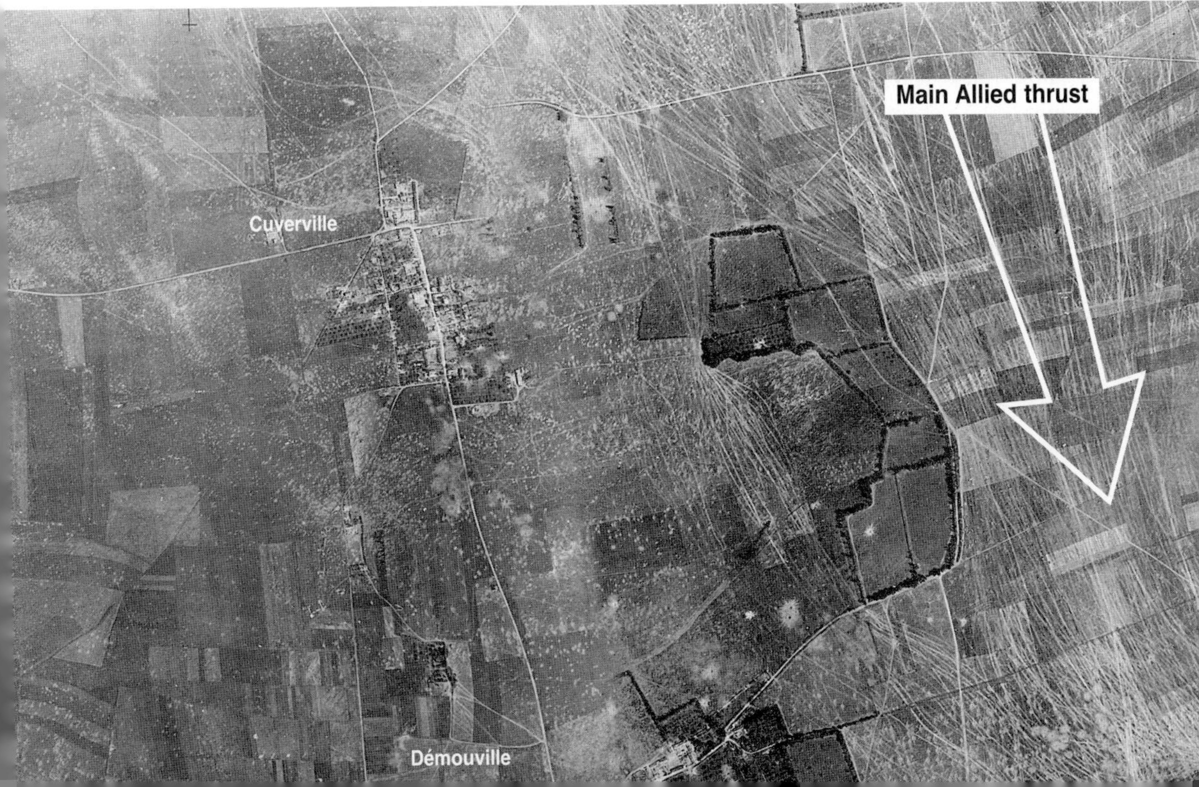

achieved against a point target by fifty British heavy bombers) would obstruct a heavily built up area, achieving the same effect in open countryside would require up to forty bombs per acre of villages and fields. Such truths were counter-intuitive. And in July, 1944, these truths had yet to be evaluated. Even after ORS disseminated their findings, it was hard for the generals to accept that the awesome sight and sound of heavy bombers pulverizing the battlefield might not be achieving all that was hoped.

Nevertheless, some lessons were already being learned. An army accustomed to the 'rolling barrage' could easily accept the importance of advancing closely behind the bombardment. Troops might find 'leaning on the barrage' uncomfortable (the impact on advancing infantry of live shells bursting ahead has been likened to being punched in the body and face). Losses to 'friendly fire' occurred: worn barrels and faulty shells did lead to a proportion of rounds falling short. Nevertheless, it was recognized that these were minor concerns compared to the saving of life that could be achieved if the enemy's positions could be taken before defenders emerged from hiding. Increasingly sophisticated artillery tactics were invented (or often, revived from the First World War). Artillery bombardments would stop long enough to tempt defenders out of their bunkers before renewing their fire; rolling barrages might end with smoke or noise-makers over the enemy positions as friendly troops closed the final yards. From the earlier bombing of Caen, it was clear that giving the enemy hours to recover was futile. Minutes and even seconds of respite might allow defenders to recover and defences to be manned.

The ground forces of GOODWOOD were to be ready to advance immediately following the aerial bombardment. And a further lesson had been learned. The bombing of Caen a week before, and the town of Cassino in Italy the preceding March, had in each case resulted in advancing forces being held up by the devastation wrought by their own bombardment. This would be avoided. The aerial choreography of GOODWOOD assigned the British heavy bombers the job of cratering the areas either side of the VIII Corps 'corridor', using heavy, delay-fused bombs. The American bombers which followed had smaller payloads but greater numbers of bomb hooks. A B17 bomber had forty hooks, compared to a Lancaster's fourteen; one hook could drop a cluster of smaller bombs onto the corridor itself, 'carpeting' the avenue of attack with high explosive and fragmentation munitions designed to suppress the enemy without overly churning the ground. (Curiously, this sensible plan was not emulated for the Americans' own Operation COBRA, a week later. Then, the resulting craters were to prove an unwelcome obstacle, particularly to wheeled vehicles.)

THE DEFENDERS' EXPERIENCE

The first wave of bombers hit the German forces holding the western flank of the proposed advance. Lookouts posted in the Colombelles metalworks first heard, then saw the aerial armada approaching. Their worst fears were realised when the leading aircraft dropped coloured marker flares in their midst and then, even as men on the ground were being hastily roused into action, down came the first wave of bombs.

> *The men who had to submit to this carpet bombing were powerless in their helplessness, their entrenchments their only hope of survival. Most reckoned that their end was nigh.*[19]

In the open ground between Colombelles and Cuverville stood a line of tanks 'underpinning' the forward infantry. These ten Panzer IV had arrived at midnight from the *22. Panzerregiment* holding area around Emiéville to relieve the previous company there. The experienced tank men denied themselves the luxury of occupying their predecessors' positions. Assuming these would by now have become known to the enemy, they formed a new security cordon. The ten tanks formed a single line, behind the east-west Cuverville to Colombelles road (the modern D226), spaced about twenty five metres apart. Their night was quiet, the men sleeping peacefully in or under their tanks. Then in the early morning the storm broke. Huge explosions were felt and seen; and before long the view towards the nearby factory complex in the west was obscured as fountains of earth were raised into the air. The wall of explosions marched over Colombelles in the west, angling south-eastward to hide Giberville as columns of dust and smoke merged into a solid cloud. The heavy bombardment was rapidly reducing the whole area to a hellish nightmare. The bombs appeared to the awestruck tank crews to be rolling across the countryside in waves. With no time to escape and nowhere to go, they felt trapped. One wave crashed down directly ahead of the position. A pause. Then by great good fortune, the next wave of bombs fell a few metres

Fountains of earth and smoke were raised into the air.

behind. The ten tanks in the line west of Cuverville had been spared, for the moment.

Though they could not appreciate it, the ground these tanks stood on had not experienced the full weight of the Allied bombing. They were just far enough away from Target Area A to miss the worst effects of Bomber Command's cratering. This was the bombardment they had witnessed falling around their left flank and rear before they were subjected to the fragmentation munitions of the Ninth U S Air Force. So survived, more or less intact, all the tanks. The crews however did not fare so well.

> *Quite apart from the physical danger, these events had a huge psychological impact. The morale effect of the enemy's monstrous matériel superiority, bombs raining down from the air and drumfire from artillery, made even the most courageous lose heart. Our helplessness faced with such expenditure of matériel, and our own lack of antiaircraft support to counter it, could only have a depressing effect.* [20]

Closer still than the tanks to the maelstom of Colombelles were the infantry of *192. Panzergrenadier-Regiment*. Hans Höller, commanding an armoured antitank detachment, recalls men shaking with nervous reaction, hardly knowing what to do; 'We cursed this insane war.'[21]

As has been shown, the Allied armies of 1944 tended to have high expectations of heavy bombers over the battlefield. Hindsight, aided by the scientific analyses of Operational Research, was to conclude that heavy bombers were poor battlefield attack weapons.[22] Given that defending German military units might be expected to be well dispersed and well dug-in, the GOODWOOD air plan was optimistic. As it happened, in the case of GOODWOOD some of that optimism was rewarded.

To the great annoyance of some of its commanders, the principal armoured formations of *21. Panzerdivision* were positioned well forward. Given the importance of the ground east of Caen, and the extreme depth of the German defences, this was unusual. During the First World War, the Germans had evolved defensive tactics which minimized the numbers of troops exposed in the front lines. In the linear warfare of the western front, the forward trenches were 'thinned out' to the point that they were little more than a screen, or in more modern terminology, a 'tripwire'. Multiple lines to the rear contained the main strength of the defenders. Here were the reserves, intended to recapture the front lines after the attackers had expended much of their force, moved beyond their own sources of supply and command control, occupied German positions which faced the wrong way for defence, and generally been worked-over by German artillery registered on known key points. It is worth noting that the popular image of 1916 German machine gunners in forward positions 'hosing' down advancing lines of Allied infantry is somewhat misguided. On the opening day of the Somme battle, the German machine guns which so devastated the British advance were most often 2,000 or even 3,000 yards behind the front lines. As in the Allied armies, medium and heavy machine guns continued to be employed in a manner more akin to artillery than infantry; as often as not they delivered indirect, 'area' fire rather than firing over open sights.[23]

The ten *Panzer IV* stood twenty-five metres apart.

By 1944, defence in depth had proved vital on the eastern front, where the Germans and their allies simply did not have the manpower to form a homogeneously strong line across vast distances. Here it was usual to hold the mobile reserves, destined to counter attack and restore lost ground, well back from the front. Mobility and concentration of force thereby achieved local fire and armour superiority and so made up for lack of numbers. With their extensive experience gained on the Steppes of Russia and the Ukraine, the combat veterans of *503. schwere Panzer-Abteilung* had become used to operating as a mobile 'fire brigade' and became resentful if left in the front line. 'I fully realise,' wrote Tiger tank commander Alfred Rubbel,

> *that it was necessary to have tanks immediately behind the battle line as "corset stays" for the hard-fighting infantry formations that had been bled white, so as to stabilize their fighting morale... that requirement interfered with the tactically correct commitment.*[24]

Some of the *503. Abteilung* found their tactical deployment close behind the front line perplexing. *Leutnant* Freiherr von Rosen, in temporary command of the westernmost *3. Kompanie*, recalled,

The battalion was an independent battalion, of the Army reserve, and therefore came under a division for a certain period of employment at the time of the main effort. When a particular mission was accomplished, we were moved to other critical points. That was the reason why the battalion was moved in the beginning of July from the Russian front where it had been engaged in heavy fighting to Normandy. My company was in Manneville, only three miles behind the front line. We were in a state of permanent readiness to be employed as events required. In my opinion for this task the battalion was located much too far forward. We – that is my battalion commander and all the company commanders – were fully aware of this and constantly represented that we should be in as position further back from which we would be able to move to meet the weight of any enemy breakthrough. But all our representations were turned down by a higher authority. We were under the 21. Panzerdivision.[25]

***Leutnant* Freiherr von Rosen.**

Such dissatisfaction was not unknown in the British Army, whose specialist units were frequently misunderstood and misused by senior officers to whom they were attached. The Germans went so far as to produce a special handbook of guidelines for generals 'loaned' a Tiger battalion (Guderian's *'Merkblatt über Tiger-Einsatz'*), though from the comments of the 'Tiger men' this did not always lead to correct appreciation of a very specialized weapon.

A simple explanation for the tanks' unorthodox deployment so close to the front might have been the fear that without the close and visible support of the tanks, the battered and demoralized infantry of *16. Luftwaffenfelddivision* might collapse altogether. In fact, the reason went deeper. There was little love lost between *Generalmajor* Edgar Feuchtinger, commanding *21. Panzerdivision,* and his superior *Generalfeldmarschall* Erwin Rommel, *Oberbefehlshaber West.* While both individuals were favourites of the Nazi party, their career paths differed greatly. Rommel was a hero of the First World War who had again distinguished himself in the 1940 France campaign and gone on to gain almost mythic reputation in North Africa. Feuchtinger was a proud individual with an independent turn of mind who might easily resent being reminded that his own rise through the Nazi party had not been achieved on the battlefield so much as in managing the great Nuremburg *Parteitag* rallies. Visiting the headquarters of *21. Panzerdivision* on 15 July, the field marshal made critical reference to the unpreparedness of Feuchtinger's division on the eve of invasion. In Rommel's view, they had been too far from the landing areas to intervene in a timely fashion. He reminded Feuchtinger that, during the morning of 6 June, *LXXXIV Korps* commander *General der Artillerie* Marcks had personally taken command of *22. Panzerregiment*, in a nail-biting fury and before witnesses blaming Feuchtinger's absence for his division's failure to throw the British back into the sea. It was on Marcks' initiative that the only major armoured counterthrust of the day took place. As it turned out, it was too little too late.

Feuchtinger was not pleased. Nor was he awed by his superior. He rose to his own defence: showing the written orders he had received regarding his deployments and reminding Rommel of how elements of the division had been detached to other parts of the invasion front, not least his entire antitank battalion, which had been sorely mishandled on 6 June. He went further, pointing out that Rommel had neglected the opportunity to review the division's deployments during his visits on 11 and 18 May.[26] As tempers rose, Rommel may have sensed that he was losing the argument. He let slip a comment on Feuchtinger's absence from his unit on the invasion night. (It was notorious that the invasion had caught him by surprise as he spent the night in Paris with a black showgirl.) Well might Feuchtinger respond by pointing out Rommel's own absence in Germany during those critical hours. Both men parted on bad terms. Feuchtinger for his part resolved to carry out *to the letter* his superior's orders for forward deployment of the armour, regardless of the consequences. So it was that both the tank regiment of *21. Panzerdivision* and the attached Tiger battalion found themselves immediately behind the front line. Just where RAF Bomber Command was planning its heaviest concentrations.

Feuchtinger rose to his own defence against Rommel.

In the early morning of 18 July, the dozen Tiger tanks of *Leutnant* von Rosen's *3. Kompanie* of the *503. schwere Panzer-Abteilung* were dispersed under trees at Manneville. Von Rosen himself was asleep under his Tiger tank 311. While three crew members slept in the tank itself, von Rosen and *Unteroffizier* Werkmeister preferred the cool air to be found in their entrenchment dug between the tank's multiple layers of overlapping roadwheels. Von Rosen recalls that, about 06.00 hours, 'I was awakened by the thunderous sounds of aircraft engines. As I crept out from under my tank, I saw the first bomber waves approaching.' A stick of bombs impacted some distance away. The blast wave hit him like a hammer blow and he sensed the mighty Tiger tank shaking with the concussion.

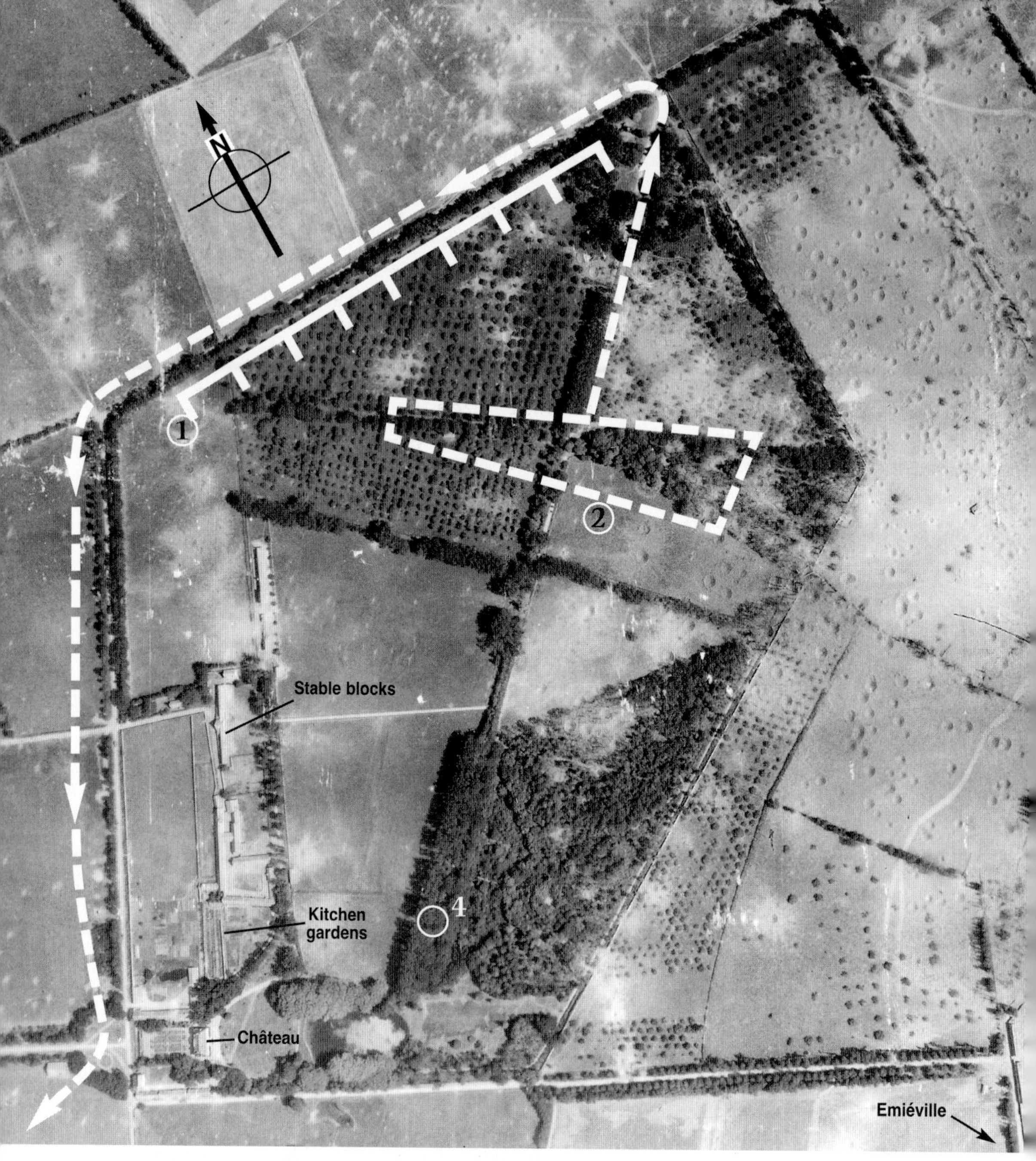

The walled, pentagonal 'haras' (stud farm) of Manneville.
1 = defensive artillery positions (see page 74).
2 = 3.Kompanie Tiger tanks initial position.
3 = route of von Rosen's surviving tanks around the haras.
4 = Tiger 213 (see page 189).

Note the concentration of bombing, affecting only the eastern side of the haras. (Details provided by R. Freiherr von Rosen.)

> *From this moment on, all concentration areas were subject to air bombardment which lasted for two and one half hours without interruption. We were located in the very centre of the bombardment area.*

This was not strictly the case, though he could be forgiven for imagining it to be true. In fact, the walled estate in which von Rosen's company of a dozen operational Tiger tanks straddled the western extremity of Target 'H'. This first stage of the bombing was broadly accurate. Most of the stream of southbound bombers flew an accurate course with few 'shorts' or 'overs'. In consequence much of the haras was spared. Few bombs from the first wave fell on the open, western half of the estate. A single line of bombs marched north to south, one leaving a crater adjacent to the main stable block. A few smaller bombs hit the kitchen gardens between the farm buildings and the château. But though rocked by blast, the château itself was spared (for the time being; more extensive damage would occur as the front lines moved over the estate). Ironically, in seeking the tree-cover camouflage of the wooded eastern half of the estate, von Rosen's company had placed themselves under the fringe of the main target area, the corner of the estate hardest hit by the bombing.

Harder hit still was the ground further east. Beyond the eastern boundary of the Manneville haras the accuracy of the bombing was marked by a five hundred yard wide avenue of devastation, beginning around Sannerville and extending southwards, east of Manneville, over Guillerville (generally referred to in 1944 as 'Cuillerville') and Emiéville. The dust and smoke from the first detonations tended to drift away south west, enabling the bombers to continue for some time before the target area became obscured. Much of that fatal avenue was left densely pockmarked by the big craters. At the northern end of the target area, a swathe of devastation extended through Banneville to Sannerville. Buildings were smashed and the single-track railway uprooted. Even so, the concentration of craters was somewhat less than at the epicentre. Consequently, though the dispersed *1. and 2. Kompanie* Tiger tanks were blasted and their crews concussed, nevertheless most of the heavy tanks escaped outright destruction. Southward, at the heart of Target H, the villages received special attention and were reduced to featureless rubble. Where had stood the stone houses of Guillerville and Emiéville, craters now overlapped one another. Roads were obliterated. And in this area was lost the greater part of 22. *Panzerregiment*.

Accounts vary regarding the total number of *Panzer IV* available to 22. *Panzerregiment* on 18 July: some suggest as few as twenty five, while most favour a figure closer to fifty. On one thing nearly all accounts agree. In the assembly area around Emiéville barely a half-dozen of the regiment's tanks survived the bombardment in sufficiently good state to have their mobility restored.

Felwebel Korflür commanded one of the *Panzer IV* relieved at midnight to return from screening Colombelles. Rejoining the main body of the regiment around 02.00 hours, he and his crew completed their routine maintenance work and by 05.30 were ready to grab some rest.

The devastated village of Sannerville. The Caen-Troarn road can just be made out, and further north traces of the Caen-Troarn railway line.

No sooner had I crawled under my tank, when suddely I heard a buzzing and growling of enemy air formations. On the horizon I could see a great number of oncoming aircraft, and I had second thoughts about my looked-for rest. Wherever they were going, someone was going to catch it! Suddenly, I saw something floating down, and thought of tin-foil strips. ["Stanniolstreifen", the device code named "Window" by the British, designed to blind radar receivers.] The squadrons came ever nearer and the "tin-foil strips" turned out to be bombs.' Korflür and his crew had only seconds to prepare for the inevitable. 'I believe my waking senses have experienced nothing like that first wave. Three of my comrades could not take it any more. They ran away and I saw no more of them. After that first wave everyone was fairly panic stricken. We wanted to get our camouflage sorted out, but quickly became aware that fighter bombers were coming, intent on finishing us off. I passed that next wave under my tank.' Around 09.00 hours, the ordeal ended. 'Emiéville and our formation area looked terrible. Some of the tanks had disappeared. The whole avenue had simply vanished. Crater upon crater made it almost impossible to make out the road. Still, it was possible to get six Panzer IV started up. Towards midday we moved off with these tanks to new positions. Emiéville will never be forgotten by those who survived...

Another survivor had a narrow escape. Hans-Jürgen Eggers was a radioman, taking shelter with seven other men under his own 4. *Kompanie* tank.

Uncounted bombers laid a carpet over the land... the bombs fell ever nearer, the earth trembled... But we were lucky and our tank escaped a direct hit, although it slid sideways. Our way out was buried and we had to dig. This went on for hours, until first one then all the rest of us were freed. I myself lost consciousness for about two hours and could hardly breathe. When I finally came around, I could no longer recognise the surroundings. Where previously an orchard had stood now there was only a lunar landscape... The dead were buried and the wounded crawled to the aid post. Our driver had lost his hearing. Weintz had injured his back. Kampsmeyer suffered a head injury. I got away with convalescing in a rest home in Jort [near Falaise].[27]

The bulk of Oppeln-Bronikowski's 22. *Panzerregiment* had been smashed by the bombing. Even among the few Panzer IV which could be restored to some sort of running order, a number were later found broken down on roadsides a short way from their assembly area. It is far from certain how many – if any – of these actually participated in combat on 18 July.

In the Manneville haras, under their tank, von Rosen and Werkmeister pressed themselves into the earth as shock waves pummelled them.

It was like Hell and I am still astonished that I ever survived it. I was unconscious for a while after a bomb had exploded just in front of my tank, almost burying me alive.

Both Werkmeister and von Rosen were hurled into a corner of their dugout, concussed and covered in earth. Only slowly did consciousness return, and meanwhile the nightmare continued with only occasional, short pauses. Von Rosen recalls that he simply lay under his tank, hands clapped to his ears, biting his blanket. He later estimated that this might have gone on for over four hours; in fact it was less than two. But the ordeal could not be measured in minutes or hours. It was impossible to hear anything. It was as if we were dead. It was so nerve shattering that we couldn't even think... One could say to oneself, will there never be an end to these explosions?[28]

Then,

the air bombardment stopped suddenly, and the following silence was uncanny.

When it was clear that the raid was ended, von Rosen emerged from his shelter, deafened and dishevelled. This part of the park with its well-tended orchards had become a moonscape of overlapping craters, the woodlands now sparse and shattered. The world was grey.

I could see that another tank, about thirty metres away, had received a direct hit which had set it on fire instantly.

This was *Unteroffizier* Westerhausen's Tiger, now a flaming wreck. *Obergefreiter* Bleidiesel had witnessed its destruction:

Finding myself outside my own Tiger 321, twenty five metres from Westerhausen's tank, I had been waiting my opportunity since the beginning of the bombardment to slip into the trench his crew had dug under his tank. Suddenly, the tank received a hit full-on. The crew disappeared.

No trace was found of Westerhausen or his crew.

Clambering over severed tree trunks, von Rosen came to a great crater, and alongside it another tank 'turned upside down by the blast.'

This was *Oberfeldwebel* Sachs' Tiger 313. Two crewmen and two of the maintenance company had disappeared under the overturned behemoth; some time later Sachs and two survivors were dug out alive.

And, when I tell you that the tanks weighed 58 tons and were tossed aside like playing cards, you will see just what a Hell we found ourselves in. It was next to impossible to see anything as so much dust had been thrown up by the explosions. It was like being in a very thick fog.

Discipline took over; von Rosen began an objective survey of the damage.

As far as my company was concerned: two Tigers were completely neutralized; two others were so badly damaged that they couldn't be employed. All the tanks were completely covered with earth, and the gun turrets had been thrown completely out of adjustment by the shock effect. Fifteen men of the company were dead; two further had committed suicide during the bombardments; another had to be sent to a mental hospital

> *for observation. The psychological shock of these terrible exchanges remained with us for a long time.'* [29]

Von Rosen's own tank, Tiger 311, which had sheltered him throughout the bombing, had received damage to the engine compartment and was unserviceable. It was later left to *Panzerfährer* Siehl, the surviving driver of the inverted Tiger 313, to take charge of 311 as a captured Sherman towed it back to the workshops (whereupon Siehl himself finally fainted and was taken to hospital in Paris).

SUMMARY AND ASSESSMENT

The Germans in the sector expected an imminent attack. They did not expect the sheer volume of bombardment that initiated the battle. The shock was numbing: both for those directly under the bombs but also for those viewing from afar, awed by the sheer extravagance with which the enemy loosed explosives across the countryside.

The Allied attack benefited enormously from the bombers' 'kicking in the front door'. The tank squadrons plunging into the narrow armoured 'corridor' made their first move untroubled by serious opposition. But further ahead, the story would be different. Key village strong points had been left largely intact. Emplaced artillery pieces remained mostly operational.

Lastly, it should be noted that two key German strongpoints lay outside the designated bomb zones. Sitting squarely across the armoured divisions' planned advance were two sturdily constructed former priories: le Prieuré, a mile north of Cagny, and le Mesnil Frémentel, a half-mile to Cagny's north west. Each was garrisoned by infantry, and around each was emplaced one of Becker's ten-gun mobile batteries. Each was to cause annoyance and delay to the armoured advance.

Within the walled farm complex of le Mesnil Frémentel lay the headquarters of I. Bataillon, *125. Panzergrenadier-Regiment* , and around the perimeter the underground command bunkers of the battalion's three grenadier companies. At his headquarters outside the north west corner of the wall, the *3. Kompanie* commander *Leutnant* Gerhardt Bandomir was just starting his breakfast when the waves of bombers appeared.

> *Our first thought was that they were on their way to bomb the cities of Germany, which depressed us. But suddenly the first wave of aircraft loosed their bombs, then the second. They fell on the Emiéville sector, over to the east… Then the gates of Hell opened up!*

Like so many others that morning, Bandomir lost track of time. Sitting in the dugout with his staff, unable to do anything but await the inevitable, he found it hard to distinguish the distant bombing from the subsequent artillery barrage.

> *Thanks to our deep and solid entrenchments, well covered, the loss of life was relatively slight. But as a demonstration of enemy air supremacy it showed up our own weakness. The psychological impact of the bombardment was severe.*

The farm buildings and the well-constructed bunkers stood the test. 'Every square metre of ground in our sector was dug-over. My bunker was hit two or three times but it held out.' Bandomir had survived bombardments in the harsh combat of the Russian front. Nevertheless, 'I came later to the conclusion that a new form of warfare was born this 18 July: a first glimpse of the nuclear age.'[30]

References

1) 'Against Odds', Dominick Graham, 1999, ISBN 0-333-66859-6, p 133
(2) General Return of the Strength of the British Army for the quarter ending 30th September 1944, AG Stats: W073/162; unpublished John Robert Peaty thesis, 'The British Manpower Crisis, 1944', King's College, University of London, p 333
(3) 'Montgomery and "Colossal Cracks" The 21st Army Group in Northwest Europe', Stephen Ashley Hart, 2000, ISBN 0-275-96162-1, p 98 & 120
(4) 'Hill 112: Cornerstone of the Normandy Campaign', Major J J How, 1984, ISBN 0-7183-0540-X, p 138; 'Comrades to the End', Otto Weidinger, 1998, ISBN 0-7643-0593-X, p 308
(5) '9. SS-Panzer-Division', H Fürbringer, 1984, ISBN 2-902171-17-X, p 227-229
(6) French, p 118
(7) Ellis, 'Welsh Guards', p 175
(8) Sources do not agree on the total numbers of bombers engaged in the three waves. Various accounts give between 942 and 1056 Bomber Command aircraft in the first wave. Data included in Staff College documentation and battlefield tours from 1947 into the 1990s contain obvious errors and inaccuracies. Moreover, the precise number of aircraft which missed targets or aborted bombing altogether due to visibility can only be guessed at. Numbers of aircraft used herein generally accord with the most authoritative study of recent years: 'Air Power at the Battlefront', Ian Gooderson, 1998, ISBN 0-7146-4211-8
(9) 'Victory in the West' vol 1, L F Ellis, 1962, ISBN 0-89839-193-8, p 339
(10) Some histories mislead over the cratering of Cagny. See Appendix 8 for this and other details of the bombing.
(11) Flight Lieutenant Linacre, quoted in 'Caen: Anvil of Victory', A McKee 1964, p 226.
(12) *Leutnant* Hans Höller, quoted in McKee, p 280
(13) Bishop, 23rd Hussars, p 70
(14) 'Operations of Eighth Corps', G S Jackson, 1948, p 100
(15) 'Taurus Pursuant: A History of 11th Armoured Division', E W I Palamountain, 1945, p 23
(16) Close, p 117
(17) A particularly good study of the Independent Air Force is 'First of the Many', Alan Morris, 1968.
(18) 'Beneath the City Streets', P Laurie, 1970, ISBN 0 7139 0114 4, chapter IV. Note that secondary effects of bombing such as 'firestorms' did under certain circumstances greatly increase the death rate. But even with the advent of nuclear weapons, explosive blast remains a fairly inefficient killer of human beings, especially those with access to shelters. Far more efficient as incapacitants of large numbers of people are modern chemical and biological agents: nerve gases, bacteria, and especially viruses.
(19) Kortenhaus diary, p 129
(20) Kortenhaus diary, p 136
(21) Höller, quoted in McKee, p 283
(22) 'Heavy and Medium Bombers in the Tactical Close Air Support Role', Ian Gooderson, Journal of Strategic Studies, vol 15 no 3, 1992, p 392.
(23) An authoritative source is 'Machine Guns of World War 1', Robert Bruce, 1997, ISBN 1 85915 078 0, see also Graham, p 36-37
(24) 'The Combat History of Schwere Panzer-Abteilung 503', ed A Rubbel, 2000, ISBN 0-921991-55-X, p 19
(25) Von Rosen, interview at Staff College, Camberley, 1979
(26) Perrigault, p 354
(27) This and other passages quoted in Kortenhaus diary
(28) Von Rosen, interview at Staff College, Camberley, 1979
(29) Von Rosen, interview at Staff College, Camberley, 1979
(30) Kortenhaus diary

Chapter 4

18 JULY MORNING: THE BRITISH TANK RUN

As German forces suffered the awesome might of the strategic bombers, some of the British forces waiting poised to attack enjoyed a brief respite.

MOVING OUT

Not in their densely packed holding areas, nor as they squeezed along the paths through the minefields, did the leading vehicles of 11th Armoured Division resemble a combat formation. Even on the far side of the minefields, the vehicles of the regimental group still had to squeeze into their tightly packed Forming Up Place: a shallow rectangle of open ground, two thousand yards wide and three hundred deep. Here the 3rd Royal Tanks regimental group awaited the moment to lead the offensive.

The dense park of vehicles seemed to offer a tempting target, but with the dawn came the aerial bombardment. The suppressive effect of the bombing was total. Not an enemy shell fell on the FUP. More serious as it turned out was the effect of the close proximity of so many armoured vehicles on the performance of the radios. It was asking rather a lot of the sensitive equipment of 1944 with its delicate components to expect it to operate at all within an armoured box, alongside throbbing engines, and subjected to violent shocks transmitted through metal tracks and hard

Some tank crewmen finished a smoke as they watched the effects of the air attack.

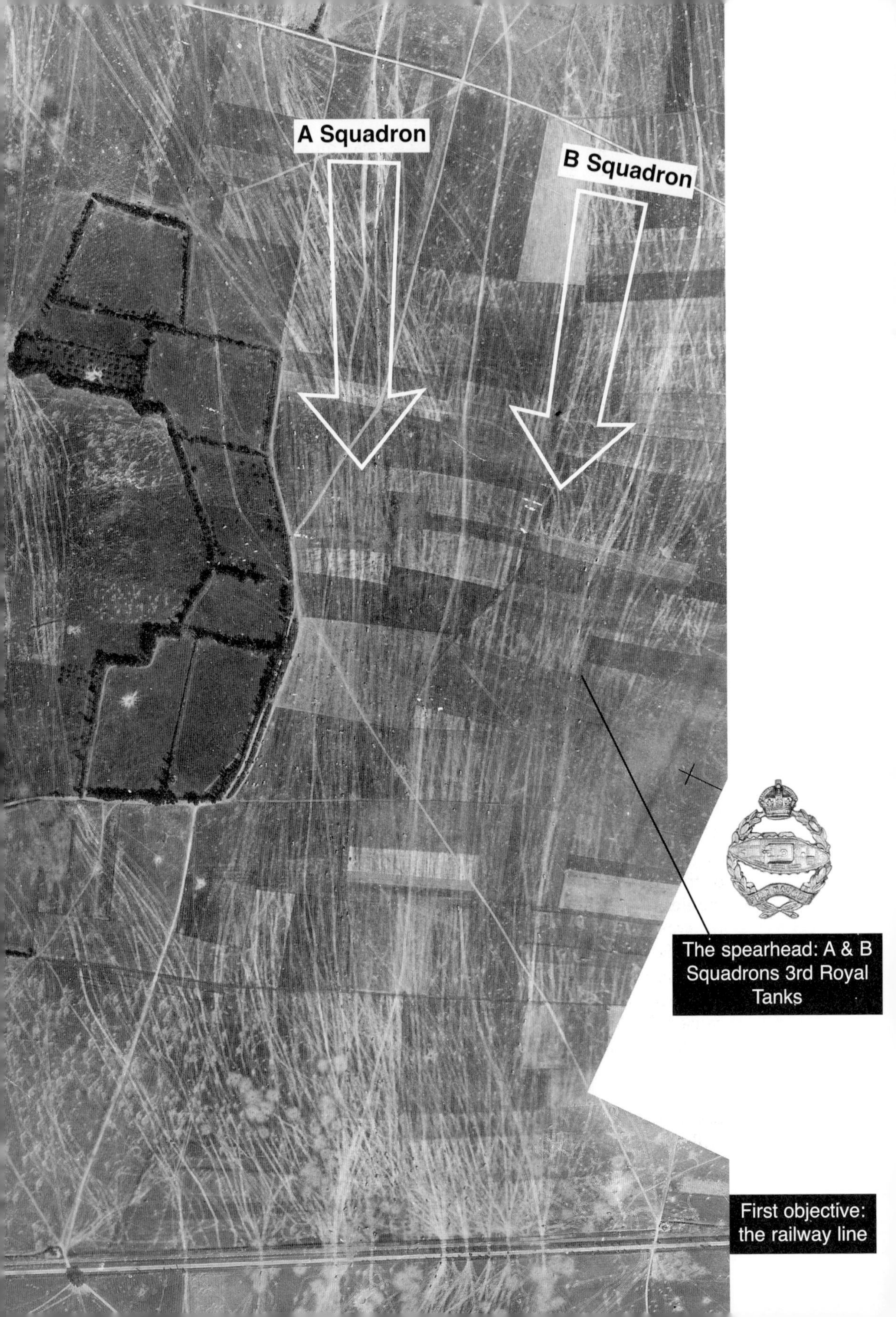

The spearhead: A & B Squadrons 3rd Royal Tanks

First objective: the railway line

suspension. Operators took care to 'net' (or fine tune) their sets to squadron frequencies at the last possible moment before going into action, and tank commanders dreaded receiving a 'netting call' from the CO's wireless operator whilst engaged in combat. Today the netting proved particularly difficult, and some consequent communications problems were experienced as the morning progressed. Meanwhile, other crew members took the opportunity of a grandstand view of the bombing while enjoying a last cigarette. (Officially smoking was banned within the tanks; some units or individual commanders turned a blind eye to this while in action.) The day was going to be warm. Even surrounded by a growing cloud of exhaust fumes, the 'open air' was preferable to the atmosphere inside a tank.

H Hour approached and crews slid into their vehicles. At 07.45 hours, the artillery commenced a rolling barrage directly ahead. Eight field regiments (192 guns) began to beat a two thousand yard width ahead of the Start Line. Many of the field guns had been in action for weeks, firing many thousands of rounds. Before major actions, large quantities of shells were typically dumped at gun positions, and despite attempts to 'segregate' production batches, ammunition from different sources was inevitably mixed up. What is more, as the official British artillery historian recognized, 'Even if the ammunition was all the same, guns were apt to develop considerable differences in wear during periods of prolonged activity.'[1] By July, the rifling of some of the 25 pounder field guns was already so worn that shells fitted loosely into the breech. Barrels wobbled loosely in their mounts due to worn trunnions. One 13th RHA officer recalls seeing a single gun's shells fall 80 yards apart on the same laying. In the absence of spare parts and the time for calibration of muzzle velocities of individual guns, the net result was variation in accuracy. Some shells fell short. And some tank crewmen, finishing a cigarette or lingering to watch the view, were too slow getting behind armour. 3rd RTR's A Squadron lost Lieutenant Philip Pells, commander of 3 Troop. Major Close quickly ordered Sergeant Freddie Dale to assume command of the troop, with command of Pells' Sherman assumed by its corporal wireless operator. On the right of the squadron, Lieutenant Osbaldeston too was killed and had to be replaced as troop commander. Further back the C Squadron commander Major Peter Burr, a desert veteran awaiting promotion to Brigade Major, had his head blown off. There was time only for hasty command reassignments, and considerable disruption was caused. By the time the tanks and accompanying carriers were off and moving, the artillery barrage had already moved on some distance. It was an inauspicious start.

BATTLE FORMATION

Hitherto, the division's tank fighting in Normandy had largely taken place in very close country. In a landscape where impenetrable hedgerows lined small fields, where stone walls enclosed dense orchards

The dense Normandy countryside restricted mobility.

of low-hanging trees, interspersed with sturdy stone buildings, the desert veterans of the Royal Tanks found themselves having to learn new tactics as quickly as the inexperienced tank crews of the Yeomanry and the Hussars. As German tankers in Normandy had already realised, the ground rarely permitted the effective deployment of tanks in groups of more than two or three: Troop (or '*Zug*') strength. Only briefly, on the rolling, open country between Hills 112 and 113, had there been much opportunity for the British tanks to deploy in whole squadrons. And even there, Montgomery had made the decision to withdraw the tank regiments of 11th Armoured from the open battleground before the armoured assault of *II. SS-Panzer Korps* had fully developed.

This was all unexpected. 11th Armoured Division's pre-invasion training *'courtesy of Roberts, its new GOC, embraced tactics that corresponded to best practice in North Africa.'*[2] After his division's (most commendable) first battle, Pip Roberts became somewhat depressed about the outlook for the armour in this new theatre, commenting to a colleague *'I fear that the outlook for armoured divisions doesn't look too good.'*[3] As the German tank forces had also begun to discover, the dense terrain simply did not lend itself to manoeuvres of large tank formations. But perhaps GOODWOOD might signal a return from the bocage fighting to what had been foreseen.

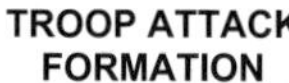

Having negotiated the tortuous route around the beachhead and across the waterways, the armour was looking forward to open country ahead. For 3rd RTR open country meant 'good tank country', where the veterans of the regiment hoped to enjoy the benefits of room to manoeuvre.

Now clear of the minefield lanes, the regiment 'shook out' into troops and squadrons, and its battle formation began at last to take shape. The plan for the attack was reminiscent of the open desert. The regimental group would form an armoured 'box', with tanks on its outer faces and other units within. The tanks led. The first wave comprised A Squadron on the right and B to their left. The two nineteen-tank squadrons moved each with two troops 'up' and two following. Each troop adopted an arrowhead of three Sherman Vs about thirty yards apart and the troop Firefly tucked in a similar distance behind. In the centre of each four-troop square was the squadron headquarters with its three tanks, the squadron commander attempting to regulate the speed and maintain the formation of his unit.

As close as possible behind followed the second wave of the regimental group. Colonel Silvertop's Headquarters Squadron was accompanied by the infantry and artillery commanders: Major Noel Bell of G Company, 8th RB; and Major Bill Smyth-Osborne of H Battery, 13th RHA. Both maintained position alongside the colonel's tank, while Silvertop himself concentrated on keeping in contact with the two tank squadrons ahead. Also with this wave advanced the flails, the AVREs, the carrier platoon of 8th RB, and the regimental reconnaissance and antiaircraft troops.

The third wave comprised the remainder of the task force. Leading the self-propelled artillery and the half-tracks

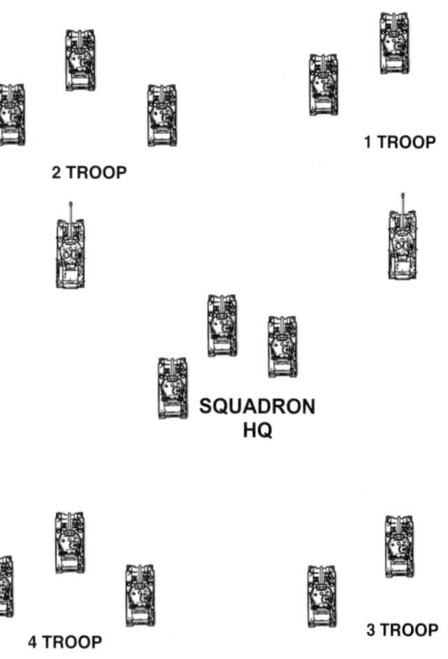

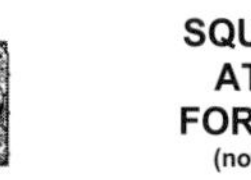

of the motor infantry were the tanks of C Squadron. As soon as they were clear of the minefields the tanks sprinted forward, two troops to each side of the box, to screen the flanks of the mobile formation. Altogether, the reinforced regimental group comprised upwards of 140 assorted vehicles, most of them armoured, moving on a front which quickly narrowed from two thousand metres to barely a kilometre.

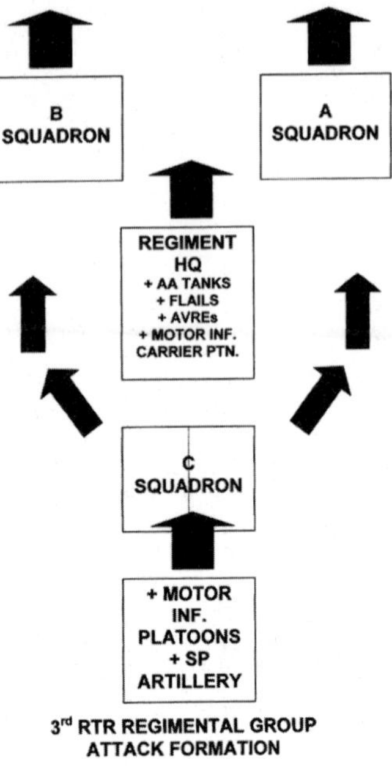

3rd RTR REGIMENTAL GROUP ATTACK FORMATION

Further back, eight more armoured regiments waited their turn, each accompanied by similar numbers of vehicles, edging forward in a traffic jam which reached back far to the west of the Orne bridges. And these were not the only traffic jostling for places in the advance. Intermingled with the armoured regiments and their accompanying artillery and motor infantry were great numbers of specialist vehicles: the brigade headquarters, the divisional 'Tac' headquarters, divisional assets including sappers, signallers, and of course medical personnel. Each division had its armoured car regiment, with troops of cars anxious to struggle through the tight mass of traffic towards the front, there to probe for gaps through which to penetrate and fan out behind enemy lines. And of course, each of the three armoured divisions had also its entire brigade of lorried infantry and a (towed) Field Regiment, RA. Though these were not involved in the initial planned breakthrough, each divisional commander was understandably keen to bring them up as soon as practical to enable his division to function as a whole unit.

INTO THE CORRIDOR

After hasty attempts to sort out the confusion caused by short artillery rounds, the leading tanks rolled forward, hoping to catch up with the barrage which had already begun to move south. Bill Close later confessed, '*We had orders to try and remain one hundred yards behind* [the barrage] *but we set off in some disorder.*' If the symmetry of the planned 'regimental box' was not achieved, there were few to witness the fact. The earlier bombing had raised a murky pall over the entire landscape into which the tanks were plunging, and the advancing artillery barrage raised a curtain of smoke and dust in the immediate vicinity. It was all the two squadron commanders could do to make out the tanks closest to their own. '*We roared on through boiling clouds of dirt and fumes, thirty eight Shermans doing their best to keep up with the rolling curtain of fire. I could see tanks either side of me slowly picking their way through the ever increasing number of bigger and bigger bomb craters. I only hoped that B Squadron on my left was keeping up… I kept willing us on.*' Though the bombing here had avoided 'cratering', the loose earth turned by the later fragmentation

Taken just before 12.15 hours, this photograph of the armoured corridor shows the traffic jams forming around the railway as German fire begins from the east.

The view west from Lirose towards Cuverville: the armoured corridor barely a kilometre across.

bombs and the immediately preceding artillery barrage were trial enough. On a clear day, these obstacles would have been easily surmounted. But with a brown fog limiting visibility and fumes from the shells lingering in the hollows, it required constant vigilance to avoid hitting an unseen hole at the wrong angle and toppling the tank. Drivers changed down through the gears to retain control as tracks thrashed dry, powdery soil.

It is normal in any battle for order to descend into confusion. This time

The tank killer silenced: an abandoned Pak 40.

German casualties: slit trenches became graves.

confusion had arrived somewhat earlier than expected. Fortunately for tank commanders now preoccupied with uneven terrain and low visibility, their difficulties were a small price to pay for the near-total suppression of nearby enemies. For the time being, there was no serious opposition to deal with. A thousand yards beyond the Start Line, there were few defenders still active in the path of the advance. The guns positioned to cover this ground were in Cuverville (now substantially rubbled) and Touffréville (spared by the bombing, but so screened by shellfire that any guns still manned lacked a line of sight into the smoke). The battery of mobile antitank guns sited in the area, open topped and lightly armoured, was neutralized, either in their emplacements or as they attempted hurriedly to displace southwards. Of towed antitank guns, the tanks encountered only a handful in this first stage of the battle, three of which were later confirmed to have been destroyed by tank shells rather than bombs. But the bombardment had worked. Most of the guns were uncrewed, the gunners shocked into insensibility and taking refuge in shelters.

Tank crews in combat are not well placed to take infantry prisoners. The few Germans appearing out of the mist in front of the tanks were in no mood for resistance, and were briskly waved to the rear by tank commanders in their turrets. Some Germans were observed to be incapable even of walking in a straight line; more than half of these prisoners remained stone deaf for the rest of the day. Less fortunate were the many, unable or unwilling to leave their trenches, who were despatched by grenades dropped from the passing vehicles. Their slit trenches became their graves, filled-in by the following British infantry. Lieutenant Robin Lemon, then 2ic in 3rd RTR's Reconnaissance Troop, shot down an enemy soldier who misguidedly approached his Stuart tank clutching a grenade. So, the confusion caused to the advancing force was outweighed by the distress inflicted on the defenders. Much later and with the benefit of hindsight, tank crews interviewed by Operations Research were unanimous in their approval of the overall effect of the bombing in this first stage of the tank run.

The artillery barrage continued relentlessly, advancing at a steady five miles per hour, drawing still further away from the tanks. Consequently, the tanks found their visibility somewhat improved as some of the dust had time to settle. Struggling to keep up the pace, the squadron commanders were able to tidy their formations. Each squadron now reduced its frontage to about six hundred yards as the corridor narrowed between Démouville and Sannerville. As A Squadron skirted the woods north west of Démouville, a few of the right-flank tanks could discern enemy movement and even some firing. Without stopping, commanders turned their turrets and the tank gunners 'brassed up' the treeline with their co-axial 0.30 calibre Browning machine guns.

THE FIRST RAILWAY

Pressing on still further south, the leading elements reached the first major landmark: a single track railway between Caen and Troarn. Even this early in the battle, precise timings begin to present problems. Still, it seems that the leading elements of 3rd RTR reached the railway some time after 08.30 hours and soon after, as the rest of the regiment arrived, the first tanks began to cross. An advance of two miles from the Start Line had already taken the best part of an hour.

From this point, the 3rd RTR war diary becomes decidedly unreliable. Following an anomalous and inaccurate 08.00 hours entry *'LE MESNIL FREMENTEL reported clear'* (by whom, one wonders, since no Allied forces were yet anywhere near the place), five further entries take us to

The Caen-Troarn single-track railway. The level crossing at Lirose was just south-east of spot height '21'. The present-day photograph on page 74 was taken from spot 21, facing west, on 18 July 2005.

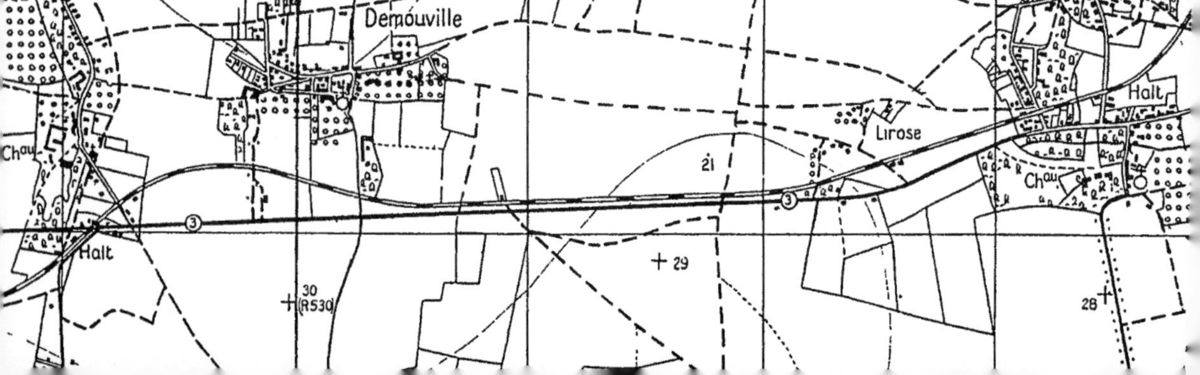

Instructions regarding War Diaries and Intelligence Summaries are contained in F.S. Regs., Vol. I. and the Staff Manual respectively. Title pages will be prepared in manuscript.

Month and Year July 1944

WAR DIARY
or
INTELLIGENCE SUMMARY
(Erase heading not required).

Army Form C. 211

Unit 3 R Tks.

Commanding Officer Lt Col D.A.H. Silvertop, M.C.

Place	Date	Hour	Summary of Events and Information	References to Appendices.
			after unit has left barrage.	
		1500	H Bty joins Regt Gp.	
		2130	G Coy joins Regt Gp.	
945756	17	0100	Unit leave area. Line ahead.	
		0415	RHQ reaches new area 059758. Leaguer in wood. Heavily camouflaged.	
		0630	Complete Regt Gp arrives in new area.	
059758		1500	26 Assault Sqn RE joins Regt Gp.	
		1600	Orders Gp. Fuller details Op GOODWOOD. Orders for march to conc area 1173 issued. Ready to move 2400 hrs. A Sqn 22 DG joining Regt Gp 0545 hrs 18 Jul. in conc area.	
		1900	Orders Gp. Orders given. Ready to move 2400 hrs.	
059758	18	0100	Moved to conc area.	
		0230	Arrived in conc area 122746.	
		0430	Reveille.	
		0500	Orders Gp. A Sqn 22 DG joined Regt Gp.	
		0530	Message from Bde by LO. H Hour - 0745 hrs.	
		0610	Regt Gp moved out of conc area to forming up area by 2 routes.	
		0700	Forming up area reached - 103703 - 120703 - 120700 - 103700.	
		0745	H hr. Unit advances due SOUTH behind 25 pr barrage. Owing to speed of barrage and nature of country tks commenced falling behind barrage line of barrage.	
		0800	LE MESNIL FREMENTEL reported clear.	
		0805	Reached MATILDA. Experienced difficulty in crossing rly line due to unexpected depth of cutting. Resulted in temporary loss of barrage.	
		0810	Barrage lifted. Opposition slight. Small number of inf in platoon posns.	
		0830	GRENTHEVILL byepassed on WEST side.	
		0930	Crossed rly line at 074624.	
		1000	Reached 070623. Engaged enemy a tk guns and tks ib area HUBERT FOLIE - 072618.	
		1400	Posn at 070623 covered by enemy A tk guns and tks. Withdrawn to 072628.	
		1500	2 NY took up posn on the right in area 070628.	

3043 - PMED - 500,000 - 4.42

10.00 after which we find a four hour gap before entries resume at 14.00. Given the important events occurring during this precise period, it is likely (and pardonable) that the 18 July diary (at least up to 14.00 hours) is based on vague memories rather than precisely noted times. Fortunately, it is known that the first stage of the artillery barrage was due to end 300 yards beyond (i.e., south of) the railway line not before 08.15 hours (and possibly later, due to time allowed for optional pauses on pre-determined lines). Since the 3rd RTR advance had fallen well behind the barrage, the war diary's claim that the railway was reached at 08.05 and the barrage lifted at 08.10 can confidently be set aside. Roscoe Harvey's 29th Brigade Tac HQ was following close behind the 3rd RTR group, and may not have known exactly when the first tanks reached the railway. Nevertheless the 29th Brigade war diary has the more reasonable claim that by 08.37 some elements of 3rd RTR had reached the railway and were beginning to cross. The vital point is that the bulk of the regimental group took an hour to get this far forward.

The first railway was assumed in the GOODWOOD plan to be no more than a waypoint. 11th Armoured Division's APIS (Aerial Photographic Interpretation Section) had declared the single-track line to be an insignificant obstacle to vehicles. It was not.[4] The rail line that lay squarely across the line of advance ran along an embankment raised between one and two metres above the surrounding fields, with occasional drainage

The level crossing at Lirose: today no longer defended.

ditches alongside. A level crossing lay just east of the tanks' path, taking a dirt road across the rails to join the main Caen to Troarn highway running parallel to (and south of) the railway. Another crossing was to be found a kilometre to the west. Most of the Sherman tanks could clamber across the embankment, though even some of these broke their tracks when they hit the rails awkwardly. For the carriers and the half-tracks, the embankment was a serious hindrance. For wheeled vehicles it would be impassable, likewise for the Sherman flails with their cumbersome apparatus. The whole advance was delayed while the accompanying 8th Rifle Brigade carriers and half-tracks queued around the few crossing places. Matters were only made worse as wheeled vehicles came up and milled around seeking level crossings. Squadron commanders passed the word back for the AVREs to come up. These were Churchill tanks with six-man Royal Engineer crews. As well as carrying a variety of demolition charges (to be emplaced outside the tank by sixth crew member, the Demolitions NCO, who when in the tank sat on an ammunition box behind the driver), their main armament was a petard mortar hurling a massive 'Flying Dustbin' bomb containing twenty three pounds of plastic explosive. Designed to breach concrete obstacles, these set about blasting passages through the railway embankment. Congestion was eased somewhat, until later-arriving teams of sappers could bulldoze a half-dozen earth ramps over the metal tracks and create special crossings for wheeled vehicles between the existing level crossings.

Adding to the congestion on the north side of the railway line was Roscoe Harvey's 29th Brigade TAC HQ, following close on the heels of the 3rd RTR group. His brigade war diary reflected his upbeat mood, claiming that 08.00 hours found '*3 R Tks keeping up as close to the barrage as possible. The adv went according to plan.*' Even the railway, reached at 08.37 hours, '*proves not to be a great obstacle and several crossings are quickly found*'. Nevertheless, even the irrepressible brigadier had to admit that the plan was not quite being followed. At 08.45, following a pause extended by the divisional CRA, with the barrage recommenced and now angling off to the south west, the diary confides, '*Barrage moves fwd again on next phase. 3 R Tks not all able to keep up with it, but try and catch it up.*'

ROYAL TANKS PAST LE MESNIL

The hope of 3rd RTR catching up the barrage was premature. Although the map appeared to indicate open country, just five hundred metres beyond the railway line the advancing tanks encountered a significant terrain feature. A 1,500 metre length of unbroken, dense hedgerow lay across their path. With no realistic route around the new obstacle, the tanks had to select points at which the earth banks and foliage were low and thin enough for a passage to be attempted. A half-dozen such gaps were forced, including one opening which, after a few tanks had passed through, was beaten down sufficiently for half-tracks and wheeled vehicles to follow.

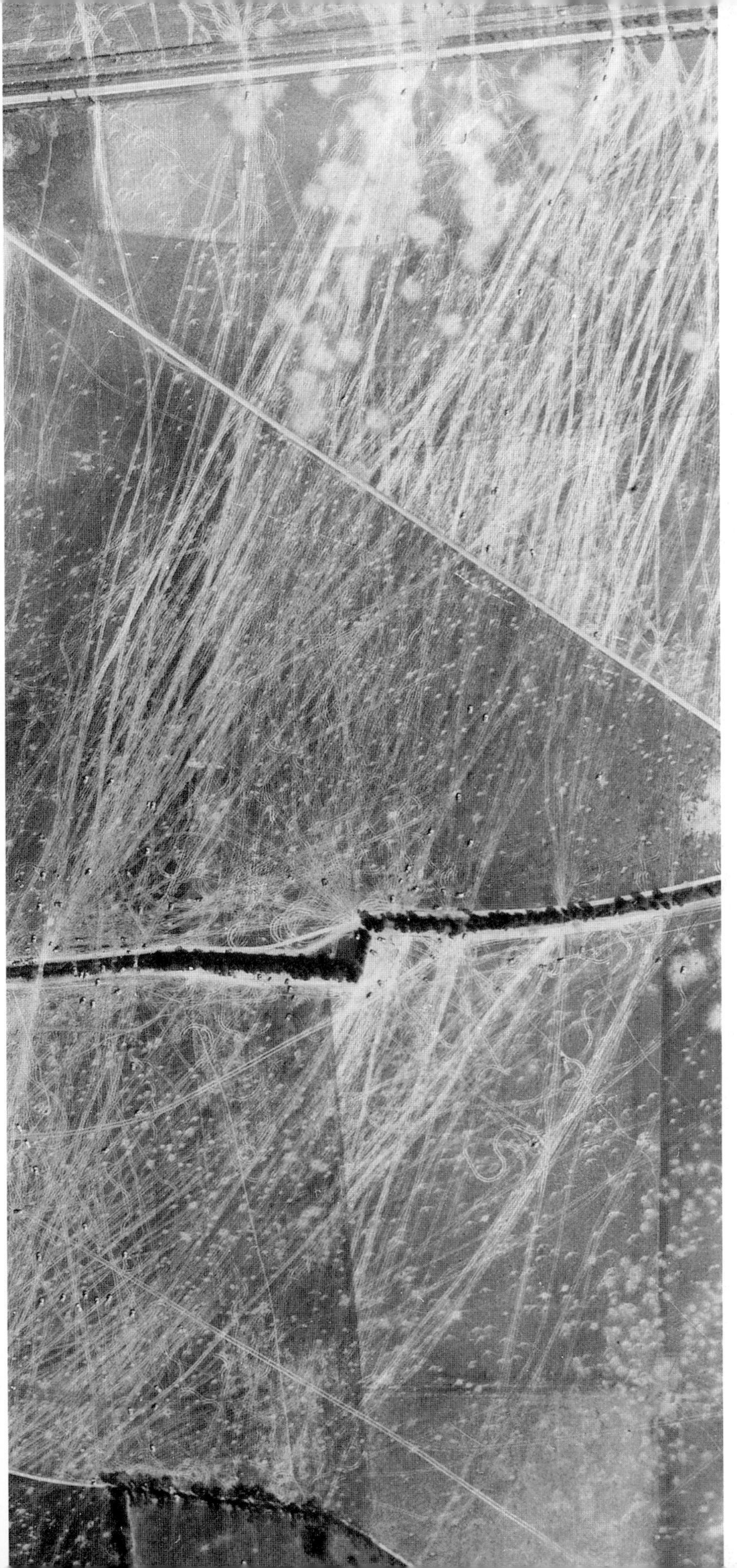

South of the first railway: the hedgerow at la Haye de Saules.

Taken about 11.50 hours, over 190 British vehicles are identifiable in this image including over 75 tanks.

Opposite: Tanks shelter briefly behind the second line of hedges before making their run around the west side of Mesnil Frémentel. Taken about 12.05 hours, this photograph includes Pip Roberts' Tac HQ of three command tanks and the four Shermans of the protection troop.

The Autoroute de Normandie today replaces the hedgerow behind which British tanks sheltered.

Nowadays, la Haie de Saules is one of the few areas of the GOODWOOD battlefield whose original terrain has largely vanished. The reason is the A13 'Autoroute de Normandie'. Nearly all the east-west stretch of bocage has been submerged under a four-lane highway. One small consolation is the bridge now carrying the D226 out of Démouville over the Autoroute, whose elevation offers a vista from Manneville and le Prieuré in the distant east around to le Mesnil Frémentel to the south. Between the bridge and the complex of le Mesnil can be seen the outline of further 1944 hedgerows. And in particular there survives almost intact a six hundred metre length of bocage just north of le Mesnil which provided 3rd RTR with solid cover until they were within very close range of its defenders.

At 09.20 hours, the barrage that had so far blazed a trail for the tanks' advance came to its end, some distance ahead of the leading tank squadrons. For the time being, 3rd RTR would have to depend for fire support on their attached battery of eight self-propelled guns. As yet, the opposition remained slight. For 3rd RTR, arriving at the second hedgerow about 09.30 hours, this further obstacle seemed an unwelcome hindrance. Unbeknown to them, it was to prove a blessing. Confronting the stout

N
3rd R.T.R. 'running the gauntlet' past le Mesnil Frémentel

le Mesnil
Frémentel

hedgerow, its branches interwoven with centuries of growth and its roots sunk deep into the high earth bank, the first tanks probed for a possible way through. Commanders in their high turrets gaining a line of sight through the foliage were able to make out the walled priory complex of le Mesnil Frémentel with its surrounding orchards, a mere five hundred yards ahead. The place was evidently enemy-held, as was confirmed when various weapons opened up on the advancing tanks. The A Squadron commander recalled,

I stopped and looked through my glasses as we got closer to the village. I could see considerable activity among the walls and the houses, and it was pretty obvious that the village was strongly occupied. I wanted to stop and use my squadron properly and put down a shoot but I was being told by my CO in no uncertain terms to get on, get moving, and go to the west of the village.[5]

Hitherto in Normandy, many a British offensive had ground to a halt as leading units paused to deal with a thin German defensive screen. Colonel Silvertop and his brigadier were both conscious of the need to press ahead, bypassing pockets of resistance which the follow-up infantry could deal with. Harvey was becoming dissatisfied with the pace of his armoured brigade's initial advance, but at least the regiments had kept moving. The plan assumed that resistance would have been crushed by the preparatory bombardment. Sure enough, there had so far been little or no serious opposition from the natural strongpoints the tanks had bypassed. A racing man, Harvey was still determined that his tanks' role in GOODWOOD should be a gallop through the enemy lines. At the sharp end, two miles ahead of Harvey's Tac HQ, Major Close realised that the opposition was stiffening. And this was not the way he had been trained to deal with defended villages.

I was somewhat reluctant to present the flanks of my tanks to an obviously well-defended village, but gave orders to my troops to fire on the move as we passed to the west.[6]

The combination of these orders and the fire emanating from the walls and orchards of le Mesnil caused the tanks to edge westward along the thick hedgerow. Charging in ones and twos through thinner parts of the obstacle, the tanks forced two major breeches, which were progressively widened and flattened as three squadrons of tanks took their turn. There were casualties. One A Squadron Sherman to Close's left rolled to a halt and began belching dark smoke. Next, two tanks of B Squadron were hit. Dark shapes could be seen rolling out of their crippled mounts, tanks and crewmen alike setting the uncut grain on fire. The tanks fired as they moved across the face of their tormentors. Now, true to their role, some of the regimental reconnaissance troop had pushed their way forward to join the leading squadrons. Two of these lightly armoured Stuart tanks were promptly hit and knocked out.

The Shermans charged on, now due south, ever closer to the wall of le Mesnil. They presented their vulnerable flanks; barely an inch and a half of armour stood between the enemy and their fuel tanks and ammunition racks; turrets turned to nine o'clock spraying bullets and firing High Explosive rounds in the direction of gunflashes amongst the buildings and trees. Even at this range, fire from the moving tanks could hardly be accurate.[7] But even inaccurate fire at close range was enough to suppress most German gunners and put others off their aim. And even a tank as tall as a Sherman was a difficult target when racing obliquely across the front of a gun at 200 metres range or less. More important, most of the defenders of le Mesnil Frémentel were ill-equipped to meet this threat. As close as any of the garrison to the advancing enemy was *Leutnant* Gerhardt Bandomir, in his command dugout on the outside north-west corner of the priory wall. His experiences on the Russian front had conditioned him to emerge from cover as soon as possible after an attacking barrage lifted, in order to repel the waves of infantry which invariably followed. Today, however, he emerged to find at first… nothing. Only some time after the barrage, as defenders found time to congratulate themselves on their survival, did a mass of tanks appear in the north, directly to the front of the company position. 'To our great surprise, they were not accompanied by infantry. We were helpless with just our rifles and our machine guns.'

Whether the defenders of le Mesnil Frémentel had any surviving antitank guns at this moment is not known. The infantry of course had their *Panzerfäuste*, though it would have taken a brave man to emerge into the open to engage enemy tanks moving at speed with such a close-range weapon. And as far as Bandomir could tell, there were no survivors of his unit in the fields in front of his company position. The main antitank defence around le Mesnil was mobile, and by the time the main body of the 3rd RTR group erupted onto the scene, passing between 09.30 and 10.00 hours, the surviving self propelled guns had already moved out.[8] As will be seen, the fourth battery of Major Becker's mobile battalion had left its carefully camouflaged positions on the eastern flank of le Mesnil, initially falling back towards alternative positions to the east. From that direction, it is most likely that this battery accounted for the 3rd RTR tanks lost on the approach to le Mesnil. It was the good fortune of the leading 3rd RTR tanks that they had first edged westward before crossing the hedgerow, then charged rapidly across the north-western face of the priory complex. By so doing, they minimized the time they would be exposed to fire from a kilometre to the east. Once past le Mesnil, the south-westbound tanks descended a slope and crossed a hedge which effectively put them into dead ground, out of sight from le Mesnil or Cagny. Even so, standing in his turret in the comparative calm, Bill Close noted spent shells still coming from that direction.

> *As I crossed over that fairly open country, there was some AP shot, 88 millimetre, coming from the areas of Cagny and le Prieuré, and it was quite extraordinary: they were 'overs' and had no effect on my tanks; and as they came across the top of the corn you could actually see them coming as they left a wake rather like the wake of a torpedo…*[9]

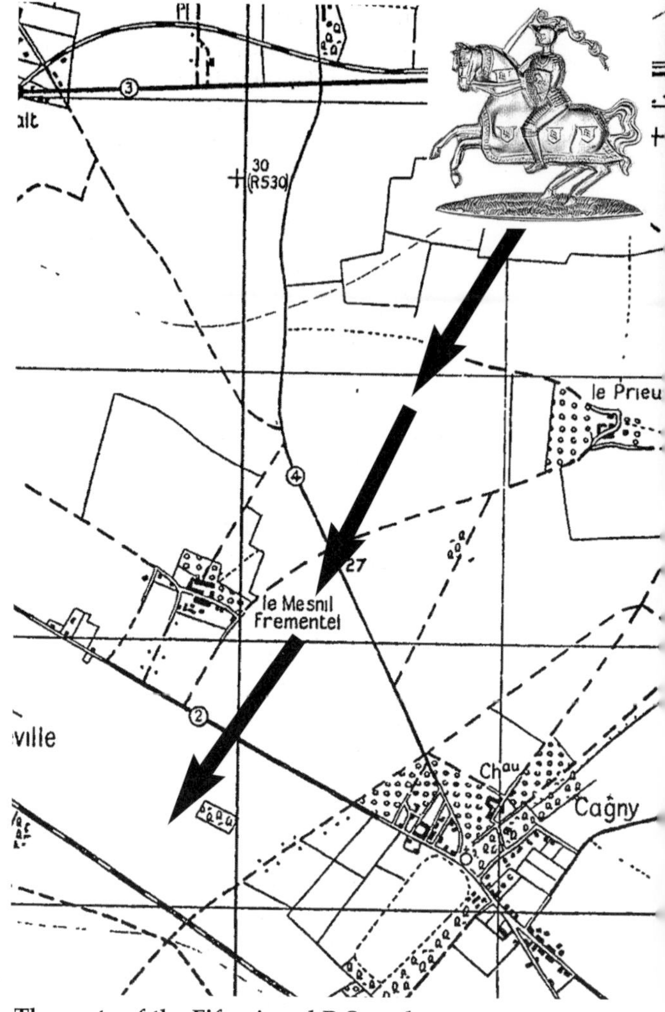

The route of the Fifes A and B Squadrons.

In the relative quiet, at the forefront of the 3rd RTR advance, Bill Close had moments to take stock. His own squadron's losses had so far been slight: since leaving the Start Line, only one tank lost. Descending a gentle slope from le Mesnil Frémentel south west towards the main Caen to Paris highway and parallel rail line, his squadron found itself in a wasteland of splintered trees and dead cows, the aftermath of the American fragmentation bombing. On the move, with occasional hold-ups, for two hours, his squadron had now pushed forward four miles, with nothing on the open flanks of the advance save enemy-held villages and farms, in various stages of suppression. According to the briefing, this should have taken them clean through the German lines. On the contrary, Close realised, the German defences were deeper than predicted. And they were waking up. As the armoured formation roared on south, over the main road and the second railway towards the next objective of Grentheville, enemy movement could be seen in the treelines ahead. The fight was far from over.

FORWARD THE FIFE AND FORFAR

Having set 3rd RTR again on the move from the first railway crossing, Harvey then turned his attention to the second regimental group coming down the corridor: the 2nd Fife and Forfar Yeomanry. So far, the Fife and Forfar were having an uncomfortable day. Having crossed the waterways after 3rd RTR, they had arrived in their final concentration area only at 04.00 hours. There was little chance to rest before reveille. Then came the din of the aerial bombardment, and soon after the call to move out. The regiment had more difficulty than the Royal Tanks negotiating the paths through the minefields, as did every successive tank regiment that day with competition for the available road space increasing. Only four paths were allowed them. Also inconveniencing the regiment was an unfortunate accident with their water supply. Something putrid had unaccountably got into the regimental water bowser, and in spite of the customary heavy treatment with chloride of lime, most of the tank men were suffering varying degrees of dysentery. [10]

The Fifes' formation was similar to that of the RTR. Along with their accompanying I Battery, 13th RHA, and F Company, 8th Rifle Brigade, they formed a multi-arm regimental task force arranged in three groups with two sabre squadrons in the lead.

Once over the railway, the advance would be free of the constraints of the initial, narrow corridor and able to open out onto a wider front. Though determined to push 3rd RTR forward as quickly as possible, Harvey was hopeful that if the Fifes could be got quickly over the railway they might catch up and the two leading regiments sweep forward more or less in line abreast. In the half hour it took 3rd RTR to advance from the railway crossing, through the first hedgerow, and past le Mesnil Frémentel, a distance of about two miles, the two lead squadrons of the 2nd Fife and Forfar Yeomanry did indeed manage to struggle across the railway and jostle past the tail of the 3rd RTR regimental group, still negotiating the Haie de Saules hedgerow breeches. From here the two regiments' paths diverged. As 3rd RTR ran westward around the north and west of le Mesnil Frémentel, the Fifes were to angle left and sweep down past the eastern flank of the farm and its small orchards.

Having left behind the single track railway and hurdled the Haie de Saules hedgerows, the Fifes' leading two squadrons continued to make good time. As early as 09.12 hours, as Harvey saw the leading elements of the Fifes rolling southwards, 29th Brigade confidently reported to 11th Armoured HQ the welcome news: '*2FF Yeo 800 yds from CAGNY*'.[11] From this point, a mile of completely open ground beckoned. The Fifes' two leading squadrons opened out, A to the right and B to the left, a total frontage of 700 yards. The tanks thundered unopposed across the grain fields, with the second wave of regimental Headquarters, the Recce Troop, and the carriers of F Company, 8th RB racing close behind. Abandoned enemy equipment was observed, and many prisoners attempting to surrender were simply ignored in the headlong rush.

By 09.20 hours, as the artillery barrage reached its conclusion, 29th Brigade reported to division, '*3 R Tks and 2 FF Yeo cross main rd CAEN – VIMONT.*' In the case of 3rd RTR this was a trifle optimistic, but it is likely that the Fifes had indeed caught up. Certainly, by 09.35 hours brigade HQ reported that the leading Fifes had reached the main, dual track Caen – Paris railway, and by 09.46 they were across. Lieutenant William Steel Brownlie, commanding 4 Troop, A Squadron was exhilarated.

> *We had never before driven in formation for more than a couple of hundred yards, except on exercises. Was it all over bar the shouting?*[12]

It was not.

References

(1) 'The Development of Artillery Tactics and Equipment', A L Pemberton, 1951, p 197. (Unpublished 'official history' of the Royal Artillery in the Second World War.)
(2) 'Military Training in the British Army, 1940-1944', Timothy Harrison Place, 2000, ISBN 0-7146-8091-5, p 171
(3) Roberts, p 167
(4) Roberts later called this *'the only mistake they made in the campaign.'* (Roberts, 173) For their part, the interpreters pointed out, with some justification, that it was sometimes hard to tell the GOC what he did not want to hear.
(5) Close, interview at Staff College, Camberley, 1979.
(6) Close, p 119
(7) The gyrostabilizers provided in some American tanks, designed to facilitate firing on the move, had so far proved unreliable and were not favoured by the British authorities nor by the tank crews.
(8) Gerhardt Bandomir diary. Bandomir claims to have witnessed one of Becker's self propelled 10.5cm howitzers which had been knocked out and half-buried by a direct hit. This might have been in the vicinity of le Mesnil Frémentel, but it is equally possible that he made the sighting further north, as Bandomir was led into captivity with the survivors of his garrison.
(9) Close, interview at Staff College, Camberley, 1979. It is correct that these rounds were almost certainly 'overs' directed at British units further back. The term 'eighty-eights' was commonly applied by the British to any antitank fire; in this case it is equally possible that the shells were 7.5cm, or else from 8.8cm guns at greater distance, since true 'eighty-eights' would not have become so innocuous after a mere 1,500 metres.
(10) 'A Soldier's Tale', personal diary of Trooper John Thorpe. The effects of dysentery on fighting men encased in armour throughout a hot summer's day are not to be dwelt upon. Supplies of toilet paper were strictly rationed and wholly inadequate for such eventualities. Suffice to say that as the day progressed some of the men took every opportunity to leave their tank to clean up. And as a consequence most of them were to suffer dehydration far beyond the 'dry throat' which commonly accompanied battle. The previous day, a surprise issue from the ration truck of one bottle of Whitbread beer and one tuppeny bar of Cadbury's chocolate per man plus a white loaf to each crew (*'only one side mildewed!'*) had been welcomed by some. The War Diary cheerfully records that *'morale was improved by the arrival of the N.A.A.F.I. and the first rations of* beer.' Cynics reflected wistfully: *'Coo! What have they got lined up for us?'*; and *'I wonder what happened to our rum. I have only ever had one rum ration since we landed.'* The cynicism was sadly justified.
(11) An interesting example of how confused signals can intensify the fog of war. 11th Armoured recorded at 09.15 (their signals log rounded minutes to 5s and 10s), *'3rd R Tks half way between CUVERVILLE and DEMOUVILLE. Leading Tps 800 yds NORTH of CAGNY.'* Any officer taking time to interpret this information might have thought it strange for 3rd RTR to be back *north* of the railway when the bulk of the regiment was over a mile to the south of Démouville and advancing still further south. Clearly, someone's wireless procedure had been imperfect and 'le Mesnil Frémentel' had been mis-recorded as 'Démouville'.
(12) Steel Brownlie diary

Chapter 5

18 JULY, MORNING: THE GERMAN RESPONSE

Whether in slit trenches, command bunkers, huddled under vehicles, or pressed against the bare earth, the men beneath the aerial bombardment suffered alone. Each individual's ordeal was relieved only by solitary prayer, numbed shock, or in many cases unconsciousness. Only when the nightmare ended could any sort of order be restored. Even then, wires had been cut and delicate radios rendered unserviceable. In the early hours of the battle, effective counter measures depended on the initiative of isolated groups. While much of the 'infantry veil' melted away before the ground attack, pockets of resistance from Colombelles to Manneville stood like rocks against the incoming tide.

BECKER

Major Alfred Becker is remembered more as an engineer than as a charismatic fighting soldier. For all the sophisticated wireless equipment with which he equipped his unit, he was unable to exert 'hands on' command of all his mobile batteries throughout the battle of 18 July. His accounts of those batteries not under his direct control are sketchy at best. However, he had worthy deputies. The facts remain: throughout the

French Hotchkiss H-39 chassis with a 7.5 cm Pak 40 anti-tank gun.

morning of 18 July, the surviving mobile guns of Becker's *Abteilung* underpinned the German resistance to the armoured onslaught; on every corner of the battlefield, the batteries Becker had extemporized in his Paris workshop played an active part.

Various accounts have reported Becker's own claims that the only 'important' loss suffered by his *Abteilung* on 18 July was the near-total destruction of *Hauptmann* Eichorn's *1. Batterie* during the bombing. This has always appeared unlikely, given both the prominent role of the other batteries in the fighting and the relative weakness of their vehicles' armour. It is now clear from photographic evidence that the other batteries did indeed suffer losses on various parts of the battlefield.

Before dawn, by 04.30 hours on 18 July, Becker was in the field to the north of Cagny in his armoured scout vehicle. To either side of his position were his third and fourth batteries, and he was in touch with his mobile headquarters and its antiaircraft screen of 2cm Flak 38 (six

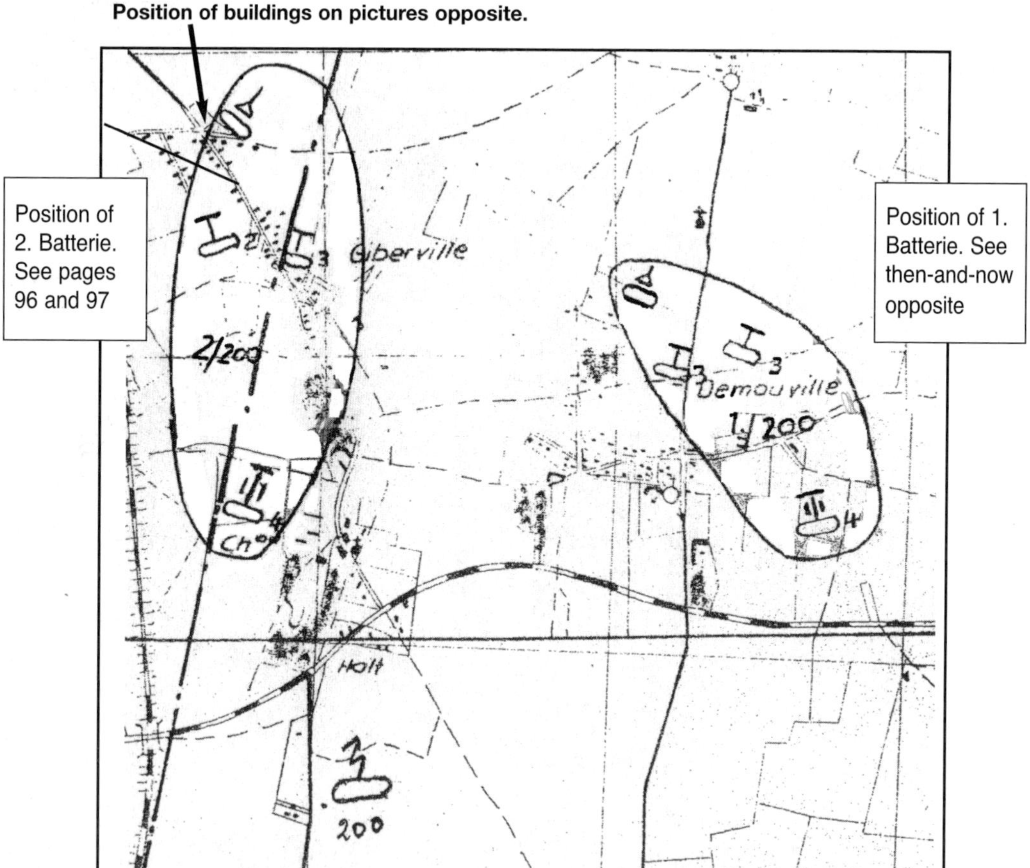

Major Alfred Becker.

Position of buildings on pictures opposite.

Position of 2. Batterie. See pages 96 and 97

Position of 1. Batterie. See then-and-now opposite

'2' Batterie 7.5 cm gun disabled and destroyed by retreating Germans.

The'Russian bakery', with a battery observation post on the top floor. This building and the adjacent gable are visible on page 95.

N

Position of SP gun in 1944

single guns and two four-barrelled *Flakvierling,* all mounted on French half-tracks) a kilometre to the south, using short-wave radio messages relayed by his accompanying armoured radio car. When first the Colombelles and Mondeville area to the west erupted in smoke and fire, followed shortly after Banneville and Emiéville to the east, Becker realised that an assault from the north was likely, and concentrated on keeping in touch with Eichorn's *1. Batterie,* closest to the expected avenue of attack. The precise position of this battery is unclear: Becker locates Eichorn's guns at midnight, 17 July, just on the north-eastern side of Démouville. However, photographs of antitank guns and howitzers wrecked in open ground not far from Touffréville reveal that at least part of this battery was lost on the opposite, eastern side of the 'armoured corridor'. Becker lost radio contact with Eichorn just before 07.00 hours, as the American medium bombers carpeted the whole area of the corridor. When Eichorn reported back to Becker's command bunker later in the morning, it was to report the near-total loss of his battery's vehicles. Even so, many of the crews had survived the immobilization of their armoured vehicles, to be taken prisoner by the advancing British.

Also forward was the second battery, under *Hauptmann* Förster. From his battery lookout post on the top floor of the Russian bakery at the northern end of Giberville (which served the immigrant labourers of the metalworks), Förster had a grandstand view of the opening battle. His five operational Pak 40 were deployed either side of the main street, his four howitzers 500 metres south, in open ground between the chateau and the railway. Much of the second battery story is conjecture, since Becker had no further contact that day. The battery probably underpinned the infantry garrison of Giberville, resisting the assault of the Canadian 8th Brigade. Advancing over open fields of wheat and turnips, the infantry of the Queen's Own Regiment of Canada had lost their barrage, and even when supported by tanks of the 1st Hussars they experienced 'a slow and painful fight through the village, constantly hampered by continuing fire from the factory area.'[1] No doubt Förster's howitzers supplemented that fire from the west. He left at least two antitank guns abandoned at the top of the village, apparently destroyed by their crews after becoming immobilized. After the fall of Giberville, it can be supposed that the surviving mobile guns moved west through the underpasses of the Minier railway embankment and on through Cormelles, taking up antitank positions in front of Ifs, between Cormelles and Bras. Quite possibly, these were the '5 Panthers' reported moving across the rear of 3rd RTR, and firing away towards the north east, shortly before 13.15 hours. Panther tanks they certainly were not.

Of the remaining batteries, more is known. All three played their part in slowing the initial British advance. Alerted by the bombardment, they began to engage enemy tanks shortly after 08.00 hours, the battery commanders relaying back to Becker the interesting news that no infantry appeared to be accompanying the advancing tide of British tanks. The

Two views of a 2.Batterie 7.5 cm gun in Giberville; a second was destroyed across the road (page 93). A third view of this same vehicle is shown on page 96.

batteries then conducted phased withdrawals to prepared positions from which their thinly armoured vehicles could keep up an effective long-range antitank fire. *Hauptmann* Nösser's *3. Batterie* supported the garrison of Grentheville before falling back to the orchards around Soliers. *Hauptmann* Röpke's *4. Batterie* engaged 3rd RTR from the eastern flank of le Mesnil Frémentel before falling back to the south of Four (where it took up positions masking the emplacements of the greater part of the field artillery of 16. LFD). *Oberleutnant* Schreiner's *5. Batterie* began the day with one three-gun section either side of le Prieuré, using orchards for cover, and the battery howitzers south of the farm. From these positions, the sections withdrew in bounds to the woods between le Prieuré and Manneville, engaging the oncoming tank squadrons (who mistook the guns for 'Tigers' in the

Another view of the gun on page 95.

10.5 cm howitzer of 1.Batterie destroyed in open ground between Démouville and Touffréville.

Touffréville church

Nearby, a 1.Batterie 7.5 cm gun destroyed in the open.

woods) before moving on to end the day in firing positions straddling the railway west of Frénouville. Many GOODWOOD histories unaccountably confuse the movements of these two batteries; their true destinations are clearly shown in Becker's personal situation maps (*Stellungs-Skizzen*) of the day's events. As will be seen later, the precise timing and paths of the two batteries' moves south can only be conjectured. Nevertheless, it is certain that *4. Batterie* was well clear of le

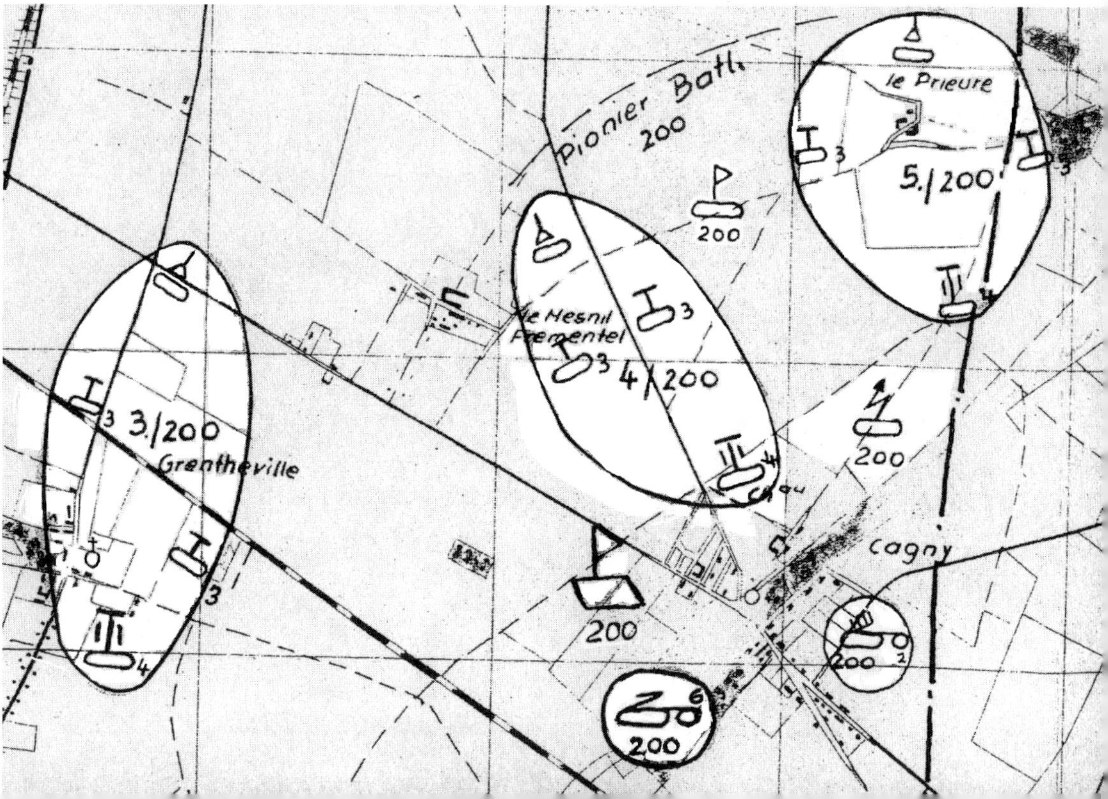

Mesnil Frémentel before the Fifes' lead squadrons passed through that same area, so it can confidently be inferred that Röpke was installed south of Four by 10.00 hours. The journey of *5. Batterie* involved passing around or through Cagny: of that, more later.

VON LUCK

Returning from leave in Paris, von Luck's car travelled overnight to reduce the risk of air attack. Others too were making use of the precious hours of darkness, and the Mercedes was held up by the nightly supply convoys. Only some time after dawn did von Luck's car approach his Frénouville command post. (He later estimated the time to be around 09.00 hours; shortly after 08.00 is much more likely, and by that time the sun was well up in the sky.) As ever in daylight, he scanned the skies while his driver covered the last few kilometres. Other than a certain haze in the west, nothing seemed amiss. The major looked forward to changing out of his dress uniform and having a little breakfast before reviewing his forward units.

Von Luck's tranquillity was rudely shattered by the news of the early morning's aerial bombardment. According to von Luck, he found his headquarters staff paralyzed by indecision. Abandoning thoughts of

Major von Luck (still wearing his 'little pistol') briefed by _Leutnant_ Bandomir.

Von Luck surveys the scene; in the foreground is his adjutant, *Oberleutnant* Liebeskind.

breakfast, von Luck quickly assessed which of his headquarters staff were coping with the emergency. One of these, his adjutant *Oberleutnant* Liebeskind, was despatched to divisional headquarters; another liaison officer was sent north to contact von Oppeln's tank regiment. Von Luck then summoned his personal command tank and set out to see for himself what was happening.[2] Von Luck tried to calm his crew by showing his own coolness: he offered cigarettes and together they set off along a minor road into Cagny.

> *Crossing Cagny very slowly, which was half destroyed, and coming to the western corner of Cagny I was absolutely upset about what I saw. About fifty to sixty British tanks already crossed the main road Caen – Vimont, direction south west, and some of them already over the railway, and further tanks were following from north east. It was quite clear to me that the British had started to move through our lines. It was clearly impossible to reach le Mesnil Frémentel.*[3]

In moments, von Luck realised the seriousness of the situation. It was now around 09.00 hours and already strong enemy armoured forces were over six kilometres behind what had been the German front line, and streaming south. Von Luck's first battalion, its headquarters in le Mesnil Frémentel, was cut off and for all he knew already overrun. The status of his second battalion, deployed to the north of Cagny, was unknown. Major Becker's batteries and the division's tanks were not in communication. There was nothing between his Frénouville headquarters and the enemy, nor any German forces close behind to reinforce the front.

What happened next is one of the best-known stories of the Normandy campaign, told many times with minor variations. Yet von Luck's account remains the only known source. According to him,

> *'I decided to drive back to my headquarters to organize new defence lines or counter attacks. Driving slowly through Cagny I suddenly saw a single antiaircraft battery of the air force with their guns in the air. I went over to the CO and informed him about what I have seen. And I gave a clear order to get immediately involved in this battle by fighting the British tanks. But, I got a flat refusal telling me that he was under air command and had nothing to do with our battle on the ground. So, I took my little pistol and asked him whether he would like to be killed immediately or get a high decoration. He decided for the latter. So, he got a clear order to get in position with his battery at the north west corner of Cagny, not to deal with the advancing tanks but with the following tanks coming from the north east.'*[4]

This account raises many unanswered questions. Why was a Luftwaffe heavy battery positioned in Cagny? How had it survived the bombardment? Why is there no record of its deployment there and no trace of its presence nor of its (supposed) relocation in aerial photographs? These questions are addressed in Appendix IX.

Returning to his headquarters, von Luck began to receive a glimmer of hope. *Major* Becker was already there, bringing the welcome information that two of his batteries were in action on the far side of the battlefield, supporting surviving pockets of von Luck's first battalion. Two more batteries were already in action on the eastern flank of the battle, and here von Luck's second-battalion commander *Hauptmann* Kurz had used his own initiative to construct the beginnings of a defensive line. Shortly after came Kurz's own report: he was holding west-facing blocking positions. Von Luck returned confirmation that Kurz was to hold the line between Touffréville and Emiéville. Liebeskind's return from Division also brought some relief. Feuchtinger (now back at his post) could send nothing to the western side of the battle, but was releasing the divisional reconnaissance battalion to support von Luck in the east. On arrival towards the end of the morning, *Major* Brandt's *21. Panzer-Aufklärungsabteilung* had few of its armoured reconnaissance vehicles available for combat, but its greatest value to von Luck was its infantry strength. Just as the divisional *Pionier Abteilung* of specialized combat engineers was perfectly accustomed to holding the line as infantry, its three companies now garrisoning front-line strongpoints, so too were Brandt's reconnaissance troops ready to serve as extra grenadiers. In this role they helped fill the yawning gap between Emiéville and Frénouville. They added some resilience to the fragile defensive screen of Becker's guns, and the later-arriving antitank batteries which would coalesce during the afternoon into a hasty but effective *Pakfront*.

THE TANKS

As has been seen, barely a half-dozen of the 22. *Panzerregiment* tanks in Emiéville survived the bombing in a combat-ready state. Little better off, on the fringes of that target area, the survivors of *Leutnant* von Rosen's company struggled to excavate and repair their heavy *Tiger* tanks. Their work was periodically interrupted by incoming artillery shells, and was all the harder since the company workshop technicians had been wiped out along with their vehicles with only a bomb crater marking their position. Digging out and repairing damage continued as sounds of enemy tanks and gunfire came closer. At length, by about 10.00 hours, a half-dozen tanks were more or less ready to move (estimates vary between six and eight tanks repaired). Von Rosen led the procession out through the north east gateway of the park, around the north and west walls, and onto a small rise south of Manneville. Even on this short drive, barely a mile, two of their number dropped behind with engines overheating.

Shortly after, a *Tiger* tank arrived bearing the 'I' insignia of the battalion

***Stahlfeldwagen* Hf.7, a horse-drawn carrier destroyed in the woods.**

Von Rosen's initial advance: tank tracks reveal the move to the 'small rise' south of Manneville. Later, Shermans were engaged close to the wood, before the turn south to Cagny.

commander. Sent to Paris for treatment of an inflamed eye, *Hauptmann* Fromme had returned that very morning to find his *Abteilung* in chaos. Though still unable to grasp the overall situation, Fromme was able to inform von Rosen that the acting commander, *Hauptmann* Scherf and the headquarters staff had survived in their Emiéville chateau, saved amidst the destruction by taking refuge in its narrow stairwell. Of 22. *Panzerregiment*, nothing was yet known, but its assembly area appeared to

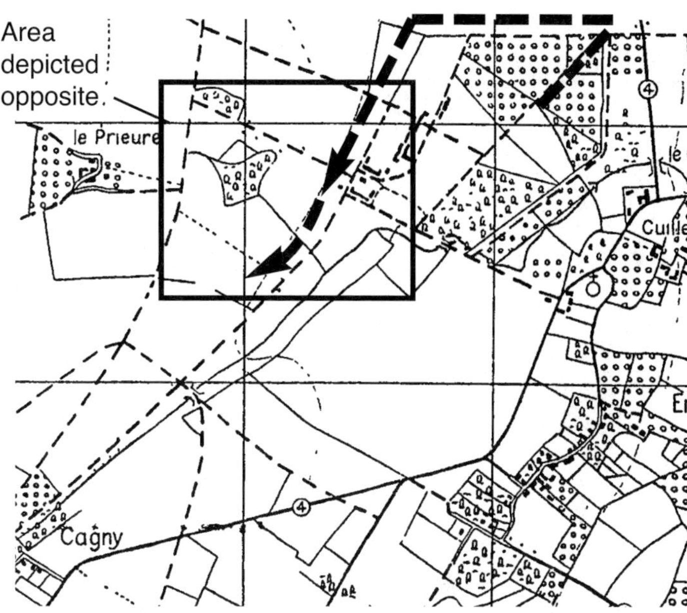

have been devastated. Von Rosen's orders were confirmed: he was to remain in command of the company, anchoring the defensive line between Manneville and Cagny. [5]

About 11.00 hours, von Rosen's tanks engaged a troop of Guards Armoured Division, probing eastwards from le Prieuré. The Shermans were driven off leaving two wrecks, one with its turret torn from its hull by an 8.8cm round. But the Tiger crews had received an unwelcome surprise. Only then did they realise the extent to which their gunsights had been affected by the bombardment. The normally reliable optics had been shaken out of alignment and 'We needed three rounds now where only one would have been adequate before.'[6] Consequently, von Rosen felt the need to open the range, to enable his guns to engage the enemy earlier. Sounds of battle were coming from the area of le Prieuré but the view in that direction was obscured by a small wood. His orders were to move south west, towards Cagny, to clear that wood before turning northwest to present the tanks' frontal armour towards the enemy around le Prieuré.

Suddenly, two of the *Tiger* were hit in quick succession. *Feldwebel* Schönrock's *Tiger* went up in flames. Its frontal armour had been cleanly penetrated. Moments later, *Feldwebel* Müller's tank was similarly hit on its thick frontal armour and left burning. This was unprecedented. The

Abteilung had lost *Tiger* tanks in Russia to mechanical breakdown, to unmarked minefields, or to flank shots which damaged engines and running gear. But losing a *Tiger* to hits on its front armour was a novel experience. Apparently facing some unknown weapon, von Rosen made a rapid decision: 'I broke off the move as I could not pinpoint the source of the fire and did not want to suffer any further total losses.'[7] Even as they fell back, a third Tiger, number 321, was hit on its muzzle brake, disabling its main gun. (See page 257)

The outcome of this probe, had it been allowed to continue towards le Prieuré, is a matter for speculation. An engagement between a half-dozen battered *Tiger* tanks and 5th Guards Armoured Brigade would have been an epic contest. At the very least, consternation would have been sowed *behind* 11th Armoured Division, threatening all the gains so far made and potentially imperilling the survival of 29th Brigade. As it was, von Rosen's *3. Kompanie* took little further part in the battle.

SUMMARY

The initial response to the British assault of 18 July was uncoordinated. Units directly in the path of the assault were stunned by the aerial bombardment. Dietrich's *I. SS-Panzerkorps* was wrong-footed, with one division on its way to leave the area and the other facing west and some hours from the field of battle. Feuchtinger was absent at the outset, and indecisive on his arrival. Von Rosen was absent at the outset, and highly energetic on arrival, albeit within a fairly narrow command span. Fromme was absent at the outset, while his deputy Scherf started the battle walled-up with von Oppeln-Bronikowski and the *22. Panzerregiment* staff as their chateau command post was destroyed around their ears. Scherf lost touch with his *Abteilung* for much of the morning, and von Oppeln soon found that his tank regiment had been effectively neutralized. Everywhere, the aerial bombardment severed effective communications. But deprived of high-level command and coordination, junior officers on every corner of the battlefield rose to the occasion, defending tenaciously with whatever means were at hand.

References

(1) 'The Victory Campaign, vol III', C P Stacey, 1960, p 171

(2) Von Luck states that this was *'a radio Panzer IV that the Panzer regiment had put at my disposal.'* While there is no reason to disbelieve the statement of an experienced soldier, if this was truly a specialized command tank, with reduced ammunition storage to accommodate extra radio equipment, it is not impossible that it was actually one of the *Befehlspanzer III* on the strength of *22. Panzerregiment.*

(3) Von Luck, interview at Staff College, Camberley, 1979

(4) Von Luck, interview at Staff College, Camberley, 1979

(5) Rubbel, p 242; '45 Tiger en Normandie', Didier Lodieu, 2002, ISBN 2-84673-015-6, p 70-71

(6) Rubbel, p 241

(7) Von Rosen, interview at Staff College, Camberley, 1979

Chapter 6

18 JULY, MID-MORNING: THINGS FALL APART

Whatever the debate and controversy regarding its ultimate goal, the first key objective of the GOODWOOD plan was the Bourguébus ridge. To this end, the greatest obstacle appeared to be the initial advance down a narrow corridor, overlooked by factories to the west and wooded hills to the east, closely flanked by hamlets and villages of solid Norman stone. Previous Normandy battles had stalled due to unexpected hold-ups in the opening stages of the assault. This time it was fondly hoped that if the forward defences could be obliterated, the German front line be cleanly penetrated, and the speed of the advance be maintained over the first few miles, then the operation might take on a momentum of its own, rolling on forward.

Between the dual-track Caen to Paris railway and the ridge, the map promised open country: gently undulating farmland with only the odd orchard-girt hamlet intervening until the ridge itself was reached. Surely this was 'good tank country' *par excellence*, in which the armoured divisions could employ their mobility and manoeuvrability as never before in the campaign to date. Shortly after 09.30 hours, the first tanks of two regiments, moving more or less abreast, reached that railway line. And from that point the nature of the battle changed.

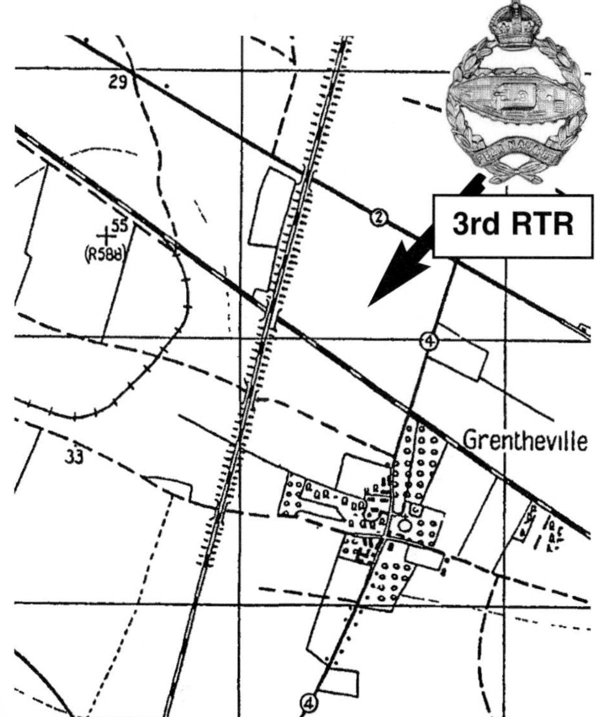

3rd RTR AT GRENTHEVILLE

A and B Squadrons of 3rd Royal Tanks had a little time to draw breath after running the gauntlet of German resistance at le Mesnil Frémentel. Advancing south-west, a slight downslope put them into dead ground as viewed from le Mesnil Frémentel. Ahead a hedgerow-lined rectangular field blocked the line of sight to the south, while due west appeared the raised embankment of the Chemin de Fer Minier. As the lead tanks rounded the north-west corner of this field they saw ahead the main Caen to Paris railway line, at this point an insignificant obstacle only slightly above the level of the

3rd RTR
advance
around
Grentheville
Chemin de Fer Minier
Caen-Paris Highway
Caen-Paris Railway
Rail spur to
Cormelles industry
N

Grentheville

surrounding fields. And just beyond the dual tracks lay the next objective: Grentheville. Ahead, to the tanks' left flank, a mass of orchards reached out from the village as far as the railway; straight ahead and set back from the railway was a 150 metre long wall, ominously loopholed. And beyond the wall, nestling amongst orchards, stood a chateau, farmyards, and houses of the hamlet itself. Only this outer wall of the chateau was so far visible amid the as-yet largely untouched tree cover. The advancing tank commanders' attention was caught by movements along the wall and in the treeline. Suddenly, as the range closed, the ground immediately ahead erupted in columns of fire.

Grentheville: woods and orchards west of the village led almost to the railway embankment.

From the wall and even closer from emplacements hidden in the crops ahead, salvoes of rockets howled skywards. These were the notorious *Nebelwerfer*. Large-calibre rockets launched from light six-barrelled mounts, they constituted an important part of the German artillery in Normandy. Relatively inaccurate and short ranged, and hugely demanding in their consumption of scarce ammunition, nevertheless their massed salvoes could be devastating against unprepared troops. Many a platoon of British infantry having advanced to seize an enemy hedgerow or orchard was mercilessly cut down in its moment of victory by a coordinated hail of pre-plotted mortar and rocket fire. And the unearthly wail of the *Nebelwerfer* rockets ripping the sky led the troops to loathe them as 'Moaning Minnies' or 'Sobbing Sisters'. For tanks, and especially against tanks charging headlong, they were no match. The screaming warheads rocketed steeply upwards, over the tanks, bound for somewhere in the rear, tails of smoke clearly revealing the positions of their launchers. Some of the advancing Shermans now fell victim to true antitank guns camouflaged in the distance. But most pressed on, raking the nearest *Nebelwerfer* emplacements with bow and turret machine guns; and as the

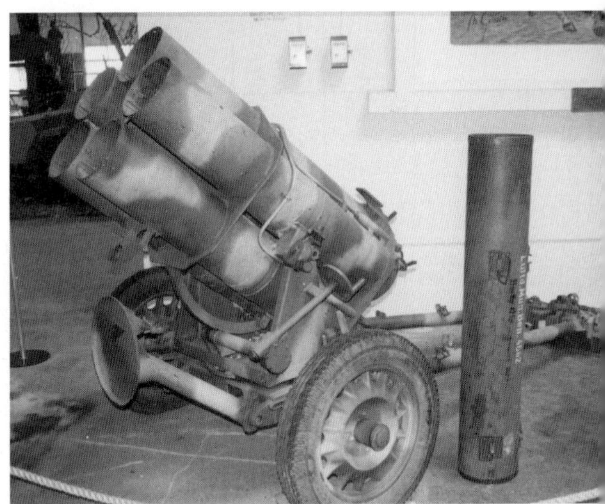

21 cm, six-barrelled 'Nebelwerfer' and its ammunition.

range rapidly closed, they physically overran the positions, crushing the flimsy launcher carriages beneath tank tracks.

Still, tanks as yet unaccompanied by infantry were not about to venture into orchards and buildings. Once again, the first wave of the armoured tide flowed around the obstacle, turning westward while attempting to return fire on the move. Bill Close was on the right flank of this movement.

> *As I reached a little cornfield a few hundred yards from Grentheville we were engaged by antitank guns on the forward edge of the village. And some of the tanks in my troops on the left, about four of them, went up in flames. I could also see several of the tanks further left, in the left hand squadron, were also brewing. There was quite a lot of AP shot coming from the bushes and trees in Grentheville and also where the farm buildings are. Obviously antitank guns in very well concealed positions.*[1]

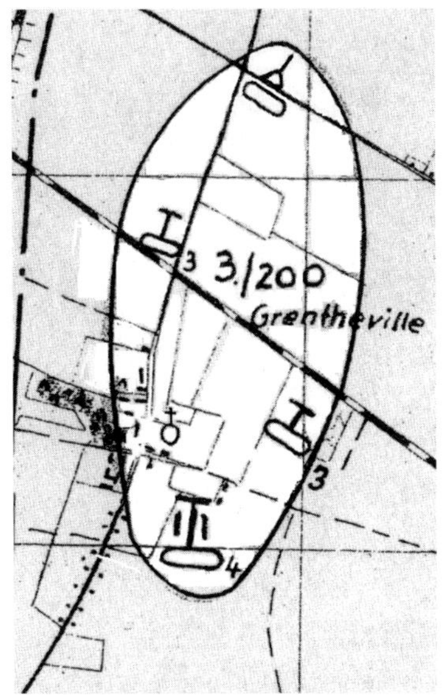

The initial deployment of Becker's 3.*Batterie*: armoured command vehicle to the fore; two troops of 7.5 cm Pak; one troop of four howitzers.

It is just possible that some self-propelled guns of Becker's 3. *Batterie* were still at this moment within the orchards of Grentheville. However, it is more likely that the antitank fire aimed at Bill Close was coming from guns emplaced outside the village. Before the British advance, the mobile battery had been deployed with one section of three 7.5cm guns due north of the village, along the railway, facing north; a second to the east, facing le Mesnil Frémentel; and the section of four 10.5cm howitzers south east of the buildings. The battery observation post was positioned north of the railway, and would have given early warning of tanks streaming around le Mesnil Frémentel. By 10.00 hours, it seems certain that the northern section would have displaced southwards, through the orchards north of the village, under cover of the battery's other guns. Given the policy of the lightly armoured *Abteilung* to fall back well before coming under effective fire, this was probably a fairly hasty manoeuvre performed as soon as the first British tanks appeared, barely one thousand metres distant, offering little immediate opportunity to inflict damage on the attacking force. Hardly surprising, therefore, that when Becker's guns did deliver fire from south east of Grentheville, the forward elements of 3rd RTR should seek some relief from the enemy by moving to the opposite, north-western, side of the village and orchards. Still on the right flank, Bill Close's A Squadron was now suffering badly, and,

> *within a matter of moments there were five or six tanks brewing up. I told my two right hand troops to tuck themselves down along the line of the embankment and get some HE fire on the forward edges of the village as quickly as possible. I had an OP with me right from the start. He was in a sawn-off Honey [see Appendix VI] and I had given him*

instructions to stick close to me. I tucked myself in behind a small ridge, called him over, and told him, "For Christ's sake get a stonc [a standard concentration of artillery] *down as quickly as possible."*[2]

Road and rail underpasses below the Chemin de Fer Minier.

With 3rd RTR temporarily held up north and west of Grentheville, a few words are needed about the immediate lie of the land. Without revisiting the details of the Chemin de Fer Minier railway embankment (see Appendix I), it should be pointed out that the only shelter to be found by the tanks in front of Grentheville was the slight down-slope to the north of Grentheville and the low embankment along which ran this stretch of the dual-track Caen – Paris railway (turning further east into a shallow cutting). Together with the remaining crops, this did not amount to much protection, but was better than nothing. Hence, Major Close's injunction to his troops to 'tuck in' close to the angle formed between the eastern side of the steep embankment and the northern side of the main Caen-Paris railway.

By 10.00 hours, the bulk of the 3rd RTR regimental group was passing le Mesnil Frémentel on its way towards Grentheville. Increasing numbers of vehicles were stopping short of the firing and accumulating in the area north of the railway, behind the stalled tanks. Urged on by 29th Brigade, Colonel Silvertop was insistent that the momentum of the advance be regained. Major Close was keen to comply, but recognised the essential need for some preparatory fire to cover any advance.

All the time, I was being told in no uncertain manner by my CO to get over to the west side of the embankment. And I said wait out until can get a stonc down on the village. My two right hand troops had in the meantime engaged several antitank guns and assault guns in this area. They claimed to have knocked out two or three antitank guns and at least one assault gun.[3]

With the Sherman tanks' suppressive fire against the north end of the village and H Battery of 13th Royal Horse Artillery pounding the enemy, the position north of the railway eased slightly. Close sensed that the time had come to move out.

> *I could see that the embankment was going to be rather a difficult problem, and I did not like the idea of going over the top, broadside on, within a few hundred yards of antitank guns... I wanted to get my two right-hand troops to the western side of the embankment, before I followed with the regimental group behind me. So, I gave orders for them to move. Not a tank moved. Nothing happened at all. So, I stood up in my tank, took off my beret, waved it three times round my head, and said over the air, "Conform to me." As I approached the embankment my feelings were extremely mixed. I was not quite sure what to expect, and I was very apprehensive if there were any enemy mines. In the event they weren't. And I shot through the hole, rather like a rat up a drainpipe. I emerged on the other side to see this beautiful country looking perfectly peaceful. There was no sign of any movement whatsoever. And I was an extremely relieved squadron commander, I can tell you.'*[4]

The hesitation of Major Close's troops to follow a direct order clearly made an impression on a commander with so many years of experience of fighting in tanks. The event provoked much analysis, not least from General Roberts. '*Bill Close, in order to get his squadron under the bridge going through the embankment... had to take of his hat wave it in the air, and say "Follow me!" Now, I don't believe that would have happened in either of the other three regiments in the division.'*[5] The problem was not simply lack of discipline, and certainly not lack of experience. Many of these tank men had fought together throughout the North Africa campaign. Roberts recognised better than anyone that his division included,

> *one regiment that had battle experience: the 3rd Tanks had a great deal... they had a very good commanding officer and some good squadron leaders.' However, 'The fact is that, with a great deal of fighting, all those concerned become a little more wary and a little more canny. It's more difficult to get people to go "round the corner" after that sort of experience than it is right at the outset of a campaign.*[6]

In point of fact, the chances of a Sherman tank surmounting the railway embankment at this point, even without enemy fire, would have been slim. And Major Close's 'drainpipe' was actually the widest of all the underpasses the whole length of the railway embankment: the point at which the two-track Paris railway passed under the Chemin de Fer

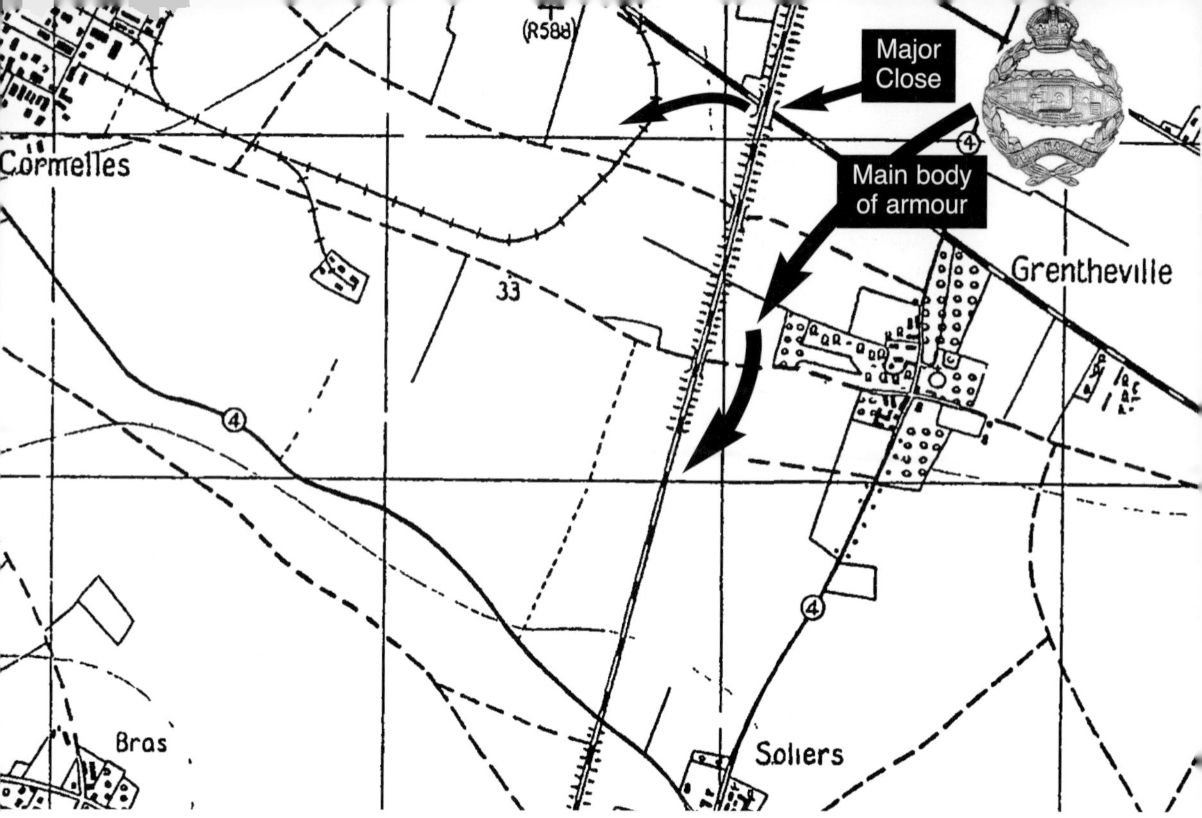

3rd Royal Tanks' advance past Grentheville.

Minier. His Sherman tank emerged on the west side of the embankment into a wholly different landscape. The distinctive intersection of two railways had proved irresistible to bombers seeking targets in the murk below, as testified by large bomb craters in its immediate vicinity. But beyond the bridge were rippling fields of golden corn, the crop awaiting harvest and mostly concealing the effects of the American hundred pound fragmentation bombs scattered over this entire sector. Left behind was the smoke and dust of an armoured engagement, its distant sounds now drowned out by the roar of the tanks' engines, the crackle of headphones, and the barrier of the embankment. The summer sun was now well up in the morning sky, beaming down through gaps in the smoke drifting downwind towards the ridge to the south.

Now the foremost element of 3rd RTR, Major Close's leading troop, accompanied as ever by the 13th Royal Horse FOO in his turretless 'Honey', pressed on to reconnoitre the territory ahead. The small band pressed some way in the direction of Cormelles, stopping to survey the factories there and seeing no enemy movement at all.[7]

THE FATE OF THE FIFES

As their leading squadrons approached the second railway line, the Fifes' progress seemed to be living up to the expectations of the optimistic briefing of the morning:

'Head for Falaise, don't stop for anything. When you come across enemy antitank guns,

> *drive at them, destroy them, run over their traces!'*

(This last comment gave some of the more sceptical individuals pause for thought.) A Squadron on the right reached the Paris railway first, and its lead tanks paused on the embankment. The way ahead appeared clear.

A Squadron briefly held position while B approached the embankment and the second wave of the regimental group closed up: regimental headquarters, the Recce Troop, and the carrier-borne infantry of 8th Rifle Brigade's F Company. Though C Squadron, some way behind, was allocated the role of regimental reserve, this was by no means intended in a passive sense. Its Major Chris Nicholls was a desert veteran, the most experienced squadron commander in a regiment which had first seen action three weeks previously. Colonel Scott's intention was to burst across the railway, pushing B Squadron left and A Squadron right. These would elbow aside any remaining defenders in order that C might, in textbook form, 'pass through' and make its run, possibly without interruption, on a single squadron front all the way to the Bourguébus ridge.

B Squadron established itself on the line of the railway, to the left of A Squadron. B Squadron had not experienced quite so smooth a run as A. Earlier, the squadron second-in-command, Captain Traherne, had been killed as he stood exposed in his turret. And passing Cagny the first tank loss was experienced when Sergeant Hogg's Sherman was hit within sight of the commanding officer. Lieutenant Colonel Scott recalled,

> *I saw him and his crew bale out. I had no real idea where the fire was coming from. We were concentrating like mad and pushing on. You couldn't stop and investigate…*

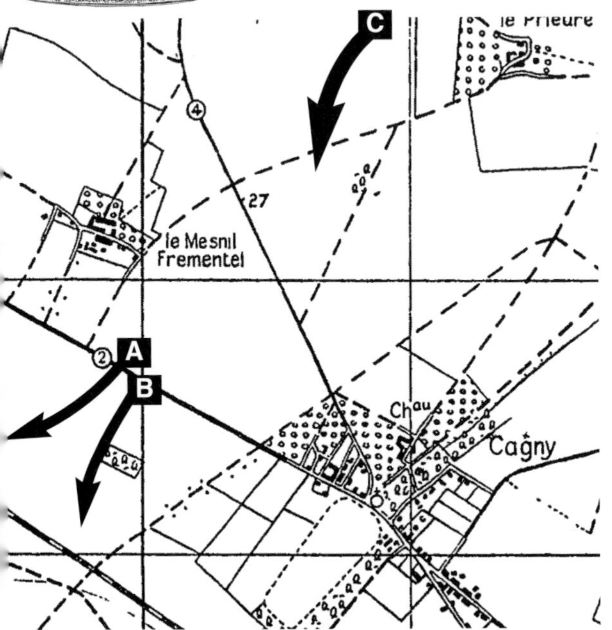

The Fifes' squadrons' advance past Cagny.

The news was passed up the line. 11th Armoured Division headquarters noted laconically, 'RIGHT just NE GRENTHEVILLE. LEFT CAGNY troublesome'.

Reaching the railway line, Scott was impatient to keep up the momentum. He needed C Squadron to shake clear of the traffic jams to the north and join the main body of the regiment as quickly as possible. Leaving a single troop behind as left flank protection, B Squadron negotiated the railway crossing while Scott tried to contact Nicholls. After repeated radio calls enquiring where the reserve squadron had got to, a careful study of the view to the north revealed the awful truth.

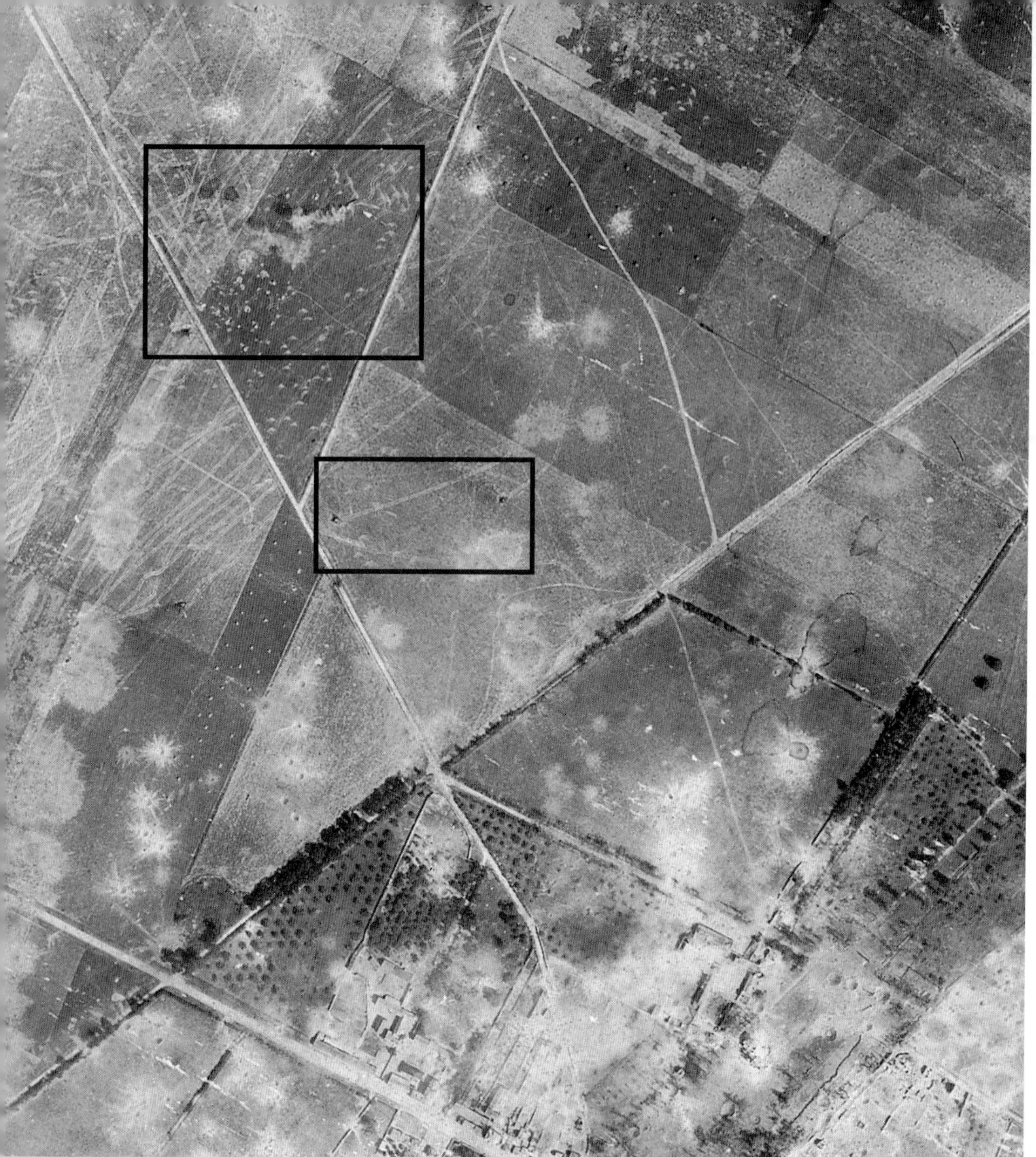

The killing fields north west of Cagny (details shown opposite).

Some distance behind, the tanks of C Squadron had indeed been held up by the traffic jam as increasing numbers of vehicles of different units struggled forward. Further back still was the final element of the Fifes' regimental group, the battery of self propelled artillery. Leaving their 13th RHA charges to look after themselves, C Squadron rushed south over the open ground, following the tracks of the leading waves of the regiment. Hearing B Squadron's report of enemy fire from somewhere in the vicinity of the orchards to the left, around the small town of Cagny, C Squadron tank commanders' eyes and turrets were turned that way. The

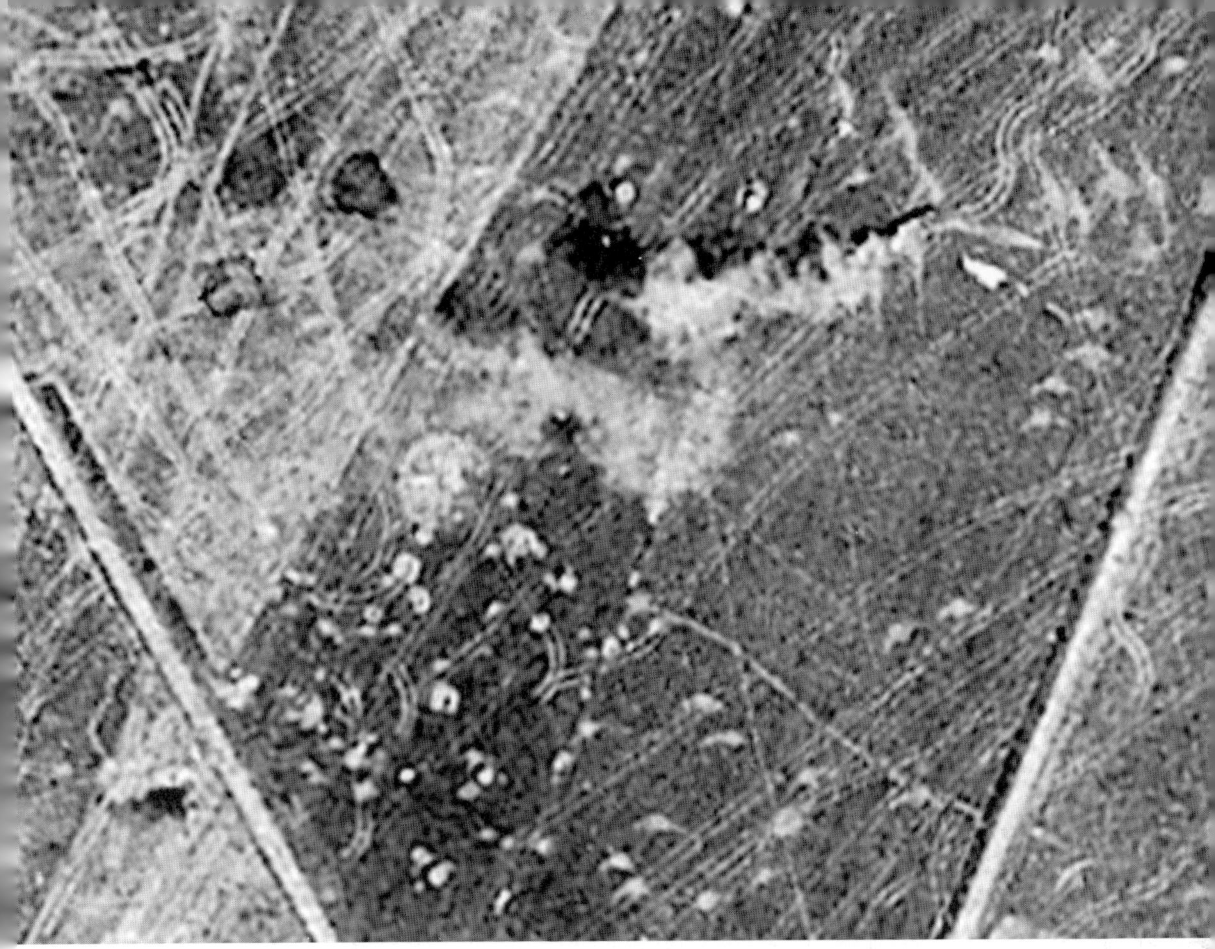

C Squadron tank belches smoke. (Stains are damage to original photograph.)

Squadron commander himself was not overly perturbed. A and B Squadron had passed the place almost unscathed, and according to his briefing Cagny had been well and truly 'Hamburged' by the RAF. The blow fell unexpectedly. Nicholls' tank blew up. Moments later the tank of Captain Miller, Nicholls' second in command, likewise crashed to a halt and began belching black smoke. One after another, the Sherman tanks of C Squadron were knocked out, some burning, some miraculously giving

Two Squadron C tanks hit as
they attempt to flee westward

their crews a chance to escape into the corn. In minutes, the squadron was put out of action. A dozen of its nineteen tanks were knocked out.

Corporal Ron Cox, an operator/loader in 3 Troop, managed to catch the destruction of the second tank in limited arc of his periscope.

> *It brewed as soon as it was hit, and the turret crew baled out, the gunner and radio operator both with their clothes smouldering. [These two would of course be last to leave the conflagration inside the turret, struggling after Captain Miller to clamber up through the single turret hatch.] Then Lieutenant Sammy Millar, our troop leader whose tank was halted just in front of us, was the next to be hit… The whole crew remained perfectly calm and almost totally silent apart from the occasional "bloody Hell!" as another tank went up.'*

Jack Thorpe, lap (or bow) gunner in the tank commanded by the sergeant of 4 Troop, left a graphic account of the scene, as witnessed through the periscope above his Browning .30 calibre machine gun.

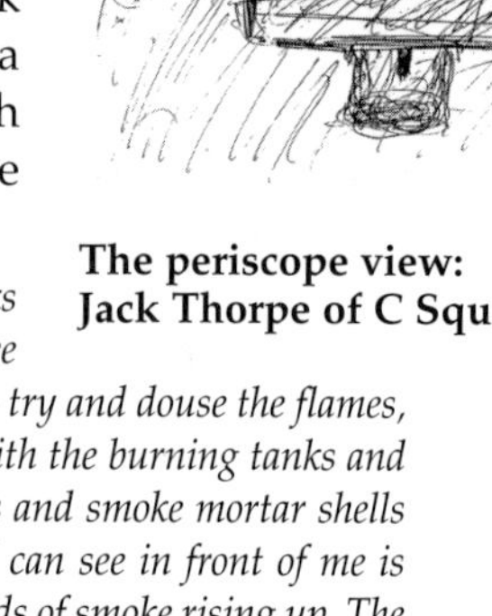

The periscope view: Jack Thorpe of C Squadron.

> *Along the column of tanks, I see palls of smoke and tanks brewing up with flames belching forth from their turrets. I see men climbing out, on fire like torches, rolling on the ground to try and douse the flames, but we are in ripe corn and the straw takes fire. Soon, what with the burning tanks and the burning men and the burning cornfield, plus smoke shells and smoke mortar shells from our tank, visibility is being shut out. Now every tank I can see in front of me is brewing, burning fiercely, flames shooting high and dense clouds of smoke rising up. The tank twenty yards away from us is hit, flames shoot out of its turret, I see a member of its crew climbing out through the flames, he is almost out, putting one foot onto the rim to jump down, he seems to hesitate and he falls back inside. Oh Christ!*

Thorpe's tank was able to stop in time to engage reverse gear and clear the scene. The sergeant in command, the only crew member with a rearwards field of vision, directed the driver as well as the gunner.

> *Cliff orders Bert to fire off more smoke shells and tells Robbie to reverse, and we go backwards, zig-zagging, right stick, left stick, right stick, gunner keep on target and keep firing, left stick, right stick, left stick".*[8]

So guided, the tank reversed, weaving its zig-zag path, all the way to the Troarn railway line, where they encountered the 23rd Hussars. With no word from the rest of their own regiment, they tagged along with the Hussars for the rest of the day.

The majority of C Squadron's tanks were knocked out. Those immobilized tanks that failed to burn were hard to distinguish from those few still manned, and continued to be hit over and over as the German gunners ran out of live targets.[9] Just as Colonel Scott tried to find out why C Squadron was not communicating, so too was Thorpe's tank commander, Sergeant 'Cliff' Jones.

> *We take stock and find we have used up most of our gun ammunition. We have lost wireless contact with the rest of the Regiment. We cannot raise our Troop Leader, nor the Squadron Leader or the C.O. There is absolutely no reply from "Red Sun" or "Sun Ray" or any other station. There is no reply as there is no one to answer.*[10]

At the railway line ahead, realising the enormity of the disaster, Colonel Scott's immediate reaction was to prevent the remainder of his regimental group from being cut off by enemies in its rear. He gave orders to his accompanying motor infantry company to prepare to dismount and advance on Cagny, less than a thousand yards distant to the north east, with a view to clearing the place. Informing Brigadier Harvey's Tac HQ of the plan, he was about to set the assault in motion when an emphatic counter order came back from Brigade.

The Fifes were not to concern themselves with Cagny but were to continue on their way south. Scott made his dispositions accordingly. The whole of B Squadron would now assume the lead; two troops of A Squadron under Captain J D ('Pinkie') Hutchison, third-in-command,[11] would face east to cover the left flank, advancing between Four and the farm complex of le Poirier, until relieved by the expected arrival of the 23rd Hussars. The rest of A Squadron would support the right flank of the advance. And behind them would come the rest of the regimental group, now virtually complete save for I Battery of the Horse Artillery who would take the safer, roundabout route west of le Mesnil Frémentel.

THE HUSSARS' DELAYS

Even before they entered the lanes through the minefields, it became clear to the 23rd Hussars that the morning was not going to plan.

> *For the first time one felt slight misgivings. Would that long tail of supporting arms ever manage to keep up with the leading tanks? One thought of the gaps through the minefield, and remembered that each regiment's "tail" was supposed to move in line a hundred yards behind the tanks, with ourselves [i.e., the following regiment] three hundred yards behind that. From the very straggled appearance of the mass of vehicles in front, even before the minefield had been reached, it looked as if the maintenance of correct distances was not going to be more than a pious hope. If we, as reserve Regiment were going to be left behind, how much more so were the Guards and the Seventh Armoured?*[12]

Like the two regiments that had gone before, the 23rd Hussars paused after emerging from the minefields to shake out into the prescribed formation: A and B Squadrons leading, left and right respectively, with C Squadron following on the flanks of the remainder of the regimental group. But the pause was only brief. Instead of three hundred yards, the tail of the preceding regiment was now a mile ahead. And in the open country, blasted by bombs and shells and littered with a confused medley of support vehicles all heading generally southwards, was the familiar figure of the brigadier. Roscoe Harvey stood in his turret, distinctive in the red beret which he refused to give up in action, furiously waving the newcomers on.

Dazed Germans were still being winkled out of foxholes and dugouts.

One corporal in C Squadron bogged his tank in a crater and while waiting to be pulled out amused himself collecting prisoners. He got up to twenty before the squadron ARV (Armoured Recovery Vehicle, see Appendix 6) arrived to tug his tank back into action. Before long it became clear that there had been little need to hurry down the two mile corridor. The traffic jam around the first railway crossings grew steadily worse as the last tanks of the Fife and Forfar regimental group left the area and their motor infantry company got their vehicles over. The first squadrons of the Hussars' tanks arrived on the scene shortly after 09.35 hours: just as A Squadron of 3rd RTR was approaching Grentheville, B Squadron of the Fifes was crossing the Paris railway towards Four, and the Fifes' C Squadron was beginning its death ride in front of Cagny.

The Hussars had even more difficulty crossing the railway than the two forward regiments, as wheeled vehicles still queuing for the few practical crossings blocked their way. Tanks sought out the paths of least resistance, and the leading troops of A Squadron strayed eastward in search of a clear passage. Suddenly from one of the forward troop commanders came an urgent report of *Tiger* tanks spotted moving in the vicinity of the large walled farm of le Prieuré. Like the preceding regimental commanders, Lieutenant-Colonel Perry Harding needed no reminding of the need to keep pressing on. But enemy tanks so close on his left flank simply could not be ignored. A Squadron was ordered to hold in place and put down suppressive fire while C Squadron came up around the left to flank the enemy force. Then, if possible, C Squadron alone would remain to 'mask' the enemy, protecting tanks and others alike at the nearby railway crossings. A and B Squadrons could thereby maintain the southwards momentum, with C rejoining as soon as relieved by the leading elements of Guards Armoured Division. Major Shebbeare's C Squadron moved into place. Formed their protective line, they witnessed a sight that was to become depressingly familiar as the day wore on.

> *Sad little parties began to come back on foot. They were the surviving members of the leading crews... They all looked smoke grimed, as does anyone who has just jumped out of a burning tank, while, beside the more active members, staggered the black-skinned figures of badly burned men. Some of the parties carried stretchers, on which still figures lay. We gave these groups a passing glance and watched our flanks intently. The sharp crack of an eighty-eight sounded as a Tiger opened up upon us from the east. It was supported by more than one Panther and, in the battle which followed, Second Troop of "C" Squadron destroyed two enemy tanks and a Nebelwerfer. Captain Hagger destroyed a Tiger, though A Squadron lost two tanks before the opposition was silenced.'*[13]

The enemies were not 'Tigers', though unseen Tiger tanks were indeed present in woods just a mile to the east. Approaching 10.00 hours, frantic efforts were being made to get these into battleworthy state. But the hour of their appearance in combat was yet to come. Nor were reports of Panther tanks any more accurate. There was at this time none on the GOODWOOD battlefield. Nevertheless, enemy fire here as well as further forward on the British left flank was now beginning to cause losses and

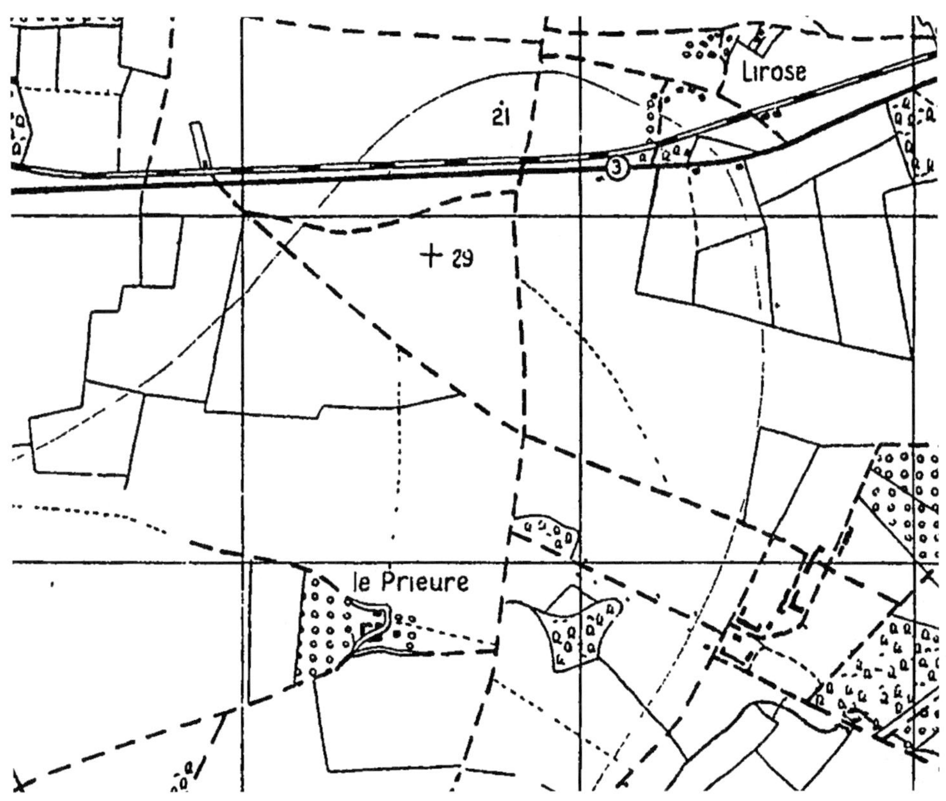

delays. Captain Heywood of the Grenadier Guards, assigned to the Hussars as liaison officer, left and hastened north to bring down his regiment's tanks to relieve the lingering C Squadron.

THE BRIGADIER

As soon as the tanks of the 23rd Hussars were past, Roscoe Harvey's 29th Brigade Tac Headquarters motored on south, over the railway, past the belt of bocage hedge, and into the cover of the hedgerows north of le Mesnil Frémentel. Here, a field appeared to offer a good position from which to conduct the next phase of the brigade's operations. The stout hedgerow running the length of the southern face of the field offered not only cover but also hidden vantage points overlooking the north wall of le Mesnil Frémentel; at its eastern end, a short stub of the hedge bent back to offer protection from the direction of Cagny.

Harvey's immediate concern was to subdue the enemy still holding le Mesnil. With the Royal Tanks to the west and the Fifes to the east both having left this German outpost in their rear, and with supporting vehicles needing to follow through, the German-held priory presented a potential threat to the brigade's operations. There are times in battle when it is hard for an attacking force to distinguish between an 'isolated enemy pocket' and a serious obstacle. Besides, Harvey had no way of knowing when or where a major German counter-attack might arise, and a British-held strongpoint would be a valuable bulwark against such a development.

Taking le Mesnil would require a mixed-arm force: heavy firepower, obviously, to suppress the defences; and infantry, the only arm capable of taking and holding ground. The brigade's infantry amounted to a single battalion, whose three rifle companies were already allocated one each to the three armoured regiments. Two of these had already passed by and Harvey had no thoughts of distracting the Hussars from their southward march. However, he had other resources. At Harvey's side were the commanders of his brigade support arms. The three 13th Royal Horse Sexton batteries under Lieutenant-Colonel Bob Daniels were no less committed to the support of his three armoured regiments than were the motor infantry companies. But also present was the young Lieutenant-Colonel Tony Hunter of 8th Rifle Brigade. Although the majority of his battalion was with the forward tank squadrons, nevertheless he still retained a small mobile reserve in the shape of his Headquarters Company plus the two machine gun platoons of his Support Company. At 09.55 hours, Hunter was ordered to 'mop up and take over' le Mesnil, with troops of the 22nd Dragoons' flails and of Royal Engineers AVREs in support. At the time, the 8th RB Headquarters troops were still negotiating the first railway; it would take over half an hour for Hunter to assemble the attackers. It appears that the AVREs were not called upon to assist, possibly because they were too deeply involved in creating crossing points over the rail embankment. But the infantry were hurried forward, alongside the troops of Sherman Crabs, the very mine-clearing tanks whose presence had been so unwelcome to Pip Roberts and which had yet to find a use on the battlefield. The GOC himself arrived in the field as preparations for the assault were being made.

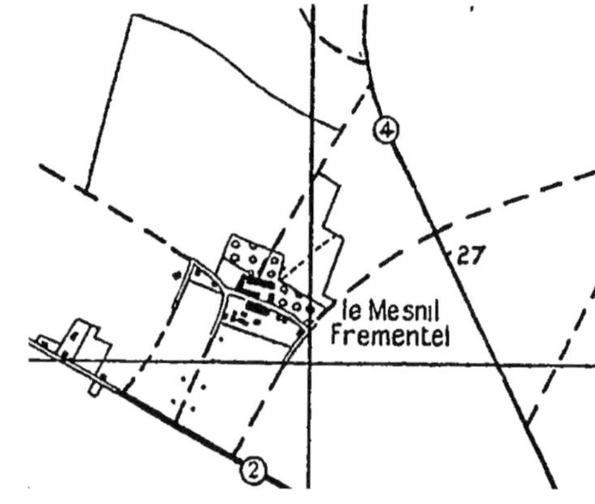

THE GENERAL OFFICER COMMANDING

Major-General 'Pip' Roberts had begun the day with his tank Tac Headquarters near the small wood west of Amfreville where 11th Armoured Division Main Headquarters was established. He was all too conscious that his division's was to begin its second battle as it had begun its first: divided. His tank brigade and his infantry brigade had different objectives and were, initially at least, to be fighting separate battles. Still, there was no doubt in Roberts' mind that his leadership would be in greatest need in support of the tanks. The task set for Jack Churcher's 159 Infantry Brigade seemed relatively straightforward. Though annoyed that

Tac HQ tanks (boxed) and Protection Troop (circled) north of le Mesnil

his own infantry had to be employed in the task of clearing Cuverville and Démouville, Roberts had given them ample support to get the job done. With the infantry brigade were the divisional towed Field Regiment (the Ayrshire Yeomanry) and the Northants Yeomanry's Cromwells (whose value in a purely reconnaissance function Roberts had come to question – they were after all *tanks*!) in a direct support role.[14]

> *In view of the tremendous hammering these two villages would have received… I thought they could be dealt with fairly quickly. Consequently, I concentrated my attention on the armoured brigade's advance.*[15]

Roberts' elevated vantage point commanded a good view of the bombing, but once the artillery barrage began the view was obscured by clouds of dust. He decided to move forward, his own tank leading (the ADC, Captain Charles Pidduck, normally navigated at the head of the column but this morning was temporarily incapacitated by mosquito stings). Roberts was mildly concerned to find no queue for the passages through the minefields:

> *'I rather hoped that the Guards Armoured Division… might be jockeying us for a place, but no sign of them.*[16]

The three Cromwell command tanks and their escort troop of Shermans stopped in the area of the Forming Up Place south of the minefields, on the slight elevation of the Butte de la Hogue. To the west could be made out the infantry advancing over open ground towards the ruins that had been Cuverville; ahead the tail elements of the 23rd Hussars were progressing south. From yet further ahead came word of the initial difficulties experienced crossing the Troarn railway line. The CRA, Brigadier B J 'Frizz' Fowler set about trying to organize a delay in the commencement of the second phase of the rolling barrage. His work was being interrupted by sudden shellbursts, so Roberts moved the HQ group five hundred yards east, only to receive a further 'stonc' which cut in two the map board on which the CRA was working (for convenience and field of vision, this board was affixed prominently to the turret top). There was no alternative but to abandon the higher ground and descend south.

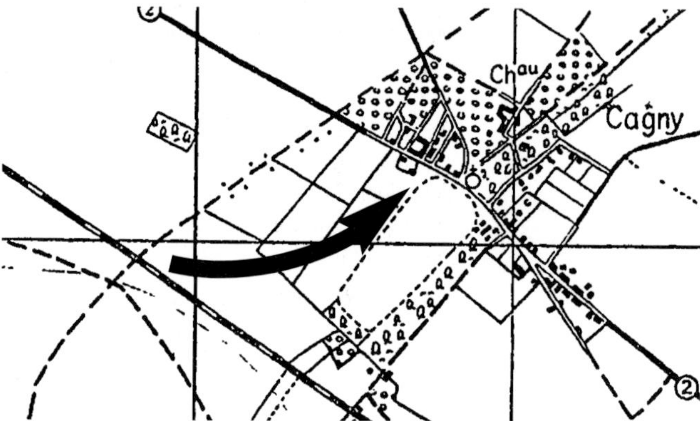

The projected assault on Cagny by F Company, 8 RB.

The significance of this move was not realised at the time. After moving south to join the tail elements of 29th Armoured Brigade, Major-General Roberts became ever more deeply involved with the affairs of that brigade to the exclusion of the wider picture. In effectively delegating control of his infantry brigade to Churcher, the British Army's most capable commander of an armoured division limited his influence over the battle to that of a brigadier. Roscoe Harvey was himself a brigadier imbued with sufficient energy and aggression to have conducted his brigade's battle with minimal direction throughout this most difficult day. Instead of retaining a grasp of events at division and corps level, Roberts' presence near the front lines throughout 18 July risked narrowing his perspective and arguably contributed little to proceedings. However, it will also be seen that other British commanders no less senior than Roberts also failed to exercise their proper scope of command.

Roberts and his followers followed the tracks of the preceding tanks and arrived at Roscoe Harvey's 29th Brigade Tac HQ a little after 10.00 hours. The position looked grim. On his approach, Roberts had not failed to note the mass of knocked out and burning tanks in the direction of Cagny. His arrival coincided with a severe mortaring. Still, he quickly found that 3rd RTR was well on the way southwards, and so too the forward squadrons of the Fifes who had evidently escaped the ambush laid for their reserve: 'I was really quite happy with the situation, except that in the rear a little trouble had developed.' Preparations were under way for the proposed assault on le Mesnil, with the Dragoons' flail tanks deployed in an arc around the west side of the walled farm, pouring in HE rounds from just four hundred yards range. Roberts did not interfere (no doubt he was pleased to see the flails being put to good use).

Overall, Roberts saw grounds for optimism. While sympathising with the plight of the Fifes' commander, his sympathy would not extend to altering the battle plan.

> *Perhaps you would like to consider what you would do as commanding officer [of a tank regiment] when, having not heard from your rear squadron for a short time, you don't get them on the air, and you look back and you find that all of these were knocked out. Some of them were burning and some of them the crews have bailed out from; at any rate, they're non-operational. Now, a little bit after this had occurred, I had come forward in my Tac Headquarters and I had gone to Brigadier Harvey who was in the outskirts of le Mesnil Frémentel. A lot of mortar fire was coming down, so I got onto the back of his tank to enquire exactly what situation was. And as I was there, I heard that it was the intention of the CO of the Fife and Forfar Yeomanry to get his motor company on their feet and to attack Cagny. Bearing in mind that I had particularly asked that we should not have to take Cagny, and bearing in mind that our objectives were further over on the right flank, I did not want to start getting involved on the left flank, as the Guards were coming forward and they were going to take over Cagny. So, I told Brigadier Harvey to cancel that order.*

Later, Pip Roberts was characteristically honest about his mistake.

> *How unfortunate was it that I had that order cancelled. Because the motor company on its own could easily have cleared up the village in a very short time.*[17]

Speculating about 'what would have happened if…' is a dangerous trap for historians. In the dust and smoke of the 18 July battle, mistakes were made on both sides. War is the province of uncertainty, and battles are not generally won by avoiding mistakes altogether, but rather by taking calculated risks in the hopes of making one or two fewer mistakes than the enemy. Sadly, Roberts' self-confessed error of judgement was

11th Armoured (Tank) Tac HQ, followed by its protection troop of Shermans.

compounded by a later action. Convinced that Cagny was held in some considerable strength,

> *when the Guards Armoured Division began to arrive I rushed over to the leading troop and warned them of the situation, and a few minutes later got hold of the CO. I fear I badly misled them.*[18]

The extent to which Roberts' warning may have influenced the Guards' caution is impossible to judge. Their performance in this, their first battle revealed the division to be somewhat ponderous in contrast to their less risk-averse 11th Armoured colleagues. Certainly, getting into and past Cagny as far as Frénouville was going to take Guards Armoured all that remained of the day and all of the next.

References

(1) Close, interview at Staff College, Camberley, 1979
(2) Close, interview at Staff College, Camberley, 1979. An 'OP' is an observation post, in this case a tank. The 'FOO' was the Forward Observation Officer in command of the post, directing and authorizing fire missions. In a British artillery regiment, the senior officers generally operated as FOOs, forward of the guns. A 'stonc' was a standard artillery concentration.
(3) Close, interview at Staff College, Camberley, 1979
(4) Close, interview at Staff College, Camberley, 1979
(5) Roberts, interview at Staff College, Camberley, 1979
(6) Roberts, interview at Staff College, Camberley, 1979
(7) In his writing and his contributions to the Staff College Battlefield Tours, Major Close refers to *'the whole of the regimental group'* following his lead across the railway. When questioned on this point, he was emphatic that his own crossing point was via the Caen to Paris railway (a landmark so clear that it is inconceivable that it could have been mistaken). He admitted however that only his small band crossed at that point; he thought that the rest of the regiment used the main Caen to Cagny road underpass five hundred yards to the north. In fact, only a small number of tanks (possibly the remaining troop of Close's squadron) crossed there. Out of Close's sight, the main body of the regimental group later moved around Grentheville on the *eastern* side of the railway embankment.
(8) This and previous passages from Thorpe diary.
(9) This was standard German procedure: a Russian study of the Kursk offensive in mid-1943 concluded that, *'German artillery, tanks, and self-propelled guns did not stop firing against tanks until they caught fire, even when the tank had stopped as a result of being hit.'* From 'The Battle of Kursk', Journal of Slavic Military Studies, March 1994, p 112
(10) Thorpe diary
(11) Not to be confused with Lieutenant G G O ('Gee Gee') Hutchison or Sergeant Hutcheson, both of the Fifes' C Squadron!
(12) Bishop, '23rd Hussars', p 72
(13) Bishop, '23rd Hussars', p 74
(14) The 11th Armoured Division history suggests that the 1943 decision to incorporate an 'armoured reconnaissance regiment' may have been *'merely a subterfuge to incorporate a fourth tank unit'* albeit one equipped with Cromwell instead of Sherman (and Firefly) tanks. Eventually both the equipment and the employment of the fourth regiment were to become *'practically identical, and ultimately quite identical, with that of the ordinary armoured regiment.'* (Palamountain, 'Taurus Pursuant', p 8)
(15) Roberts, p 172
(16) Roberts, p 172
(17) Roberts, interview at Staff College, Camberley, 1979
(18) Roberts, p 175

Chapter 7

18 JULY, MIDDAY: THE RIDGE AND THE CAULDRON

By 10.00 hours, 29th Armoured Brigade had two sharp prongs inserted deeply into enemy territory. Troops of tanks at the tip of each prong had a clear view of a crest line barely two miles distant. The order was clear: get to the ridge and complete the breakthrough. The hope in every heart was that most of the work had already been achieved.

29th BRIGADE: CLEARING THE PATH

General Roberts and Brigadier Harvey in their respective Tac HQs, just north of le Mesnil Frémentel, were truly in the midst of the battle. On every side, the fight was intensifying as the shock of the aerial bombardment wore off and the enemy began to reorganize and resist. This was not entirely bad news. In its first day of battle, three weeks before at the end of June, 11th Armoured had been ground to a halt by enemy outposts and hasty counter attacks long before reaching its (ambitious) objectives. Now, the growing volume of defensive fire indicated to the general and the brigadier that they had already penetrated the enemy's Main Line of Resistance. Confident of suppressing that resistance, relying on his general's assurance that two further armoured divisions were hurrying to secure and expand the gap punched through the enemy lines, Roscoe Harvey's single-minded goal was to press his tanks forward to the ridge. Meanwhile, around Harvey's headquarters, the work of mopping up continued.

Tony Hunter's improvised 8th Rifle Brigade battlegroup began the attack on le Mesnil Frémentel with eleven Sherman flail tanks firing against the western walls of the complex. Other tanks (possibly including some troops of the passing 23rd Hussars) added their fire against the north wall. Closing to barely two hundred yards, the flails' fire covered the advance. Most of the eight carriers of 8th RB's E (Support) Company were present, and the small carriers swept through the corn with machine guns blazing. Next, an ad hoc infantry platoon which had been scraped together from Hunter's HQ Company prepared for the assault. These advanced under cover of the fire. The enemy was by now so suppressed by the tanks' Brownings and the carriers' Vickers machine guns that the riflemen were able to cross the open ground and gain the shelter of the west wall.[1] Supported by men dismounting from the MG carriers, the small force went over the wall and began methodically to work across the farm buildings. Sensing the resistance crumble, the footsoldiers summoned a Sherman tank (possibly one of the Dragoons' 'control' tanks: equipped with one '38' and two '19' wireless sets,

The assault on le Mesnil: to the west are clearly identifiable eleven Dragoons' flail tanks (circled).
Supporting Shermans shown in squares.

flail-less but retaining its 75mm main armament). Its flanks covered by the infantry, the Sherman passed through the wall and entered the central courtyard, where it poured fire through the windows and doorways of the inner walls of the farm houses, and came to rest on top of the battalion headquarters bunker of *I./125. Panzergrenadierregiment*.

3. Kompanie commander *Oberleutnant* Bandomir (who had earlier regretted his lack of antitank weapons), now abandoned his own dugout outside the north wall, ducking through a gap in the wall and through the orchard it enclosed, in hopes of finding men of his company, or indeed anyone capable of resistance. From the edge of the courtyard, he was horrified to see the Sherman tank sitting on the battalion bunker. Recoiling, he passed again through the orchard. Collecting men both able and wounded, he determined to leave the farm and seek a place to hide up with them until dark. The band got as far as a tree-lined path east of le Mesnil. Before long, armoured vehicles rolled to point blank range and, unable to prolong the struggle, Bandomir surrendered.

Arrows mark Bandomir's path from his command bunker to eventual capture. Three half-tracks and a scout car stand by the west wall. At least one Sherman tank remains within the courtyard.

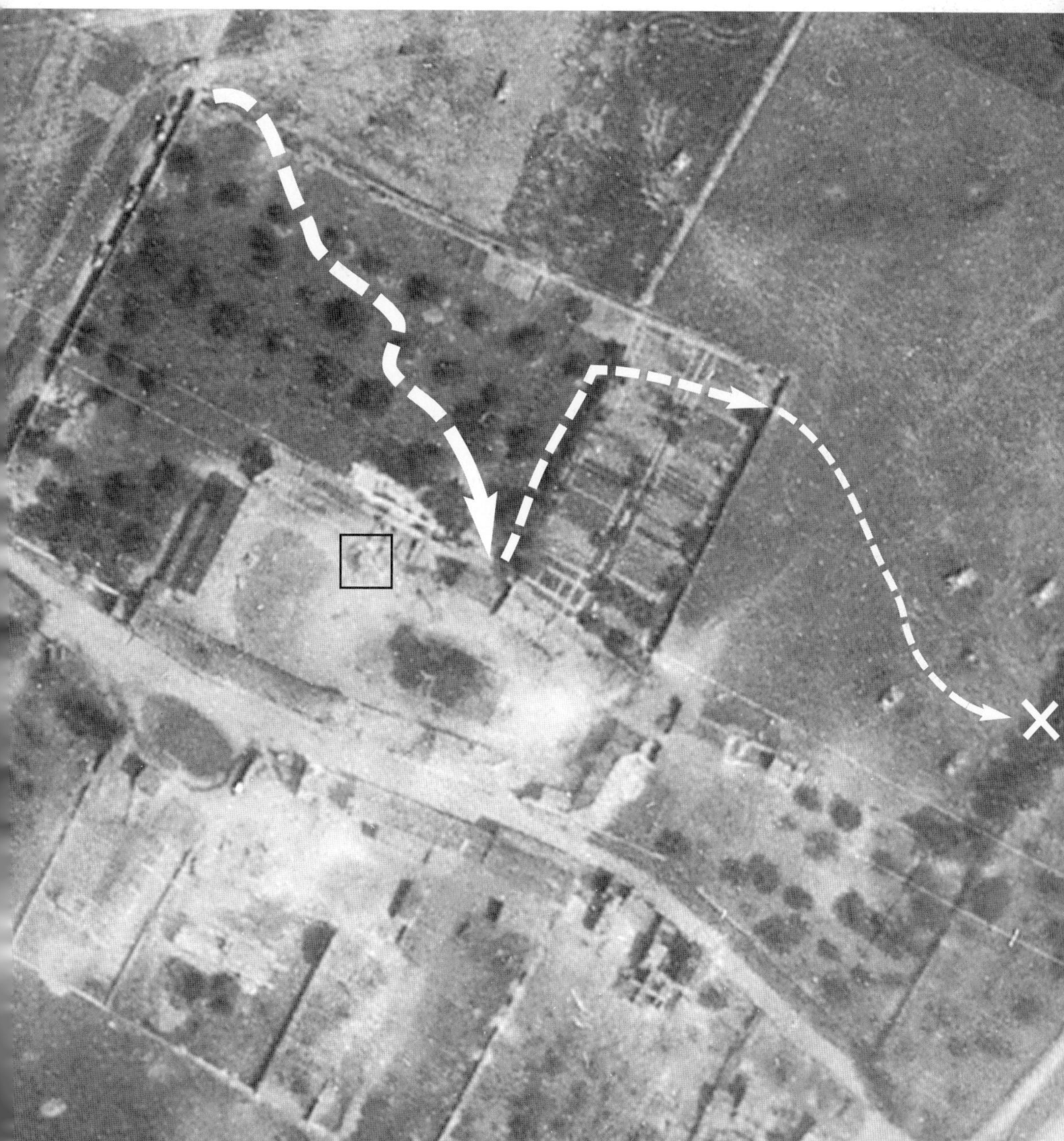

Inside le Mesnil today. Philippe Wirton indicates the position of the battalion HQ bunker.

It was about midday that the war ended for me and the survivors of 3. Kompanie. *The situation did not admit any possibility of escape. Lacking any antitank weapons and with manpower become so weak, it was impossible to maintain command of my company.*[2]

When 8th RB finally rounded up the prisoners, Bandomir counted only 134 of what had been the better part of the battalion. He noted too the abundant

The sunlit cornfields west of the railway embankment.

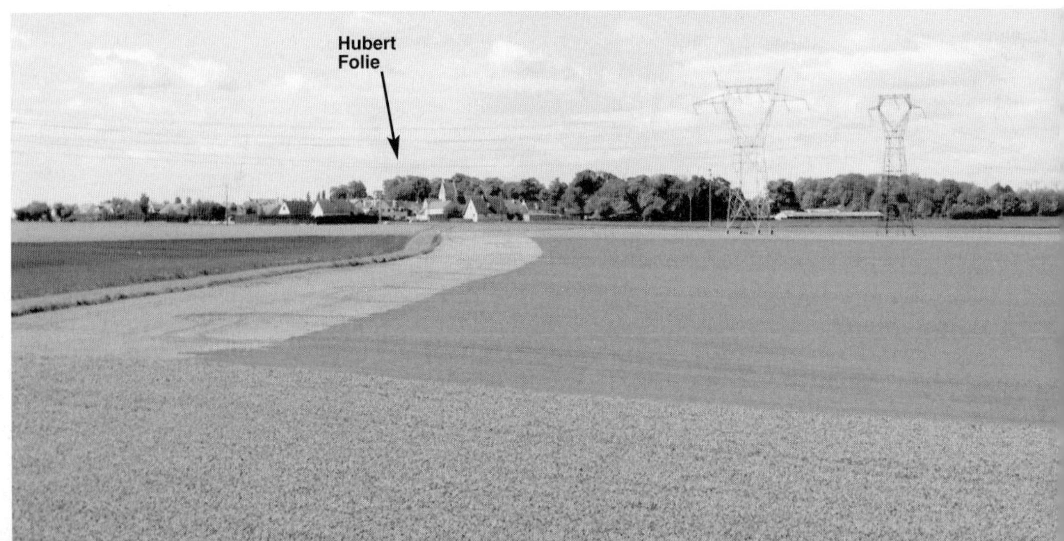

equipment and the relative freshness of the British troops, in contrast to his own weary grenadiers.

3rd RTR: ACROSS THE RAILWAY

Shortly after 10.00 hours, Major Close with his reunited A Squadron was reconnoitring west of the Chemin de Fer Minier in the general direction of Cormelles. His 1 Troop leader, Lieutenant Langdon, thought he saw a Panzer IV in Cormelles itself, which he fired upon. But any Germans in that direction were preoccupied with the Canadian threat from the north, and Langdon's superiors were concerned only with attaining the day's objective, which lay due south. Close himself had his eyes, and his binoculars, firmly fixed on the Bourguébus ridge. He scanned methodically: from the railway running straight up to Bourguébus itself, westward past Hubert-Folie with its distinctive church tower, and still further around past Bras, largely hidden in trees, to distant Ifs, shimmering in the haze on the far side of the important Caen-Falaise highway. All in that direction seemed tranquillity. There was reason to hope that success lay just ahead.

Meanwhile, the main force of 3rd RTR was pressing its advance past Grentheville. As the main body of tanks worked their way southward across the dual-track Paris railway line, progressing into the narrow passage between the embankment and the western side of the Grentheville woods, they found themselves sheltered from enemy fire. Forward elements of 8th Rifle Brigade's G Company dismounted and entered the woods. Clearing Grentheville of the enemy would not be completed for some hours, and G Company did not attempt this. For now they were directed only to screen the treeline west of the Grentheville chateau as the bulk of the regiment resumed the move south. When the regimental group moved out along the eastern side of the railway embankment, the motor infantry followed. Grentheville was not yet secured.

Progress was careful rather than rapid. Brigade HQ noted a report at 10.12 hours that '3 R Tks getting around West of GRENTHEVILLE.' While vehicles accumulated in the 'dead ground' west of the village, the tanks pressed on south in a narrow column. Emerging from the narrow gap between the

Bras
Hubert-Folie

Bourguébus
Chemin de Fer Minier

Tank tracks clearly indicate the route of 3rd RTR regimental group south from Grentheville and across the railway embankment.

orchards and the elevated railway, the leading tanks kept close to the foot of the embankment, eyes and turrets trained left towards the walled fields south of Grentheville, 500 metres distant. Of this stage of the advance, little has been recorded. The attention of Brigade HQ was elsewhere, and enemy fire appears to have been negligible. Somewhere ahead of 3rd RTR, Becker's 3. Batterie was out of touch with 200. Abteilung headquarters; on his own initiative the battery commander had broken contact with 3rd RTR and fallen back from Grentheville in the direction of Soliers.

Soliers lay even closer to the elevated railway than did Grentheville. It is not clear whether the advancing 3rd RTR group was unwilling to risk a close approach to yet another village; perhaps the leaders heard gunfire from that direction (Becker's guns and others located in Soliers were by now beginning to engage B Squadron of the Fifes, away to the east). It may be that Colonel Silvertop was simply keen to find a safe route across the Minier railway in order to expedite progress towards the ridge. In the event, before approaching within five hundred yards of Soliers, most of the regiment's tracked vehicles turned right and climbed the embankment along a short stretch where the slope was not as steep as elsewhere. Two main crossing points were established, one hundred yards apart, four hundred yards north of the bridge where the minor Soliers to Cormelles road passed under the railway. Further back, wheeled vehicles crossed under the railway using a small bridge due west of Grentheville.

So it was that shortly after 10.30 hours the 3rd RTR regimental group found itself on the far side of the embankment, in the peaceful landscape west of the railway. Increasing numbers of eyes joined Bill Close's careful scrutiny of the two villages, Hubert-Folie and Bras. Just a mile away, up a shallow slope over fields deep in golden, sun-dappled wheat, the twin objectives beckoned. The temptation to take them on the bounce may have occurred to some. By rights, according to the briefing, the morning's advance of six miles in three hours should by now have taken the regiment well into the German rear areas. Colonel Silvertop could see that seizing the two villages ahead would cap his regiment's success and provide a springboard for further exploitation. But, for all his drive, the desert veteran understood the difference between drive and folly. The villages were potential strongpoints. The advance would be uphill over open fields with only the grain and the occasional ripple in the ground offering the slightest cover. Before he ordered an all-out assault, he would have the objective reconnoitred.

When Colonel Silvertop cast about for a Rifle Brigade officer to conduct the reconnaissance, G Company commander Major Noel Bell was not to be seen. However, among the vehicles of the regimental HQ group alongside the railway bridge over the Soliers to Hubert-Folie road, was the half-track of the 11 Platoon commander, twenty year old Lieutenant David Stileman. He later recalled,

> *At this juncture, it so happened that my platoon headquarters half-track vehicle was some three yards distant from the gallant colonel, and fixing me with those steely eyes, he beckoned me over and said, "Boy, we must find out if Hubert-Folie is occupied."*

Leading squadrons of 3rd RTR fan out as they press south towards the ridge.

Soliers
Chemin de Fer Minier
Hubert-Folie

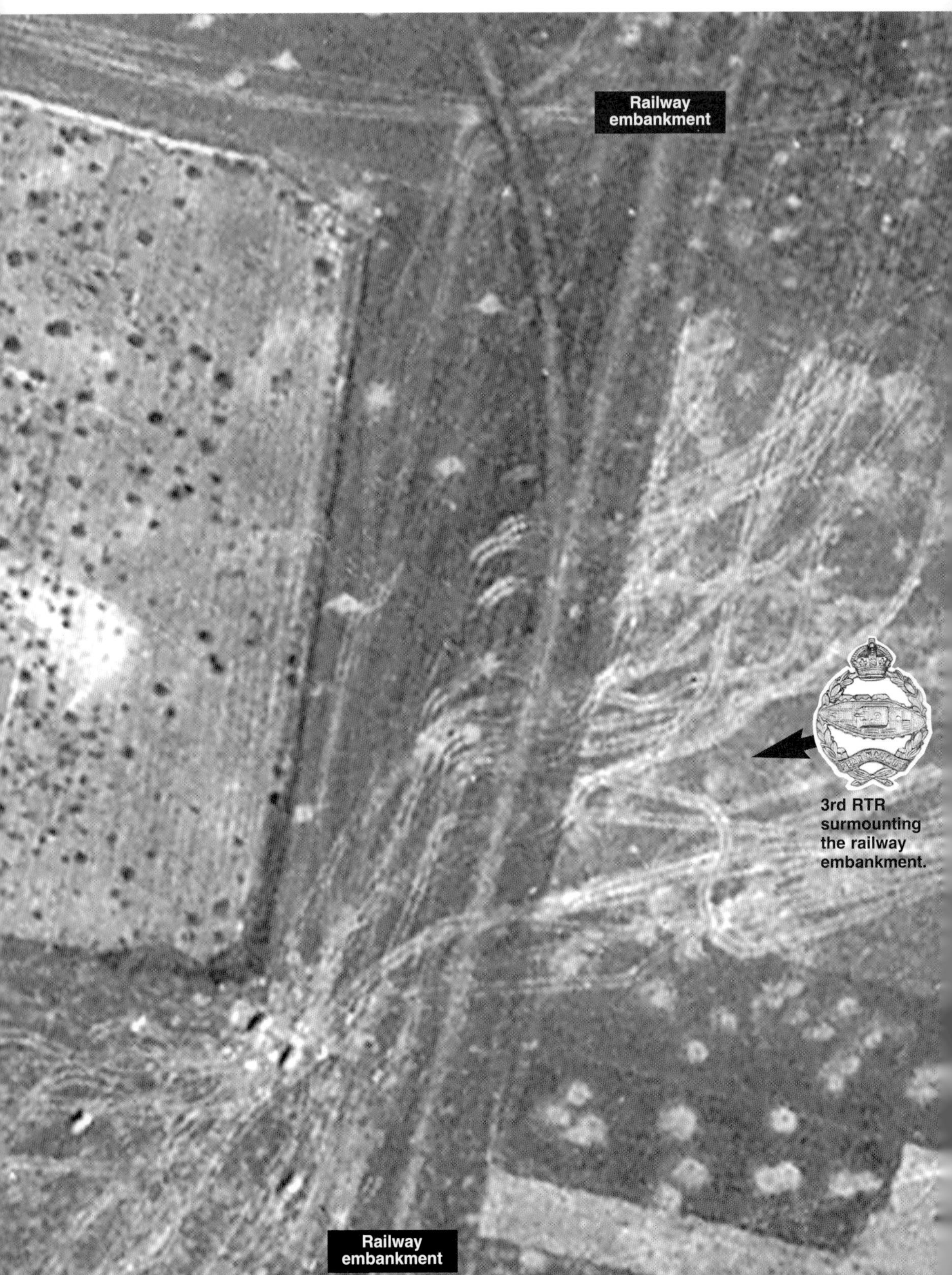
Railway embankment
Railway embankment
3rd RTR surmounting the railway embankment.

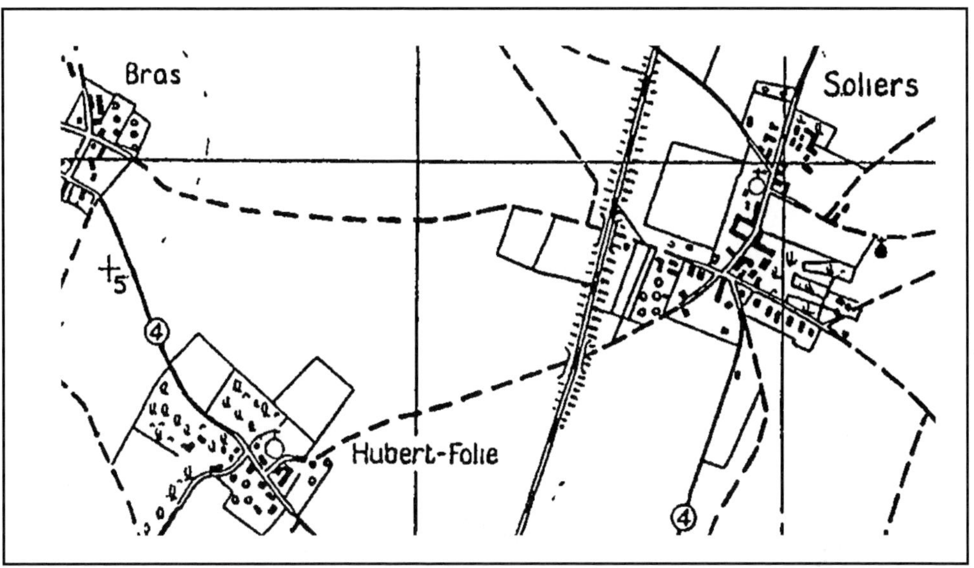

"Jolly good idea, Sir," I said or something equally fatuous. "How do you propose to do it?"

"You're going to do it," came the reply. And, as I swallowed, the ever-reassuring Noel Bell appeared at my elbow. The plan, like all good plans, was extremely simple. I was temporarily to command a section of the carrier platoon and drive hell-for-leather down the main street of the village. If we fail to appear, the chances are that the village was occupied; but if we emerge unscathed the chances are that the village was not occupied.[3]

The apprehensive Stileman received words of encouragement and more practical assistance from his seniors.

Now, it so happened that Noel Bell produced a marvellous air photograph of the village of Hubert-Folie and the surrounding area. Well of course this meant that I didn't have to fuss around with maps. And also at this moment [Major] Bill Smyth-Osborne who commanded H Battery of 13th RHA offered his services. And he decided to put a heavy artillery concentration down on Hubert Folie as we approached to the village. And the last shell was to be a phosphorous one, and this [dense white smoke] was the signal for us to start on our journey down the village.[4]

Stileman took command of two carriers of the G Company scout platoon. Following Bell's advice, the carriers were to edge as close as possible to the village under cover of the promised artillery 'stonc'. This duly arrived, and when a single white smoke shell burst on the church tower of Hubert-Folie, the party sprinted up the shallow slope to the village.[5]

Racing through the fields on the north side of the Soliers to Hubert-Folie road, the five-foot high carriers were barely visible above the uncut crop.

Believe you me, once we'd started, there was no time for sauntering and within seconds we appeared at the other end of the village and reported back to Noel Bell and told him that we had met no resistance and had seen no sign of the enemy. But how wrong one can be! Because as we discovered later, the village was groaning with enemy.[6]

In fact, the truth lay in between Stileman's optimistic reconnaissance report and his later overestimate. As was the case elsewhere, the British fixation with the village 'strongpoints' tended to blind them to significant forces arrayed around and behind. The main antitank strength of the enemy at this time was to be found in gun emplacements higher on the ridge behind and on the flanks of the villages. On 18 July, the meagre infantry reserves of 21. Panzerdivision simply did not allow for more than token garrisons in Hubert-Folie and Bras. At any rate, whether suppressed by the artillery, surprised by the sudden onrush of the racing carriers, or recognising the small reconnaissance party for what it was, the defenders of Hubert-Folie did not reveal themselves.

3rd RTR: ONTO THE RIDGE

With every indication that the way ahead was clear, Silvertop ordered the ridge to be stormed. The regiment was ready. The brief hiatus while the

Stleman began his reconnaissance mission from here, up the gentle rise to Hubert-Folie church.

Opposite, Hubert-Folie: arrows show Stileman's reconnaissance, up the hill, around the church, and through the village.

reconnaissance was ordered and executed had given time for some reorganization. Each of the three sabre squadrons had lost a half-dozen tanks: squadron commanders profited from the time to re-structure troops. Now, the squadrons were spread out in a crescent-shaped front line: from the regimental group's headquarters by the railway bridge on the Soliers to Hubert-Folie road, north alongside the railway embankment, and then north west along the Soliers to Cormelles road. On the far right flank was A Squadron, roughly on the mid-point of that road, a mile due north of Hubert-Folie.

Shortly before 11.30 hours, the tanks began to roll: up the slope towards the ridge. The tanks of A Squadron moved off first, advancing in a south-westerly direction aiming to pass around the eastern side of Bras. Echeloned behind to their left followed B and C Squadrons. The tanks of A Squadron ground steadily uphill: a dozen Shermans on a three hundred yard front, their treads leaving dead straight tracks in the uncut corn. In the vanguard of the advance was 1 Troop commander, Lieutenant 'Johnny' Langdon.

The quiet country scene erupted into violence as carefully sited guns let loose a torrent of Armour Piercing shot. The foremost Sherman was just short of the road leading south-east out of Bras towards Hubert-Folie. Its driver instinctively hauled the tank in a sharp left turn, then pulled back to the right in an attempt to throw off the enemy aim. But in vain. The tank was hit as it reached the road and crashed to a halt before erupting in a dense column of smoke. Langdon's tank was hit, and somehow he managed to extricate

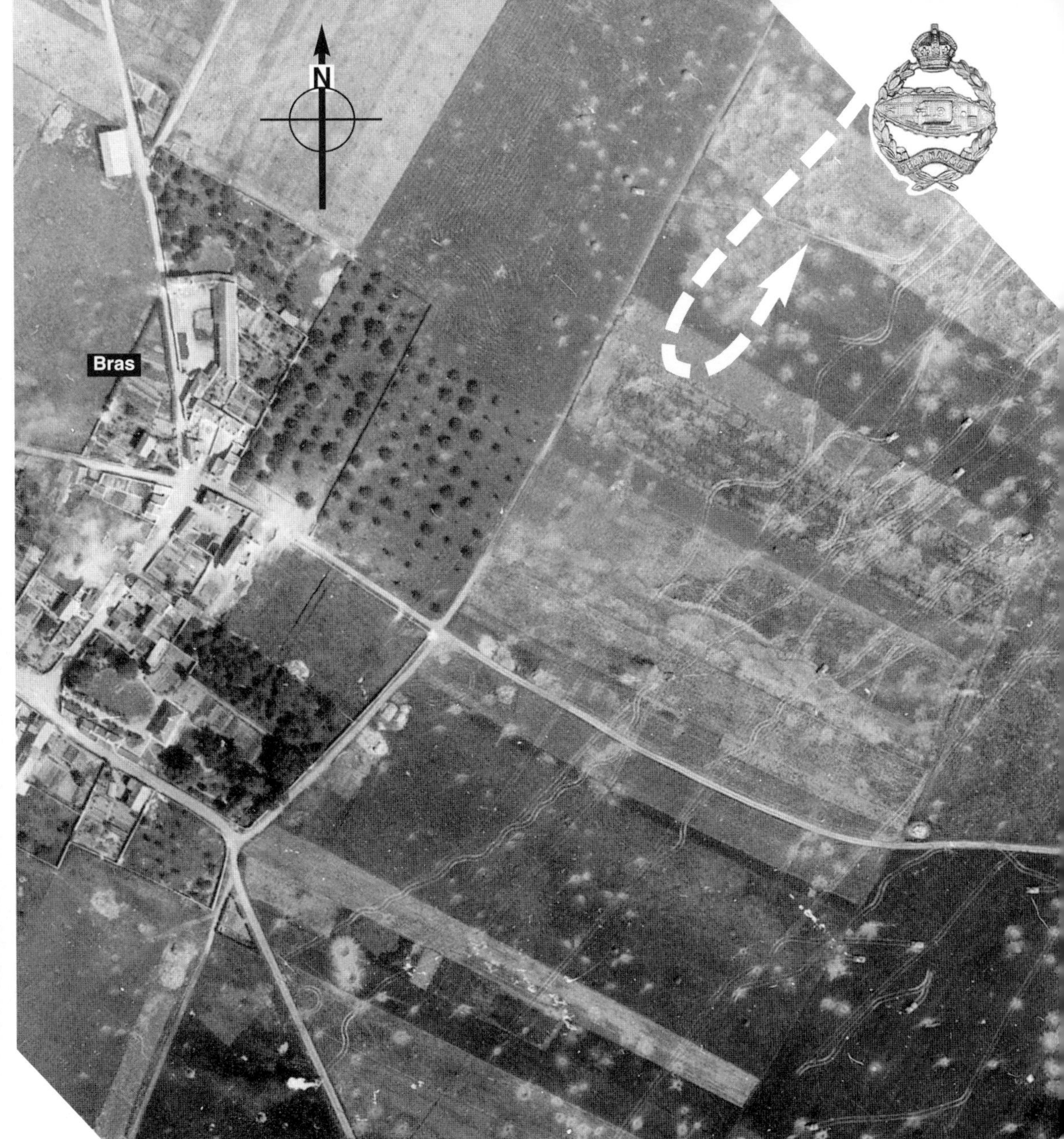

The failed assault on Bras: 3rd RTR falling back, shortly before noon.

himself and his crew as the ammunition went up and the tank burst into flame, though his gunner was mortally wounded. As smoke billowed from the stricken Sherman, Buck Kite watched from the following tank.

> *Bras is at the top of a slope beside a small wood. We started copping it there and I fired back… before the Sherman on my left brewed up. The crew baled out and came over to my tank carrying the gunner, a Scots lad called Hume who used to play for the battalion football team.*

With extraordinary bravery, Kite's tank halted alongside long enough for

N

After its drive straight up the hill this tank reversed 'left stick – right stick' until it was hit and burned.

Langdon's stricken crew to clamber aboard.

> *I thought, "My God, Hummer, you'll never keep goal again." Both legs were hanging on by threads of sinew. They got him on the back of my tank and I handed him morphine as I had other things to do... When I had reversed to the bottom of the hill Mac* [the regimental Medical Officer] *came up in a half-track and took Hummer away but I heard that he died in hospital.*[7]

Burning crewmen rolled on the ground to extinguish the flames. Blackened survivors helped each other back through the corn. Some were lifted on to the engine covers of a reversing tank, where the turret might offer some protection. The more fortunate were picked up by a regimental ambulance or by 8th Rifle Brigade half-tracks and carriers to be rushed back to an aid post.

The surviving tanks of A Squadron needed no instructions. Facing an insurmountable deluge of fire they changed gear and reversed down the hill, drivers hauling on their steering columns, 'left stick, right stick', zigzagging back the way they had come. As his squadron fell back, Bill Close's own tank was hit with a crash. Fortunately it did not brew.

> *There was a hell of a crack and someone shouted "Bale out, sir", so I hopped down and saw that a shot had neatly removed the rear sprocket and the track was cut in two.*[8]

The crew baled out unhurt and Close sent the four crewmen back to the cover of the rail embankment where an advanced aid post was to be found alongside regimental headquarters. Close then dashed over to take over his sergeant's tank. He was 'rather disconcerted' to find this tank had already been hit and abandoned, so he carried on to resume command of the squadron from the troop corporal's tank. Covered by the two surviving Shermans of Buck Kite's troop (one a Firefly) and accompanied by the faithful artillery officer in his Stuart, Close organized the survivors of his squadron.

A Squadron regrouped, taking what shelter they could find from vegetation, folds in the ground, or abandoned tanks (whose growing numbers helped by attracting a proportion of the Germans' fire). B and C Squadrons also took losses in the opening salvoes, and their advance angled away eastwards, away from Bras, skirting Hubert-Folie in their search for a way forward. The fire appeared to be coming from all directions. From directly ahead, not only guns hidden within Bras and Hubert-Folie but also several concealed in previously unseen emplacements were unmasked behind and above the villages, with a field of vision over the battlefield hindered only by smoke from burning tanks. It is likely that one of Becker's mobile batteries had moved into positions to the west, just short of Ifs, where still more guns were emplaced, enfilading the British advance. And shortly after, the few tanks to penetrate as far south as the Hubert-Folie to Bourguébus road found themselves also exposed to flanking fire from the south east.

Jim Caswell, commanding one of the forward B Squadron tanks, 'could only see two Tigers or Panthers in a wood at Bourguébus. Until then everything had gone well.'

Langdon's tank was hit as it reached the road.

Then, disaster.

Tanks reversing away from Bras.

Several B Squadron tanks were knocked out, some burning. I ordered Barney (Trooper Barnes) to turn left to face the enemy tanks and then reverse… We were now firing at the enemy, but I could tell they were ranging on us. We had reversed about 25 yards and we were hit in the front and the shell killed our gunner, Bill Slater, outright. Stan Duckworth (wireless operator/loader) was seriously wounded in the legs and slumped onto the turret floor.[9]

Though himself wounded in the knee, Jim tried unsuccessfully to open the two forward crew hatches, before giving up and hauling the wounded operator out of the still-reversing tank. Jim carried the operator for an hour to an Advanced Field Dressing Station where he himself collapsed with wounds that ended his Army career. Only twenty years later did Jim learn why the tank had continued moving. Throwing the tank into reverse gear was an instinctive response.[10] Barney the driver had gone a step further by inventing a device to keep the accelerator compressed if he were wounded while reversing. The gadget served its purpose; with its driver dead at the controls the tank continued its unrelenting backwards voyage across the battlefield.

About this time, an enigmatic signal was recorded by 29th Brigade: '11.30 3 R Tks report their flanks rather exposed to AP fire from area BRAS 0663 and SOLIERS'. Almost simultaneously, 11th Armoured Division noted the position of 3rd RTR: '11.35 On line of road BRAS – BOURGUÉBUS'. This was optimistic but soon to become actuality. Before midday, three troops of B Squadron tanks did indeed reach the Bourguébus road at the point where it bridges the Chemin de Fer Minier (here the embankment became a deep cutting as the ridge steepened and the railway ascended more gradually). Individual tanks (possibly elements of the Reconnaissance Troop) had probed even deeper, south of that road. But this was to be the high-water mark of the regiment's advance. By the time the reports were received, the surviving tanks of 3rd RTR had recoiled northwards down the slope before intense fire. At 12.01 hours, VIII Corps still believed 'Battle going very well. 11 Armd Div pushed on extraordinarily well but beginning to feel a little naked.' 'A little naked' was something of an understatement.

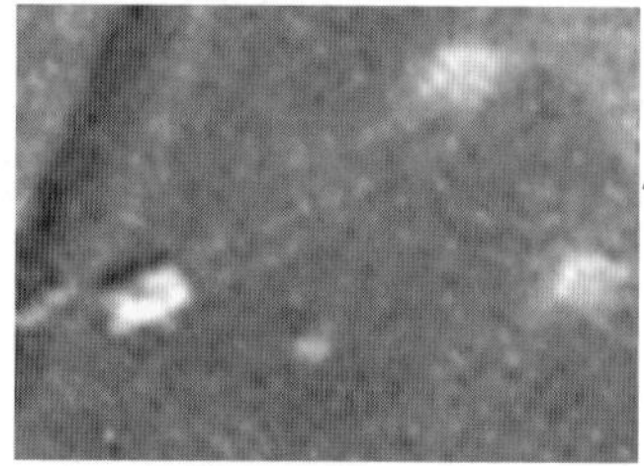

3. One lone tank progressed this far towards the Falaise road before being hit, its turret facing enemy fire from 8 o'clock.

THE CAULDRON OF FOUR

The Fife & Forfar's Colonel Scott quickly revised his plans to take account of both the apparently total loss of his reserve squadron, and also the prohibition against sending an avenging force back to clear Cagny. (Though, truth be told, the attached H Company of 8th Rifle Brigade could probably have been

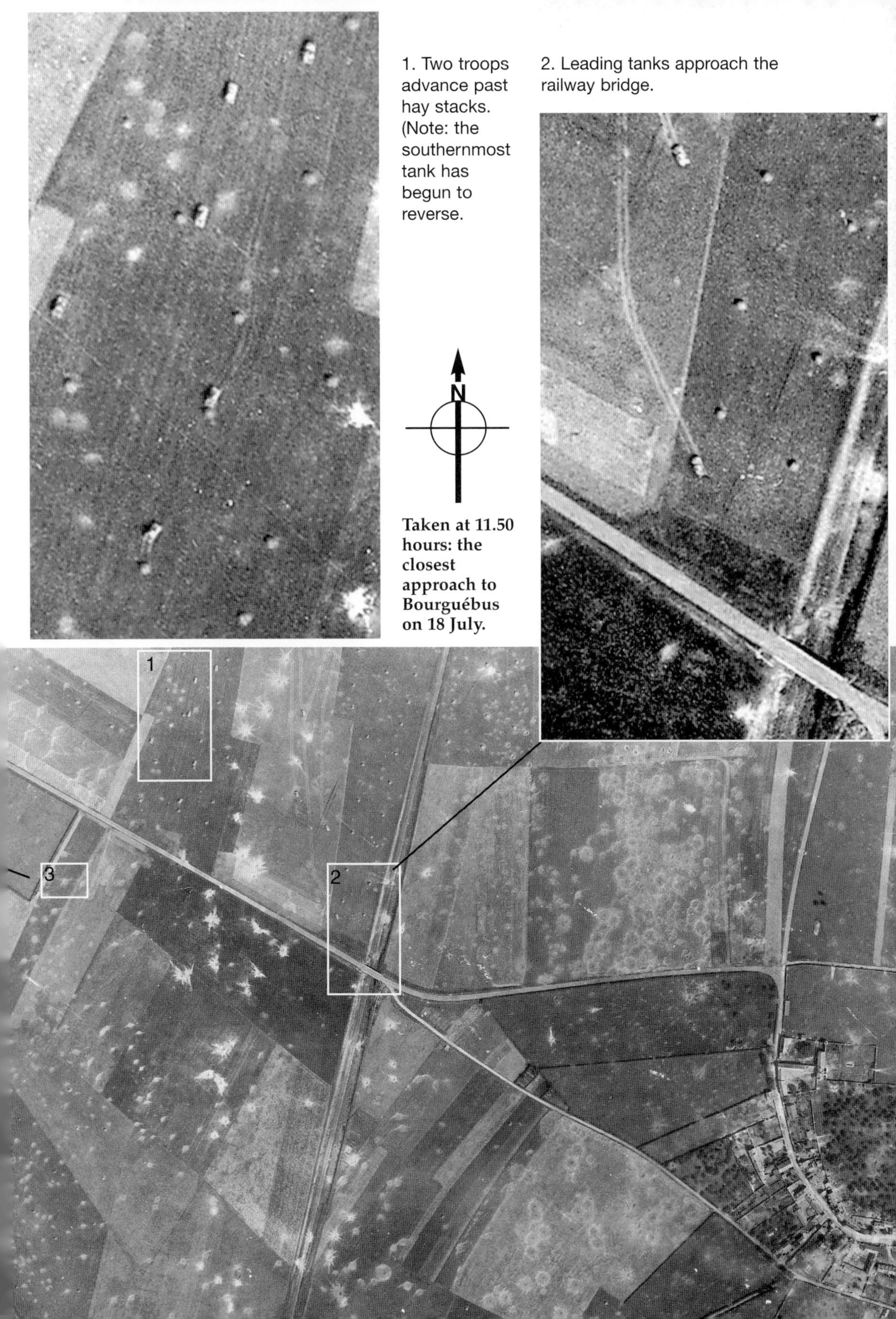

1. Two troops advance past hay stacks. (Note: the southernmost tank has begun to reverse.
2. Leading tanks approach the railway bridge.
N
1
2
3

Taken at 11.50 hours: the closest approach to Bourguébus on 18 July.

spared to accomplish this.) His regiment's route up to the Bourguébus ridge ran between Soliers and Four, a corridor barely a thousand yards wide. Scott remained convinced that this was a single squadron front, and so chose to send B Squadron forward, to be followed by A Squadron in support, less two troops protecting the left, a sensible precaution, since most of the opposition so far seemed to be coming from that flank.

B Squadron set off in a south-westerly direction. Scott recalled,

> *'We shook out into a tactical formation, passed Grentheville on our right, shooting up a number of Nebelwerfers in the woods there, and pressed on.'*

(The defenders of Grentheville were by this time too concerned with pressure from the western orchards to offer effective return fire.) Meanwhile, the Fifes' flank guard moved out south east, around the other side of Four, the farm of le Poirier on their left. Steel Brownlie recalled being,

> *given the job of looking left and covering that flank, while the rest of the regiment went*

> *on, down into the valley in front. We had no cover, except for the shape of the ground, and simply sat in the corn. I was at once fired on by what appeared to be a self-propelled gun in the valley, and two tanks to the right of me went up in smoke.To the south-east was an artillery position, a row of guns, maybe 105mms. They were firing. I did an HE shoot on them, until they shut up, and there was no movement except wisps of smoke.*[11]

Steel Brownlie's judgement (or hindsight?) was exceptionally accurate. The two tanks of Captain Hutchison's 3 Troop had indeed been brewed by fire from Becker's *4. Batterie*, now occupying positions to the south east of Four. Behind these self-propelled guns was a complex of artillery emplacements containing heavy batteries of the *Luftwaffen-Artillerie-Regiment 16*, equipped with captured Russian 12.2cm howitzers.[12]

One of the great attractions of open country for the British tank squadrons was the possibility of employing the fire and movement tactics in which they had practiced so extensively in England. The principle involved troops of tanks moving alternately: some using speed and manoeuvre to make themselves difficult targets while others behind gave covering fire. The moving elements would seek protection, ideally hull-down behind hard cover or simply using the folds in the ground, stop, and in turn open fire to cover the advance of the rear units. Unfortunately the ground over which the regiment now advanced was very open indeed. Opportunities for the leading tanks to 'go to ground' were few. Even the crops hereabouts in the triangle of fields between Grentheville, Soliers, and Four would steadily become flattened. So it was that after a very few 'bounds' forward beyond the railway line, the whole of Scott's force was in country more 'open' than they might have desired.

B Squadron was spurring forward. Before long the Soliers to Four road was reached. Tanks were within a hundred yards of the hedges and orchards around Soliers when a volley of antitank fire was loosed from the village. Becker's *3. Batterie* had successfully disengaged from its positions around Grentheville and was now well placed to meet the new threat from the north east. One tank was knocked out just outside Soliers on the Four road, opposite the little hedged roadside calvary. Others reversed away in haste. The following troops of tanks edged away from Soliers, still taking losses but now at slightly greater range, and using bursts of speed to give the Soliers gunners tricky deflection shots. Crossing the Soliers – Four road just 500 yards west of the centre of Four, tanks crept in close to a hedgerow and took measure of the situation. There was little that could be done: the Soliers guns were too well camouflaged to be picked out. To the south, more emplacements were visible on the ridge, looming above the exposed tanks. (In fact, the nearest battery was over a kilometre away, and only eight metres higher in elevation, though on that flat terrain eight metres was sufficient to give the Fifes the impression of being at the bottom of a fire-ringed bowl.)

The unequal struggle continued. At last, goaded by demands from brigade to press on, another push forward was attempted. The precise story of the Fife & Forfar's midday battle between Soliers and Four is generally glossed-over as one of those frantic exchanges in which no one could keep track of events. However, some idea of the development of the action can be gained by following the sequence of signals recorded by the parent unit, 29th Brigade Headquarters.[13] The following list includes all signals recorded by 29th Brigade as received from the 2nd Fife & Forfar Yeomanry in the three hours following 10.00, together with comments made at leisure by an author not engaged in battle and blessed with the wisdom of six decades of hindsight. (For interpretation of map references, see Appendix II)

10.02 hr: *2 FF Yeo report enemy inf and guns in SOLIERS 0862.*

10.38 hr: *2 FF Yeo in FOUR 0962*

This is misleading. Individual tanks of the regiment may have approached the northern edge of this map square around this time. But the Fifes were *not* in Four!

10.48 hr: 2 FF Yeo report SP guns in BOURGUEBUS and unspecified guns in FRENOUVILLE. Leading sqns between these two places.

Bourguébus appears to have been used to indicate the approximate direction (south) rather than the precise location of enemy batteries; 'Frénouville' likewise appears to indicate fire originating from anywhere south of a line from Four to Frénouville. The two troops of A Squadron (now reduced to six tanks) might have been approximately half-way between the two villages, but the rest of the regiment was still north-west of Four.

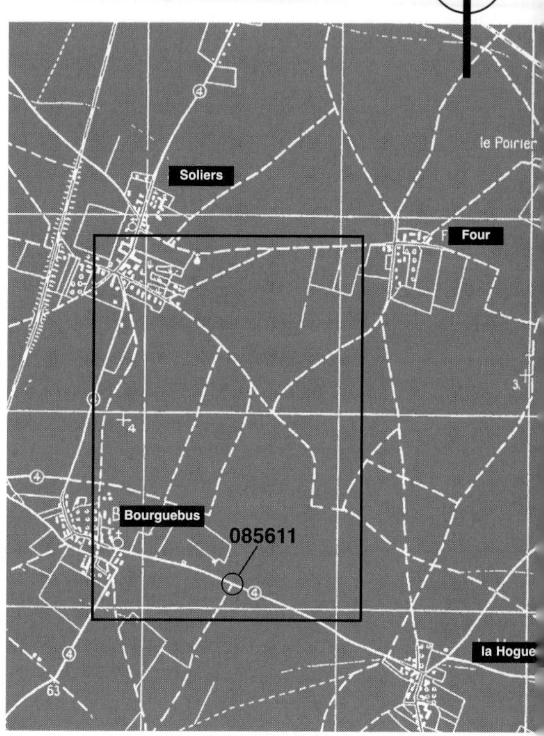

11.15 hr: *2 FF Yeo reach 085611 near BOURGUEBUS*

This is the most contentious of the signals purportedly sent by the Fifes. If true, it would have meant that tanks had reached the mid point of the road between Bourguébus and la Hogue. Far from reaching the Bourguébus to La Hogue road, it seems that no Fife & Forfar tank passed further south than the little track leading south-east out of Soliers. No explanation can be offered for this signal save that it was mistaken by someone.

11.23 hr: *2 FF Yeo report one Panther engaged on left.*

It is unlikely that any *Panther* tanks were engaged in the area so early. In the distance, an enemy vehicle firing from cover would be hard to identify.

11.30 hr: *2 FF Yeo pushing on to BOURGUEBUS*

11.38 hr: 2 FF Yeo report heavy AP fire from FRENOUVILLE 1162 which is

Calvary
Four
Soliers
Fife's advance along hedgerow
Killing field
German batteries
Bourguebus
085611
la Hogue

pinning down their left sqn

By this time, losses to B Squadron had reached the point at which A Squadron's two unengaged troops and the squadron headquarters troop had to be called forward. So B now became the 'left' squadron. Its survivors had again attempted an advance southwards (and so towards, though still very far from, Bourguébus) from the Soliers to Four road, along their sheltering hedgerow. As soon as the tanks passed the end of the hedgerow, they were immediately exposed to fire from west, south, and east (the batteries from the east only now unmasked and joining in the fight, hence their mention in this signal). By the time the signal was received, a number of tanks were burning furiously in the field less than a hundred metres beyond the hedgerow's end. This is almost certainly the furthest the squadron penetrated south.

In this newly-harvested field, map reference 087625, aerial photographs taken between 11.45 and 12.00 hours reveal at least seven vehicles burning within a fifty yard circle; it is possible that more knocked-out vehicles may be concealed by the billowing smoke drifting downwind.

11.42 hr: 2 FF Yeo told not to go for FRENOUVILLE which will be dealt with by the 5th Gds Armd Bde. Told to go to objective via BOURGUEBUS and TILLY-LA-CAMPAGNE 0760

Hearing of the heavy losses being incurred and checking the map reference, Brigadier Harvey drew the incorrect conclusion that the Fifes were deviating eastwards, towards Frénouville. Like General Roberts, Harvey was determined to stick to 11th Armoured objectives and leave Frénouville to the Guards. His attempt to put the Fifes back on a southbound track was ill informed. By the time this message was sent, all of the Fifes' tanks west of Four which were still capable of moving were falling back in a northerly direction.[14]

11.52 hr: 2 FF Yeo report four unidentified tks moving SOUTH area 1162

11.55 hr: 2 FF Yeo report four camouflaged enemy

The leading tank was knocked out by the tree-lined calvary east of Soliers. **(See page 151)**

Two views of the Fifes' killing fields taken seconds apart allow some estimate of tank casualties

One lone armoured vehicle just north of the German battery. Unidentifiable but lacking British white top. Perhaps a Becker gun *tks at 083605*

12.00 hr: 2 FF Yeo report tks moving into BOURGUEBUS

12.14 hr: 2 FF Yeo report eight tks probably Tigers moving into BOURGUEBUS from SE

According to the pre-battle briefings, reports such as these were supposed to bring down a rapid response from Typhoon fighter-bombers orbiting ready to offer close support. The response was slow in coming, and lacked the hoped-for coordination with the needs of the ground forces. By midday, the guns of I Battery, 13th Royal Horse Artillery had come up and the two four-gun troops were in firing positions nearby, south of the Paris railway and ready with a rapid response to urgent calls. But there was a limit to what eight twenty-five pounder guns could achieve against ever more numerous enemy tanks. During this period, Colonel Scott concentrated on attempting to reduce enemy resistance in the village of Four: the remaining tanks of A Squadron attempted to shoot F Company of the motor infantry into the place, with any covering fire the beleaguered tanks of B Squadron could add.

12.40 hr: *2 FF Yeo 800 yds short of BOURGUEBUS and keeping West of LA HOGUE 0960. Mot coy in FOUR 0962. Held up by the 8 enemy tks.*

Once again, this entry is potentially misleading. The best explanation offered is that, from the vantage point of tanks seeking what cover they could find west of Four, Bourguébus loomed twenty metres higher, and (like the closer, lower batteries) its height advantage might have foreshortened its actual distance of a mile. As for the motor company, they were certainly attempting to close Four, but any suggestion that they held the place was wide of the mark.

12.45 hr: *2 FF Yeo report that they have now only 20 tks left; heavy fire from Cagny was stated to be the cause of most of these losses. Later a few tks which had got lost rejoined the regt. Five appeared at Tac Bde HQ at 1250 and were sent on. 2FF told to clear SOLIERS.*

This interpretation is interesting. 29th Brigade Tac HQ was close to the wreck of C Squadron and remained under the impression that Cagny was the main source of the Fifes' problems. Still failing to appreciate the strength of the defences on the Bourguébus ridge, Harvey believed the ridge could be reached. But far from breaking through to the distant ridge line, the Fifes were struggling merely to hold their ground. Now in the attempt to maintain the momentum of the advance there appeared the 23rd Hussars.

At 12.05 hours, 29th Brigade had recorded: '*23 H ordered to move up area GRENTHEVILLE.*' Though the author has no direct evidence, it seems highly likely that 23rd Hussars passed from le Prieuré around the *west* side of le Mesnil Frémentel. It is almost inconceivable that they would have proceeded across the killing ground between le Mesnil and Cagny, where C Squadron of the Fifes had so recently been massacred. Certainly, the tail elements of the Fifes' own regimental group took the roundabout route, and since the Hussars' leading B Squadron crossed the Paris railway near to Grentheville, a roundabout route and approach from west of le Mesnil is indicated.

The fire of optimism still burned at Roscoe Harvey's 29th Brigade Tac HQ. Hard on the heels of the 12.45 order to the depleted Fife & Forfar to *'clear SOLIERS '*, 3rd RTR was signalled at 12.50 hours to *'try and clear up BRAS 0663 and if possible HUBERT FOLIE 0662 as well.'* In similar vein, at 12.55 hours 23rd Hussars were ordered to *'move up to 2 FF Yeo area and clear up BOURGUEBUS and prepare to move on TILLY-LA-CAMPAGNE.'* These orders appear to assume that the main enemy line had been breached and that all the tanks needed was a direction in which to head. As the Hussars' B Squadron emerged onto the Fife & Forfar battleground, the truth was quickly revealed.

Minutes later a more realistic order followed. At 12.58 hours, Brigade told the Hussars 'not to come further South than SOLIERS.' Unaware of the plight of the Fifes, the Hussars might well have wondered at this sudden curtailing of their task. In blissful ignorance of what had gone before, the Hussars quite naturally used the same tactics, advancing from the Paris railway towards the gap between Soliers and Four on a single-squadron front. From the railway just east of Grentheville, the Hussars struck south with two troops up: 1 Troop on the right, 2 Troop left. The advance continued almost to the centre of the triangle formed by Grentheville, Soliers, and Four. Then it was stopped short by enemy fire. The troop Fireflies were among the first losses. Lone tanks manoeuvred desperately, releasing smoke and firing at anything resembling an enemy, until the welcome order came to fall back on the rest of the regiment. The survivors of the Fife and Forfar were meanwhile clustered close to the hedgerows west of Four, not far away across open ground but unseen through smoke and dust. No contact between the Hussars and the Fifes had yet been made.

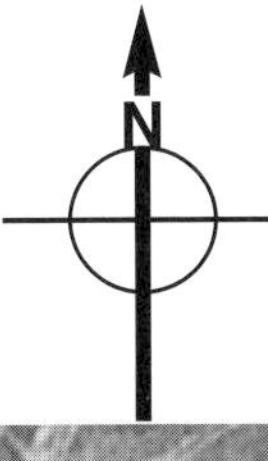

Taken about ten seconds apart, these two images reveal the northern (rearwards) direction of the Fifes' tanks at 11.50 hours.

References

(1) In this author's previous work on the subject, he believed the infantry had crossed the open ground in three M3 half-tracks. He now has photographic evidence that these vehicles, followed by a Dingo scout car, only arrived at the west wall between 11.40 and 12.00 hours, i.e., *after* the infantry had moved into the buildings.
(2) Bandomir diary
(3) Stileman, interview at Staff College, Camberley, 1979. It was typical of the banter that grew over the years between speakers on the Staff College tour that Major Bill Close took to referring to the – then – inexperienced young lieutenant as the *'florid cockerel'*. To which Stileman's self-effacing response was that *'At the prospect of this charade I must confess that I felt more like an anaemic broiler!'*
(4) Stileman, interview at Staff College, Camberley, 1979.
(5) 29th Brigade noted at 10.58 hours that *'3 R Tks ask for arty conc on HUBERT FOLIE'*. It seems most likely that this was for information only, and that the concentration was fired by the eight 25 pounder guns of Smyth-Osborne's H Battery alone. Nevertheless, in a confused battle and lacking an accurate 3rd RTR record, the signal is useful in pinpointing the time of Stileman's reconnaissance to shortly after 11.00 hours.
(6) Stileman, interview at Staff College, Camberley, 1979.
(7) 'Panzer Bait', William Moore, 1991, ISBN 0 85052 3281, p 147
(8) Close, interview at Staff College, Camberley, 1979.
(9) Caswell diary
(10) Jim Caswell recalls that later, when Bingo callers announced the number '88', the audience would roar out in unison *'driver reverse!'*
(11) Steel Brownlie diary
(12) The artillery regiment of *16. Luftwaffenfelddivision* was also equipped with batteries of Russian 7.62cm guns. Neither calibre had particularly impressive armour piercing capability, and the 12.2cm guns may even have lacked AP ammunition. Becker's guns were generally sited in well camouflaged prepared positions, from which they hoped to open fire before being spotted and then displace away from any situation before it became threatening. Becker himself was at this time in his armoured command vehicle close to the front, and according to his own account coordinating *all* the artillery in the area of Four via his *200. Abteilung Gefechtsstand* [mobile headquarters] currently south of Frénouville.
(13) Though invaluable to the historian, signals logs need to be studied with some care. Where either the sender or the recipient of the signal is in a combat area, many interruptions may occur: the sounds of battle or poor reception, to say nothing of the sending or receiving signaller being distracted by actual combat. The 29th Brigade signals officer sat in the bow gunner's position of Roscoe Harvey's command tank, frequently distracted by urgent communications from and to the brigadier himself via his brigade major sitting between the two, in the gunner's seat. A former officer gives the warning that, *'timings recorded are more often that not those when the messages were received at the battalion, brigade, or divisional H.Q., instead of those when the action really took place.'* (Scarfe, Assault Division, 1947 Preface) Nevertheless, signals logs are a great help, especially when, as here, the battalion, brigade, and divisional records can be compared!
(14) Since British aerial reconnaissance photographs were taken with considerable overlap (to permit stereoscopic viewing), the direction of moving vehicles can easily be ascertained from successive images.

Chapter 8

18 JULY, AFTERNOON AND EVENING: TWILIGHT OF AMBITION

By the end of the morning, the three 'prongs' of 11th Armoured Division's assault were losing strength and momentum. The chances of any further penetrations by the three armoured regiments were fading as their attacks were blunted against a thickening defensive wall. Help was slow in forthcoming. Meanwhile the German defences were organizing and counterstrokes being prepared.

LEIBSTANDARTE

When the enemy assault he had so long predicted became reality, *I. SS-Panzerkorps* commander 'Sepp' Dietrich was quick to recognise the threat. Even though elements of his *1. SS-Panzerdivision* were already occupied with the defence of the Orne river line south of Caen, he responded with alacrity to orders from Panzer Group West to shift a major part of the division to defend the Bourguébus ridge. Reconnaissance elements of the *Leibstandarte* reached the ridge line about noon, and soon were shoring-up the small garrisons of Hubert-Folie and Bras. (Though equipped with armoured reconnaissance vehicles and able to move rapidly across country, the companies of this *Aufklärungsabteilung* were well accustomed to being asked to hold the line in an infantry role.)

Behind the infantry would follow the self-propelled guns of the divisional *Sturmgeschütz* battalion, after it could disengage from its positions west of the

Assault howitzer (*Sturmhaubitze*). As the *Sturmgeschütz* battalions equipped with long 7.5 cm antitank guns, a proportion of 10.5 cm StuH 42 were included – typically three per ten-gun battery.

N
Soliers
Bras
Hubert-Folie

Bourguébus
Note: forward heavy antiaircraft battery in hedgerow-lined field with no ground line of sight

The Leibstandarte arrive. Assault guns on the western ridge, Panther tanks coming off the eastern ridge into the 'cauldron' of the village of Four

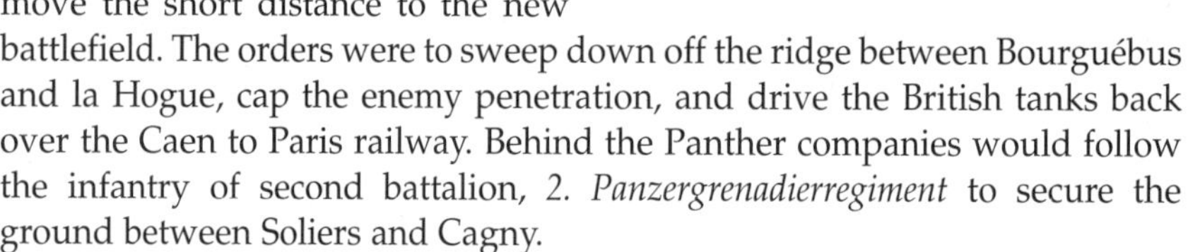

Outclassing Allied tanks in hitting power and protective armour – The *Panther*, Pzkmpf Mk V.

Orne River. Its batteries would arrive to stiffen the defence of the ridge south of Bras by about 17.00 hours. Meanwhile, it was on the eastern flank that the primary strike force of the division led the counter attack. The Panther battalion of *1. SS-Panzerregiment* was in divisional reserve around the village of Rocquancourt, on the Falaise road just four kilometres south of Bras. Once mobilized, its forty-six Panther tanks required only to turn north and move the short distance to the new battlefield. The orders were to sweep down off the ridge between Bourguébus and la Hogue, cap the enemy penetration, and drive the British tanks back over the Caen to Paris railway. Behind the Panther companies would follow the infantry of second battalion, *2. Panzergrenadierregiment* to secure the ground between Soliers and Cagny.

The main thrust of the Panther battalion attack was east of the Chemin de Fer Minier. Reaching their line of departure between Bourguébus and La Hogue about midday, the *Abteilung* enjoyed not only a height advantage over the British tanks they faced, but also some cover granted by sunken roads and foliage running across the upper reaches of the gently sloping ridgeline. Below, the ground was open. For once in Normandy, the coming battle might have permitted whole tank companies to manoeuvre together. Still, this was not the Russian steppe, and in Normandy the tactics had been changed. For German tank commanders in Normandy, open country also meant exposure to air attack, and as small groups of Panther tanks descended from the ridge, commanders' eyes scanned the sky above. Grenadiers huddled in their shallow foxholes as the armour rolled by:

> *suddenly our Panthers rolled over our positions toward the front. The Kommandants were only looking out for fighter bombers... Our Panthers took off at top speed across the open terrain. They were headed for Soliers and they soon disappeared from view.*[1]

Predictably, the Typhoons descended. By this stage of the campaign, German tank crews had a horror of rocket attacks from the air. At that time, neither Allies nor Germans had come to terms with the extreme inaccuracy of air-launched antitank rockets; their morale effect remained very great indeed. Nevertheless, the attacks were not as well co-ordinated as had been planned. Direction of fighter-bomber aircraft by ground observers was a science in its infancy: the attachment of a Forward Air Control Post to 29th Brigade Tac HQ was somewhat experimental. Today's experiment was compromised as early as 12.15 hours. As calls came in for air strikes against tanks advancing across the Bourguébus to la Hogue road, the single Contact Car (a turretless Marmon Herrington armoured car) was hit and the RAF Air Liaison Officer incapacitated.[2] The 29th Brigade war diary charitably records that the ALO's deputy 'soon picked up what was required of him and coped very well indeed throughout the rest of the day.' However, many airborne sorties were left that afternoon to find their own targets. The doctrinal resistance within the British Army to greater liaison with tactical airpower is beyond the scope of this study. The

The Typhoon ('Tiffie') RAF ground attack fighter.

Visual Contact Post team: RAF Squadron leader and an Army Major.

Royal Armoured Corps had been especially resistant to painting recognition symbols on tanks, for fear that this could easily be copied by the enemy, as so frequently had been light and smoke recognition signals. The experiment announced two days before GOODWOOD that 'All tks and and armd cars will have the horizontal surfaces of turrets painted WHITE' was dutifully carried out, but appears not to have been repeated.[3]

Tank combat rapidly descended into a confused mêlée. In an area approximately two kilometres square, bounded by Soliers, le Poirier, la Hogue, and Bourguébus, bands of German tanks clashed with dwindling numbers of British defenders. As poor visibility worsened, ranges of engagement reduced. On mostly flat ground, there was little opportunity to gain hull-down positions and tanks unable to gain the cover of walls or hedges simply slugged it out in the open, relying on manoeuvre and speed of reaction. Solid shot flew in all directions; German infantrymen on the ridge above wondered at shells which did not explode, then realised that 'they were armour-piercing shells. Our Panthers were fighting up ahead with the British tanks and the ricochets were flying around our heads.'[4] Within the maelstrom of smoke and dust, British Fireflies and German Panther alike were denied their advantage of long range fire. The finest all-round combat tank of its day, its frontal armour all but impregnable, the Panther was nevertheless vulnerable to flank shots, and far from its best in such confused close combat.

TACTICS

The British attack that followed the 18 July bombing had concentrated the tank force of three armoured divisions into nine regimental groups, principally tank forces with a small leavening of armoured and mobile infantry and artillery. As has been shown, these formations were in part a carry-over from lessons learned in the open desert of North Africa. They were oddly reminiscent of the massed armour of the German Blitzkrieg tactics which had triumphed in France in 1940. By contrast, the opposing German armour tended to adopt the official tactical policy for Normandy – *Panzerkampftrupptaktik* – of breaking up armour strength into small units.[5]

From the end of June, it was laid down that German attacks in Normandy bocage were to be led by the infantry rather than armour. Even the (very few) companies of *Panzergrenadiere* retaining armoured half-tracks were to abandon their armour for the initial attack, leaving the vehicles in the rear, apart from those used to carry forward ammunition. The tanks themselves were generally to follow the infantry, advancing line abreast in *Zug* strength (platoons of four tanks) or even less (*Halb-Züge*, sections of two or three). For veteran German tankers, this was a radical departure. Previously, the ethos of the Panzerdivision had been the massing of armour. Time after time in Russia, greatly outnumbered German forces had survived and prevailed by concentrating the force available at the critical point, whether in advance or defence.

The thinking behind the new tactics was based on the early experience of combat in the bocage, the dense hedgerow country of the invasion front in which lines of sight were short, obstacles to movement many, and every small field a potential fortress. In such terrain, massed formations of tanks were generally impractical, and armour lacking the close support of infantry was fatally vulnerable to enemy infiltration and close-range fire. Additional factors influencing the new tactics were enemy air supremacy (massed armour presented an easy target) and artillery power (controlling massed armour required radio, and radio transmissions invited quick retaliation).

Not all the new tactics were practical on the relatively open slopes of the Bourguébus ridge. Here, the infantry did not lead. But the German tanks did fight in small bands, infiltrating rather than sweeping en masse across the battlefield. And, having broken cover to attack, they became locked in the struggle. Realising that his Panther tank battalion had become closely engaged, division commander SS-*Brigadeführer* 'Teddy' Wisch tried to recall his armour back behind the defensive line of infantry on the ridge. The reply was intercepted and recorded by II Canadian Corps' Special Wireless Section: the withdrawal could not take place because the battalion's tanks were too heavily engaged. Moreover, their tactical freedom to manoeuvre was severely limited by the threat of the fighter bombers overhead; better to stay locked in combat than to risk falling back over open ground.[6]

With the wisdom of hindsight, some have criticised the German counter attacks of the afternoon of 18 July.[7] Dempsey had declared himself 'prepared to lose two or three hundred tanks.' Replacement Shermans were in plentiful supply, and so long as crew casualties were not excessive, losses could quickly be made good. The precious Panther tanks were virtually irreplaceable. It is argued that the Germans would have been better advised to remain on the

Smashed and burnt-out Shermans littered the landscape.

commanding ridge rather than descending into the cauldron of Four. Pip Roberts long maintained that the defenders should have relied more on antitank minefields, and less on open space for armoured manoeuvre. Yet the immediate counter attack, when an attacking force was at its most vulnerable, was a fundamental German policy, not lightly to be abandoned. Strategically, the defence of Normandy might better have been conducted by withdrawal to the Seine. But this was forbidden. Instead, the order to stand fast inevitably implied suffering heavy losses. Operationally, von Kluge's immediate response to the news of GOODWOOD was to order the enemy thrown back by immediate concentric attack. Tactically, the Panther tanks burning in the fields around Four were a price accepted for pushing the Fifes and the Hussars back to the railway, keeping the Allies off the Bourguébus ridge, and defending the Falaise road. What is more, the habit of immediate counterstroke ('*Gegenstoss aus der Tiefe*') so deeply engrained into every field commander might – just – have succeeded.

TIGERS

After their rebuff from Cagny, von Rosen's *3. Kompanie* took little further part in the battle, busying themselves rescuing their damaged tanks from the Manneville haras before the tide of battle rolled over them.[8] By 16.00 hours only one of von Rosen's tanks remained fully operational: some retained mobility without operational guns, others vice-versa. Shortly after, Fromme ordered the remnants of the company to leave the field as best they could.

Meanwhile, *Oberleutnant* Oemler's *1. Kompanie* had been expending frantic efforts to recover from its aerial battering. By late morning the company had managed to prepare eight of its great *Königstiger* for action. With great tactical insight, they advanced out from their assembly area and north around the Manneville haras. Probing westward, roughly along the line of the modern Autoroute, this potent armoured force approached the point at which the British armoured corridor was barely one mile across, taking as its objective the town of Démouville on the corridor's far side. Between the Manneville haras and the heavily cratered Banneville the heavy tanks entered a very large wheatfield, partially cropped when the harvest was interrupted by the battle raging. Just 500 metres beyond the German spearhead lay the traffic jams of wheeled vehicles queuing to cross the Caen to Troarn rail line.

The risks inherent in speculating about 'what would have happened if…' have been discussed. Nevertheless, it seems in hindsight that this advance did have the potential to turn the entire battle into a British disaster. Had a half-dozen of the heaviest battle tanks in existence only progressed as far as Lirose and established a fire base across the narrow neck of the armoured corridor, 29th Armoured Brigade would have become effectively cut off from its lines of communication and supply. The whole thrust of the battle might have changed: from an advance into enemy territory to the desperate relief of an isolated pocket. To the 'two or three hundred tanks' which Dempsey was famously prepared to sacrifice might have been added the tank crews and command structure of an entire brigade, a shattering blow to 11th Armoured

The path of Oemler's King Tiger counter-attack.

Division at a time when it was showing signs of maturing into the Army's finest. The disaster was not to be. *Oberleutnant* Oemler's command tank *'100'* immobilized itself by slithering into a great bomb crater, unseen amid the crop. Shortly after, in the same field, *Königstiger 111* and *101* were penetrated and knocked out in quick succession (the first *Königstiger* ever to be lost in action to direct enemy fire; ironically, the Guards Firefly commander responsible for at least one of the kills, firing from the vicinity of the present-day British war cemetery, claimed to have destroyed a *Panther*). The advance was abandoned, 500 metres short of Lirose.

The *Tiger* I tanks of *2. Kompanie* went on to fight an effective delaying action northwest of Troarn (one of their number having earlier become stuck in a ditch in the Manneville haras, presumably when running blindly from artillery fire). The survivors of *1. Kompanie* remained in the general area between Emiéville and Frénouville until a 'stop line' of 8.8cm antitank guns could be established to prevent further advances by Guards Armoured. By the end of the day, all remaining *Tiger* of the *503. Abteilung* were withdrawn. The *Tiger* men went on to experience further hardships in Normandy. Every one of their remaining tanks would be lost on the retreat to the Seine, most

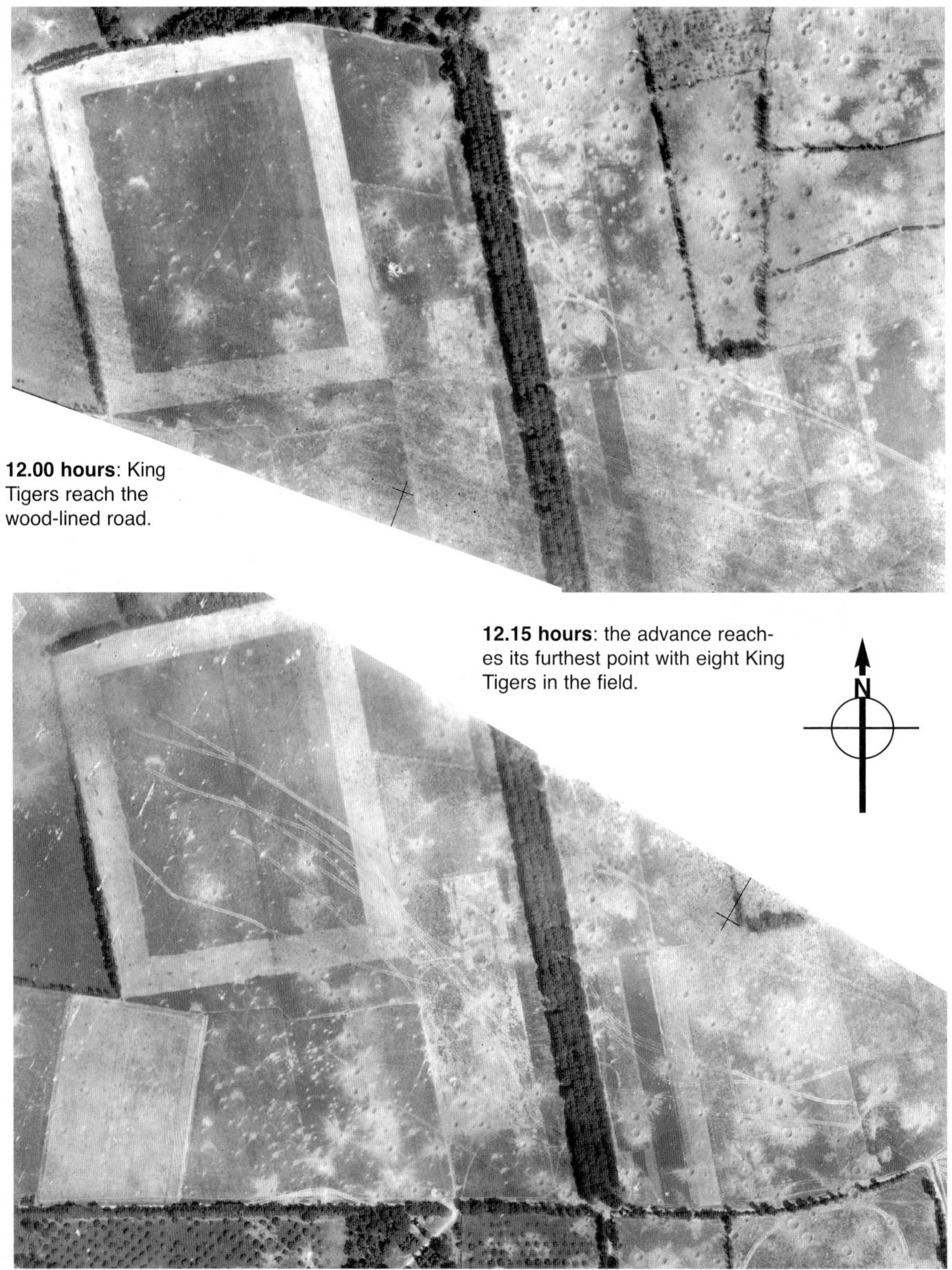

12.00 hours: King Tigers reach the wood-lined road.

12.15 hours: the advance reaches its furthest point with eight King Tigers in the field.

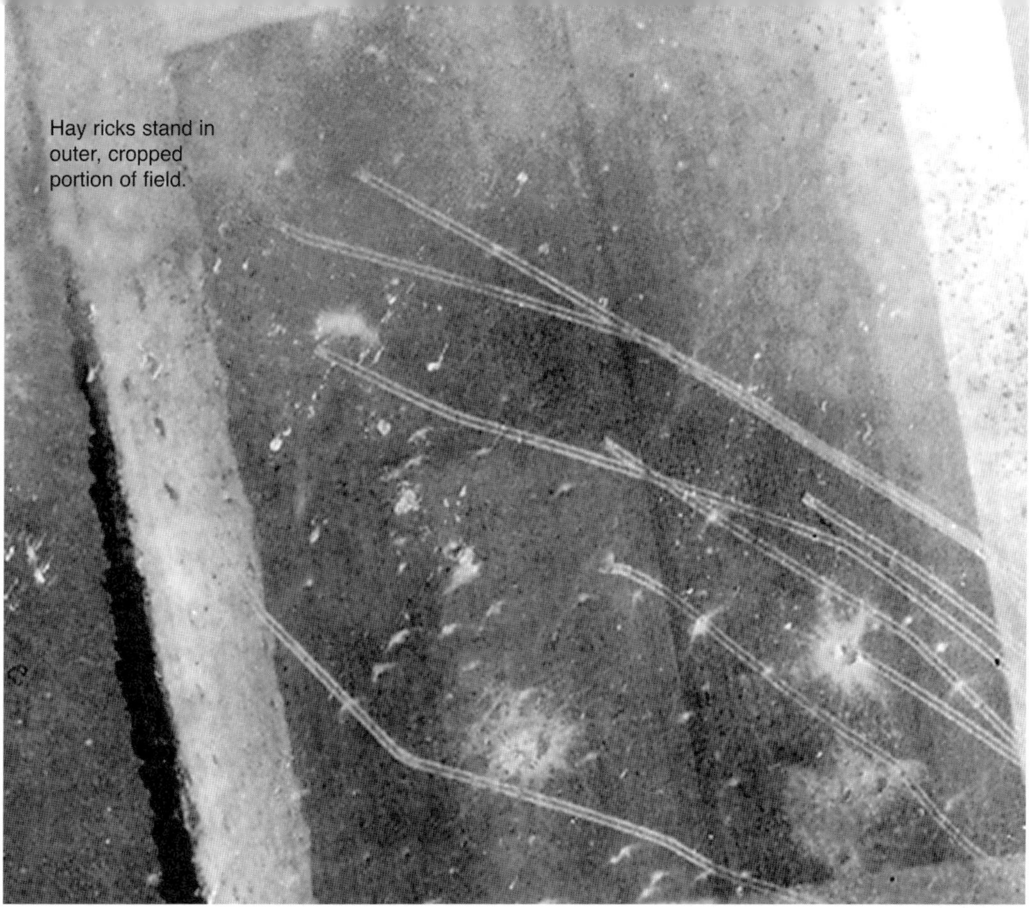

Hay ricks stand in outer, cropped portion of field.

12.15 hours: Oemler's tank is immobilized in crater while King Tigers 111 and 101 are knocked out.

destroyed by their crews after running out of fuel or breaking down where no workshop teams were on hand. But for the unit, 18 July remained their 'darkest day'.

11TH ARMOURED: DIVISIONAL COMMAND

In light of the potential (if unrealised) threats to the narrow British penetration achieved by midday of 18 July, it is worth reflecting on its leadership. Through that morning, Pip Roberts had shown a quality which set him apart from many of his contemporary British armour commanders: he was utterly determined to push his division's advance forward with scant regard for what was happening on its flanks. It has been argued that during the morning of 18 July he neglected his duties as divisional commander, limiting his perspective to that of a brigadier.[9] Roberts' judgement on 18 July was influenced by his frustration at O'Connor's interference – yet again – with the conduct of 11th Armoured Division. Roberts recognised clearly his division's task of plunging ahead to rupture the enemy lines. If he was to be deprived of his infantry brigade, so be it. Having satisfied himself early in the battle that Brigadier Churcher was making good progress in securing Cuverville and Démouville, Roberts kept a closer eye on the momentum of 29th Brigade (though hardly necessary with the dynamic Roscoe Harvey in the saddle). However, Roberts was not blind to the risk of unprotected flanks. As the morning wore on and the following armoured divisions failed to materialize on his left, Roberts became increasingly preoccupied with the whereabouts of the forces due to follow-through to exploit his penetration of the German front. In this at least, he was not acting 'one level down' at brigade level, but arguably thinking 'one level up' in terms of securing VIII Corps objectives.

Signals emanating from Roberts' Tac HQ from the late morning of 18 July had two recurring themes. His communications forward to 29th Brigade (actually, for much of the morning the two Tac HQs shared opposite sides of the same field) stressed the need for the tank regiments to disregard their flanks and press on forwards. His communications back to 11th Armoured Main HQ (and above) mainly concerned his need to be kept informed of the progress of the following armoured divisions.

Where was Guards Armoured Division? As early as 09.40 hours, 11th Armoured had demanded of the Guards' Headquarters, 'Where are your leading children?' The answer came back that the 'children' (the leading tanks of 5th Guards Brigade) were 'coming on well,' and only five hundred yards behind 11th Armoured. But were they? Ten minutes later, 11th Armoured queried,

> *Ref your information re your children – this should mean that they are about level with DEMOUVILLE. We cannot see them. Please confirm.'*

The Guards' response was hesitant. 'Wait for exact locn – sorry delay. Northing grid 68 in answer,' apparently confirming that their lead tanks were only a mile north of the first railway crossing. Any optimism raised by this

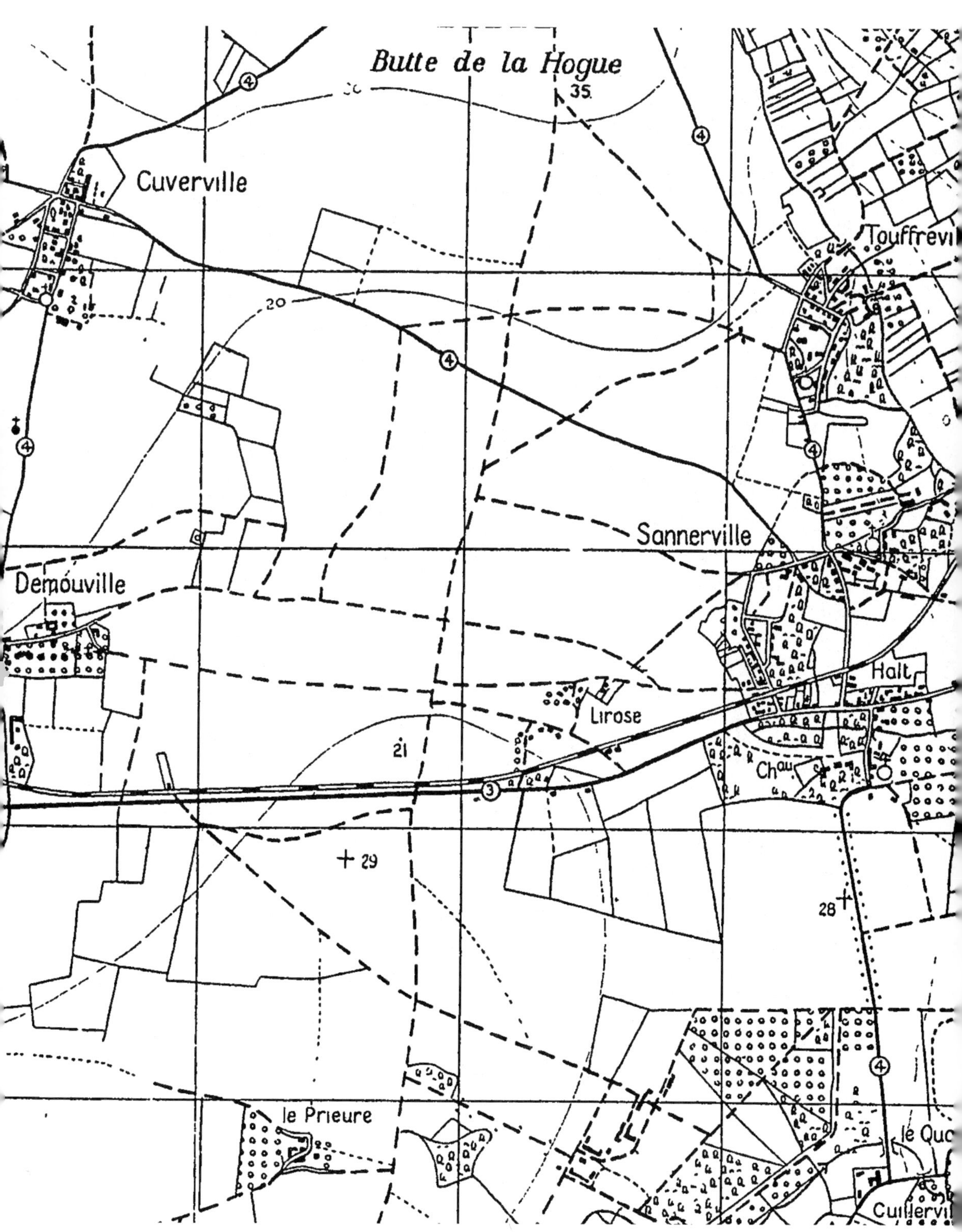
Butte de la Hogue
35
Cuverville
Touffrevi
20
Sannerville
Demouville
Halt
Lirose
21
Chau
29
28
le Prieure
le Quc
Cuillervi

reply was tempered a full hour later by the 10.40 hours report from VIII Corps that '2 Armd Coldm Gds has reached CAGNY.' And even this announcement was premature.

Between 11.00 and 11.30 hours, leading elements of Guards Armoured Division at last begun to appear in the vicinity of Pip Roberts' Tac HQ near le Mesnil, and shortly before midday Allan Adair himself arrived. The two generals 'had a few words... and he went off to do a recce of the area.'[10] Adair's departure was hastened as a previously unseen *Panzerfaust* team hidden in the crop nearby tried an opportunistic shot at the general's tank. They missed the departing Cromwell, which beat a hasty retreat, throwing back smoke bombs. For Adair, the narrow encounter demonstrated all too clearly that the area was unsecured, and further underlined Roberts' previous warning to the Guards that Cagny should be approached with caution. The warning was heeded all too well.

GUARDS ARMOURED DIVISION

About 11.00 hours, Lieutenant Heywood's squadron of the 2nd (Armoured) Battalion Grenadier Guards crossed the first railway line and moved south to contact C Squadron of the 23rd Hussars. Impatient to relinquish the task of screening le Prieuré, the Hussars were quick to take their leave, hurrying southbound around le Mesnil Frémentel to catch up with the rest of their regiment. The Grenadiers' tanks moved into the hedgerow-lined orchards either side of le Prieuré, no more aware than the Hussars had been of the German garrison still within the walled farm, lying low as no British infantry had yet approached and reluctant to engage the British tanks after the departure of Becker's mobile guns.

The Guards' plan was to advance on Cagny with two regiments up: the Grenadiers swinging west while the 1st (Armoured) Coldstream Guards bypassed Cagny to the north. But with the Grenadiers' advance already well behind schedule, and the Coldstream somewhere behind them even more so, the Grenadiers instead hurried forward on their own. Lieutenant Heywood's squadron gladly relinquished the lead to number 2 Squadron, whose troops duly set off over open fields of corn and root vegetables towards the ruins of Cagny.[11] As the squadron moved south, ominous columns of smoke rose from the fields ahead where the wreck of the Fifes' C Squadron still burned. Now began the Grenadiers' ordeal. Antitank fire from the south and east promptly knocked out two of the squadron's tanks, and the survivors scattered. The regimental commander, Lieutenant Colonel Moore, came forward to get the squadron moving. Since Cagny appeared too strongly held, the tanks should instead attempt to bypass to the north. But attempts to 'feel the way forward' to either flank proved unsuccessful. Soon after, the 2 Squadron commander's tank was hit and Major Sir Arthur Grant killed.

At last it was the turn of the 1st (Armoured) Coldstream Guards to cross the Caen to Troarn railway, and take up their assigned position to the left flank of the Grenadiers. But what was going on ahead remained unclear. While something appeared to be holding up the Grenadiers in front, behind

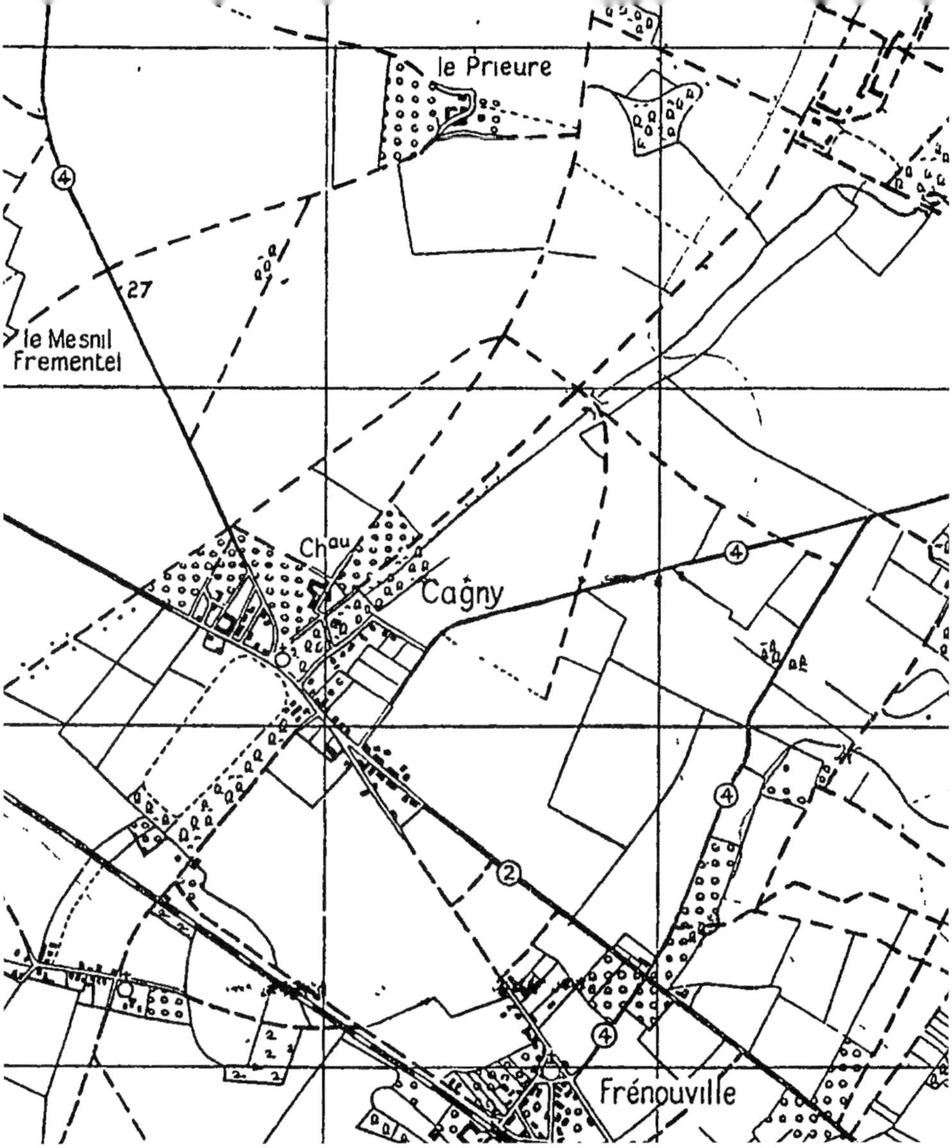

le Prieure
le Mesnil
Frementel
Chau
Cagny
Frénouville

A 21. *Panzerdivision Somua* halftrack, barely recognisable, and a knocked-out Sherman of A Squadron, 1st Coldstream Guards.

them a traffic jam of monumental proportions was accumulating as vehicles of all types crowded the few railway crossings. And making matters worse, German artillery observers were beginning to recover and re-establish communications with their batteries. The targets were a gunner's dream. Only shortage of ammunition limited the confusion caused by artillery shells and mortar bombs on the British rear. A shell falling amidst the regimental headquarters group killed Major Peter Buxton, commander of 131 Battery of the Leicestershire Yeomanry, as he left his tank to confer with the Coldstream Colonel Rid Myddleton.[12] The Coldstream's leading 1 Squadron spread out in battle formation to press the advance toward Cagny, their orders now switching them from the left flank of the attack to a move around the right of Cagny. Meanwhile, the left flank of the armoured corridor was exposed, and number 2 Squadron of the Coldstream had to be turned to face the small wood east of le Prieuré. *Panther* tanks had been reported a few hundred yards away to the east, and the crews of 2 Squadron felt exposed in the open fields. 'Our tracks were nicely covered in the tall corn, but we were a sitting target to any Panther in the woods.'[13]

5th Guards Brigade Tac HQ established west of la Prieuré. A pall of smoke from a burning vehicle drifts south west, shrouding the priory.

An abandoned Sherman belonging to the Coldstream Guards. (Also page 171)

Shortly after these events, 5th Guards Brigade Tac HQ established itself in the orchards by le Prieuré. Only when one of the protection troop tanks observed a movement within the walls, and put a few canon shells into the farm buildings, was it realised that the German garrison still remained. To the amazement of the HQ staff a number of Germans gave themselves up. 'If they had chosen to fight, Brigade would have looked very silly.' The impression of tough resistance waiting ahead was confirmed.

One of many burnt-out Shermans littering the battlefield.

When the ruins of Cagny came into view, the leading Coldstream squadron

> *saw a sight that rather shook us all… the horizon was covered with burning Shermans. I could count nearly twenty, a whole squadron, burning in one field alone. More*

Pylons marked the route eastward.

> *were hidden behind the black smoke of others brewing up, while yet others were still being hit and bursting into flames.*[14]

The Coldstream colonel quickly decided that 'We must not add to this disaster,' and the unit looped even more widely to the west, keeping as far as possible from Cagny itself until reaching the Caen-Paris railway whose earth banks and hedgerows promised the best available shelter. At this point, the regimental history relates,

> *Major Anstruther-Gray collected his squadron in a wood between Cagny and the railway and awaited further orders. Progress was impossible without infantry to destroy the antitank guns; so the battalion remained, south and west of Cagny, until it grew dark.*[15]

As an officer with the West Somerset Yeomanry (the Guards' towed field regiment) later pointed out, the Guards division was trying to operate in an unfamiliar manner. 'The general idea was that infantry made the gap and then the armour flooded through it like the cavalry of old.'[16]

At last, their arrival delayed by traffic jams until well into the afternoon, the tanks of 2nd (Armoured) Irish Guards arrived on the battlefield to confront the dismal sight of nine Grenadier Guards tanks burning directly ahead, while from the fields and woods to the east German guns were now firing with growing intensity. All visible signs confirmed the suspicion that Cagny was far too strongly garrisoned to be taken by direct assault. Instead, the Irish Guards were to advance eastwards over the open fields north of the small town. This route seemed promising. Once clear of le Prieuré, the regiment found itself in more open countryside with large, gently rolling fields intersected by hedgerows of varying density. This was the sort of country they had trained for. Lieutenant Colonel Kim Finlay directed the lead squadron to follow a distant line of electricity pylons which helpfully gave an easterly orientation. Over the open country, like huntsmen following the pack, the Irish Guards set off.

Before the open fields could be reached, the hunters had first to cross the Ruisseau de Cagny, a small stream running due north out of the devastated village. Though only a narrow trickle, the rivulet was in places surrounded by

The Ruisseau de Cagny where Ballyragget bogged.

Taken at around 12.05 hours, this image precedes the arrival of the Irish Guards. Debris in the field is a crashed German Focke Wulf 190 fighter.

patches of flat, boggy ground, and it was in one of these that Lieutenant John Gorman's 'Ballyragget' became stuck fast. Ordering his Troop Sergeant Evans to carry on the advance with half the troop including the Firefly, Gorman spent an impatient half hour supervising the freeing of his own Sherman by the troop's number four tank using a steel towrope. Then, pressing forward with all possible speed to catch up with his own tanks, Gorman came upon his own 2 Squadron commander Tony 'Dipper' Dorman.

> *"Dipper" was on his feet, evidently wounded, but gesticulating wildly forward. Since the whole strategy of our leftwards attack on Cagny had been to take it by the speed and dash which we had learned on Salisbury Plain and the Yorkshire Wolds, I took it that Dipper was urging us on and we hared up a cornfield, towards a hedge at the top of the rise.*[17]

Amid the dust and confusion of battle, Gorman's daring advance appears to have carried him past the rest of his squadron, held up by the intensity of the antitank fire to their front. Then, cresting the gentle slope and rounding the end of a hedgerow, Gorman was appalled to see just three hundred yards ahead the great bulk of a *Königstiger*.

Belonging to *1. Kompanie* of Fromme's *503.s.Pz.Abt.*, the great tank had become separated from its unit in the confusion of the battle. Its commander was an inexperienced sergeant, *Feldwebel* Gerber, who had only recently been attached to the *Abteilung* to gain combat experience and (he hoped!) the possibility of a decoration. As the *Kompanie* withdrew from its abortive attack, manoeuvring around Manneville towards Frénouville, his *Königstiger* number 122 lost contact with his company and 'the inexperienced commander lost his nerve and drove through the area in a fairly disoriented manner.'[18] Coming under fire from different directions, the gunner Hans-Joachim Thaysen tried to return fire, but the commander panicked and ordered the driver, Horst Becher, to reverse, taking the Tiger back through a hedge.

In *Ballyraggett*, Gorman ordered gunner Albert Scholes to 'Traverse left – on – fire!' In accordance with standing orders, the tank had gone into action with a High Explosive round 'up the spout'. The shell burst on the turret of the *Königstiger*, its blast deflected up into the air. Ordered to keep firing, Scholes's hollow voice replied 'Gun jammed, Sir.' Gorman hesitated a moment, found that his training did not cover the situation, then on impulse he gave the order: 'Driver, ram!' Baron accelerated *Ballyraggett* towards the behemoth, and crashed into its left rear.

Already disoriented, the German commander was further confused by the HE shell glancing off his turret, then the almighty impact of thirty tons of

The ram site in the north-east corner of the field. Note the overhead power lines.

Sherman tank. A moment later, the *Königstiger* was penetrated by an Armour Piercing round entering its left side between the running gear and the track, and taking the gunner's seat out from under him.[19] Already displeased with their commander's performance, the crew were quick to follow him as he abandoned the stricken Panzer. Gorman's crew likewise abandoned the immobilized *Ballyraggett*, and there were awkward moments as two crews faced off. Gunner Thaysen recalls his encounter with co-driver Guardsman Agnew:

> *For a moment we looked at each other in a daze. Then a rush of heroism awoke in both of us. Each grabbed for the place where he'd usually find his pistol. Heroism failed for a lack of lethal materials... We eyed each other and each tried to convince the other, with hands and feet, that the other was his prisoner. Since it turned out that each of us had opposite opinions about that, both of us shrugged our shoulders, grinned at each other, and bolted for our own sides.'*

Meanwhile, Gorman led the other three crewmen back to the shelter of Sergeant Pat Harbinson's tank, which had followed their advance, but the Sherman was destroyed by enemy fire before they reached it. Gorman pressed on across fields until he came upon a Firefly whose commander, Sergeant Workman, had been decapitated. The sergeant's body was draped over the breech of the gun and to either side the gunner and operator were in shock. Gorman took charge, the gory mess was wiped off gunsights and periscopes, and the Firefly advanced to the disabled *Königstiger* where further rounds were put into the German to ensure its destruction. By this time, Harbinson's Sherman was well ablaze, and Gorman transported the mortally wounded sergeant and his two surviving crew back to the regimental aid post.

Note the penetration of the Tiger's front-left armour, also the (later) penetration of *Ballyragget's* turret.

Attempts to bolster up the thickness of frontal armour by attaching sections of track failed to save this Sherman.

Word of this unusual encounter lifted the spirits of the regiment. But the fact remained that for all the gallantry shown and losses sustained, Guards Armoured Division was performing without distinction in its first battle. Cagny remained untaken. One officer serving with the Guards later reflected,

> *I do not think that my own division was ready for the shock of reality on 18 July, although 11th Armoured had already been through the fire on Point 112.*[20]

THE ORDEAL OF 29th ARMOURED BRIGADE

For Roberts, the appearance, however brief, of the Guards general signalled his own long-awaited opportunity to disengage entirely from the Cagny area. Trusting in the Guards to cover his division's left flank, Roberts turned again to encouraging 29th Brigade to press on. Roscoe Harvey hardly needed encouragement. Calls to 29th Brigade from all three tank regiments reporting enemy fire from both their left and right flanks met peremptory responses. To the Hussars at 11.38, 'leave someone to watch and push on'. (The reaction of 23rd Hussars' C Squadron, at that time engaging the enemy between Cagny and le Prieuré while still awaiting the arrival of the Guards, can only be imagined!) To the Fifes at 11.42, *'told not to go for FRENOUVILLE which will be dealt with by the 5th Gds Armd Bde. Told to go to objective via BOURGUEBUS and TILLY-LE-CAMPAGNE 0760'.*

And in response to 3rd Tanks worsening plight at 12.34, 'Told to get onto the main CAEN – FALAISE road.'[21]

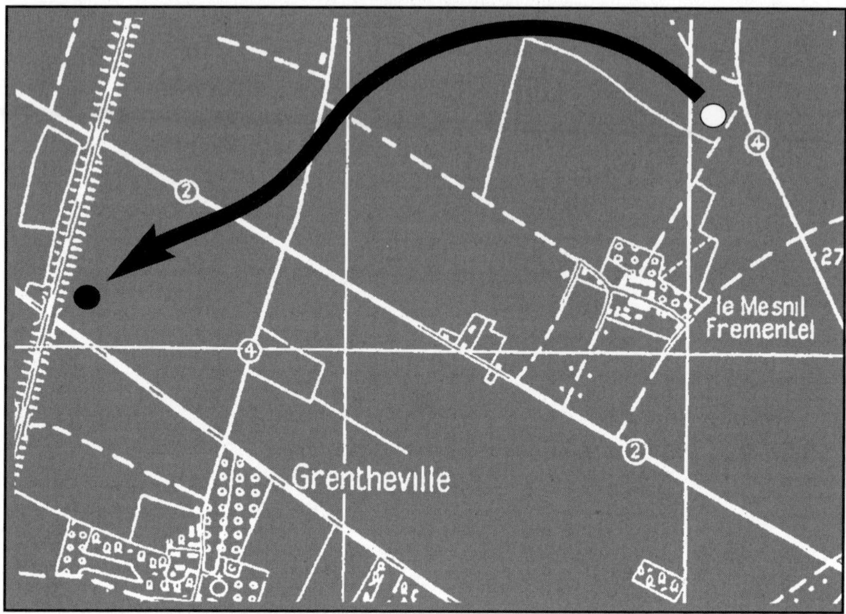

The move of 29th Brigade Tac HQ.

Shortly after midday, Roscoe Harvey had relocated his Tac HQ. The promised arrival of the follow-up armoured divisions seemed to permit a shift of 29th Brigade's centre of gravity to the west. Equally important to Harvey was ensuring he was close enough to the action – at whatever cost to his own security. The new position chosen was by the Chemin de Fer Minier embankment, just north of the Caen to Paris railway. Here, Harvey's Tac HQ could see – and be seen from – much farther afield than previously. With him in his command tank was his long-suffering brigade major who recalled,

> *Roscoe was a marvellous chap and a superb armoured commander, but he was not an easy man to work for… he was also utterly fearless. Most people have a stock of courage and in prolonged conflict that can run out – some run out quicker than others. Roscoe was quite different. The longer and more dangerous the battle, the braver he became. He really didn't seem to know the meaning of fear, and that is not always easy for those around. He would park his tank well forward and in the most obvious place. If I remonstrated with him he would say that he needed to be there so that he could see the whole battlefield. And of course the Germans could also see us, an obvious command group of three tanks and a protection troop. And they promptly shelled us. It happened frequently.*[22]

In fairness to the brigadier, the chosen site did offer the considerable refuge of the railway underpass through the embankment, though of course Harvey's tank remained exposed.

The events of the afternoon became rapidly more confused. 29 Brigade reported at 13.05 hours,

> *On RIGHT preparing to put inf into HUBERT FOLIE.* [a trifle optimistic] *Enemy in BRAS. We are not.* [incontestable!] *2 FF 800 yards NE BOURGUEBUS.* [this too was a trifle optimistic, and failed to mention that most of the Fifes' tanks within a mile of Bourguébus were now knocked out] *23H are relieving 3 R Tks.*

This last signal defies understanding, possibly indicating that the Hussars' hoped-for advance on Soliers might shelter 3rd RTR's left flank; or possibly just that the newcomers might 'relieve' 3rd RTR of their unfinished business in Grentheville. [23]

In their essentially separate battle west of the railway embankment, 3rd RTR continued with attempts to push up the slopes towards Hubert-Folie. But the high-water mark of the day's advance had already been reached at noon. Thereafter, the tank strength of 3rd RTR dwindled as the defences of the ridge were gradually increased. Several attempts were made to regain the offensive but were hopeless against stiffening opposition. The right flank remained open to fire from the ridge between Bras and distant Ifs. On the left, even the cover granted by the railway embankment was lost south of Soliers; as the ground rose above the level of the permanent way, advancing tanks were caught by crossfire from the area of Bourguébus. Lacking adequate resupply, 3rd RTR began to run low on ammunition. Silvertop bowed to the inevitable and ordered his tanks back to find what cover they could from enemy fire. In addition to fire from distant emplaced guns, increasing numbers of German tanks were appearing through the smoke and dust.

Meanwhile, the infantry of 8th RB had been offering what assistance they could to stricken tank crews. Their carrier platoon suffered heavily, though encouraged by the success of a section commanded by a sergeant which located and neutralized a German artillery observation post on the railway embankment. Noel Bell moved his headquarters behind a hedge which might offer cover from view, if not from fire.

> *We seemed to lie behind that hedge for hours, imagining every moment to be our last. I made a great mistake in passing round a bottle of gin, the effect of which lowered everyone's spirits instead of, as I had hoped, bolstering them up.*[24]

At length, as the tanks fell back, threatening to leave the motor infantry exposed in forward positions, it became obvious that there was little place for an infantry company in this essentially armoured fight. Silvertop released Bell's survivors to retire to cover until nightfall.

East of the railway embankment, mid afternoon found the remainder of 29th Armoured Brigade performing a complex dance amid a dense fog of war. To the front, even securing Soliers and Four had proved problematic, with 23rd Hussars rebuffed to the line of the Paris railway, and contact with the Fife & Forfar was now sporadic. As for the brigade's precious motor infantry battalion, G Company was still with 3rd RTR, and in no position to return to Grentheville to complete its suppression. About 12.45 hours, the advancing 23rd Hussar regimental group had detached H Company to take the village; by 14.22 hours they were reported 'in Grentheville' though the place remained unsecured. 8th RB headquarters group was ordered to move south east from le Mesnil Frémentel to prepare defences against any enemy breakthrough from the south east (a wise precaution, although the sacrifices of the Fifes and the Hussars did at least forestall an enemy breakthrough between 11th Armoured and the Guards in that sector). Later still, F Company's attempts to get into Four finally were abandoned and the company moved west to take their turn in Grentheville, while two M10 troops (119 Battery, of 11th Armoured Division's 75th Antitank Regiment; in all, eight self-propelled 17 pounder guns) arrived to form a defensive screen between

A troop of four M10s in 'finger four' formation east of the Chemin de Fer Minier.

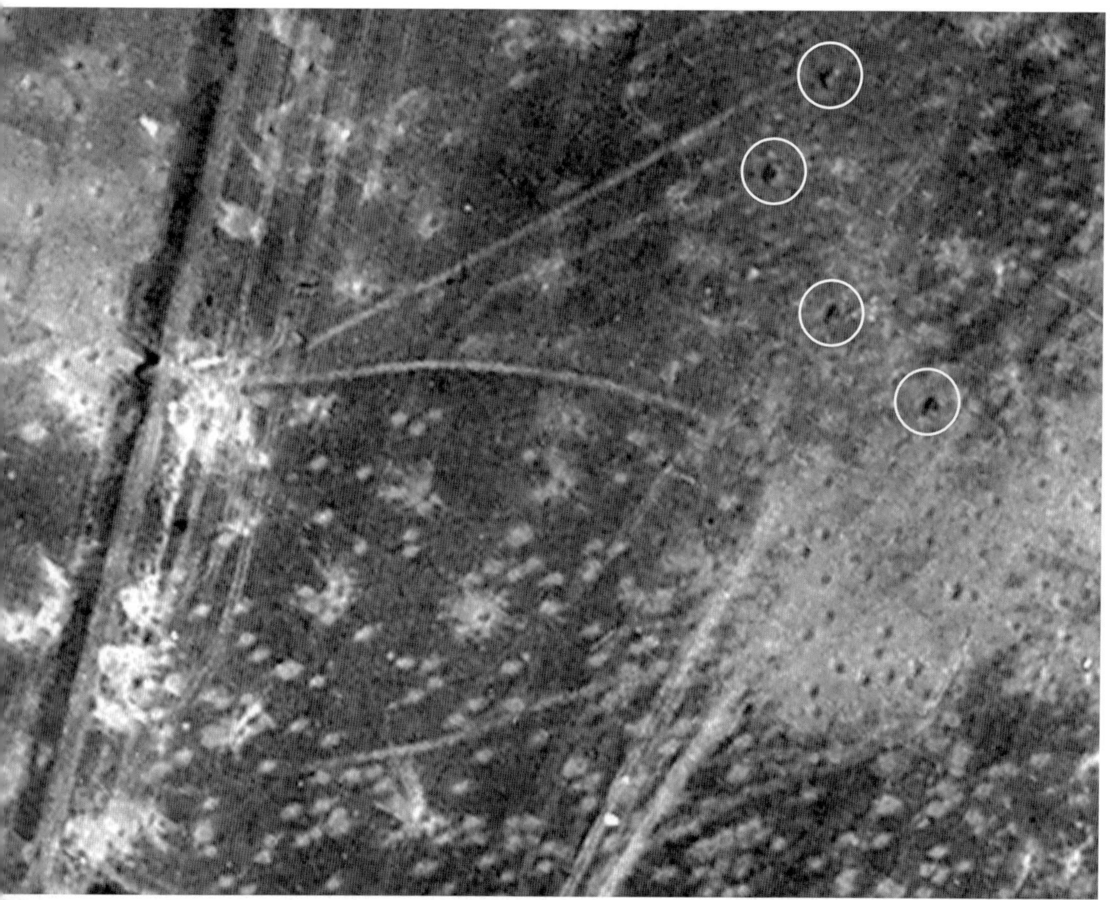

the village and the brigade HQ by the embankment.

23rd Hussars plunged again into the fray south of the railway. A desperate hour of combat is illustrated vividly in signals coming back to Brigade.

14.07 hours:

> *23 H report that their move fwd is being delayed by enemy tks. Had to pull back a little as they had 4 Shermans destroyed by 5 Panthers and could not get hull-down posns where they were. 3 more Panthers and 2 SP guns on their other flank. They could also see 2 FF Yeo getting into difficulties.* [An understatement?]

14.10 hours: '*23 H told to prepare to get up on the right flank by 3 R Tks and so make SOLIERS safe and also BOURGUEBUS.*' (The apparent afterthought of Bourguébus was wholly unrealistic; the order might as well have specified Falaise!)

And most poignantly, at 14.25 hours:

> *CO 23 H reports that it is now impossible to leave his present posn because a sqn leader 2 FF Yeo he has contacted thinks he is probably commanding 2 FF Yeo now.*

Advancing south east, the leading Hussars had come across the field in which the Fifes' earlier advance had been halted.

> *We crossed the railway line with no idea of what the true situation was. "B" Squadron advanced into the centre of the ring of blazing Fife and Forfar tanks before they saw that there appeared to be almost none left in action. One of the Fifes' Squadron Leaders ran up to say that, as far as he knew, there were only four tanks left in his regiment… While he was giving us this information, the whole of "B" Squadron's First Troop were hit and blazing in a matter of seconds. Sergeant Bateman hit a Panther and was immediately killed by a shell which penetrated his turret. Captain Blackman also scored a hit, but his tank went up in flames within the next minute. "B" Squadron began to reverse to the nearest hedge, firing back with all they had… Eventually the remaining tanks of "B"*

The armour-piercing shell that finished this Sherman tore through the track, along its breadth, before penetrating the side. All three hatches are open indicating a hasty exit by the crew.

Squadron, together with RHQ, got back to the doubtful cover of the hedge. They were still in view of the Panthers and completely outranged by their guns. It was a most helpless and hopeless situation for nearly all the 17-pounders had been knocked out, and the seventy-fives were virtually useless under the circumstances. Every five minutes there was the crack of an armour-piercing shot passing through the air, the shattering crash as it penetrated a Sherman, the shower of sparks, the sheet of flame, and then black figures silhouetted against the orange glow as they jumped to the ground, sometimes pausing to drag a wounded comrade.[25]

The Fifes' losses had been (slightly) exaggerated: the survivors pulled back north of the railway and out of the battle. Shortly after 15.00 hours, the Hussars reported that they had one squadron facing Bourguébus, 'almost completely destroyed', one facing Four, and one making its way around the west side of Grentheville, 'in a poor posn'. While 3rd RTR continued feinting towards the distant ridge, the Hussars maintained their position, giving ground only grudgingly and at cost until forced back to the line of the Paris railway. This they held. But as an offensive force, 29th Brigade was spent.

7th ARMOURED DIVISION

As early as 11.45 hours, Roberts had signalled back to 11th Armoured Division Main HQ, 'Gds Armd Bde not getting on very fast. Will CORPS let 7 Armd Div come on as soon as possible as we require them. 7 Armd Div are just short of DEMOUVILLE and could be passed through Gds.' But if the Guards' advance was slower than expected, that of 7th Armoured was more so.[26]

By midday, as Guards Armoured Division's tanks were accumulating in the area north west of Cagny, most of 7th Armoured Division was still west of the bridges. With the path taken by the preceding divisions blocked, the only forward regiment of 7th Armoured capable of manoeuvring was 5th Royal Tanks, which was edging westward towards Giberville in search of an alternative way through. Meanwhile 22nd Armoured Brigade Tac HQ

(Brigadier Hinde) was reporting back to 7th Armoured that 'a unit of HCA [the Household Cavalry armoured car regiment of 11th Armoured] says impossible to get through yet – too full of chaps'. Soon after, at 11.45 hours, Hinde reported to 7th Armoured headquarters , 'Situation obscure but FGP (11th Armd Div) sharp battle. BQT (Gds Armd Div) far further SOUTH so enemy come between own tps. No locn. We are held up behind 11 Armd Div and exact whereabouts NOT known.'[27]

At some point in the early afternoon, Brigadier Hinde pushed forward as far as 11th Armoured Tac HQ, in its field north of le Mesnil Frémentel. Pip Roberts recalled that,

> *He had been making a little recce and I thought, "This is good, we will soon have 7th Armoured Division to take over the area between us and Guards Armoured Division." But not at all; when he reached me he said, "There are too many bloody tanks here already; I'm not going to bring my tanks down yet." I was staggered, and before I could explain that a lot of the tanks he had seen were knocked out, he had disappeared.*[28]

At 12.55 hours, 7th Armoured HQ recorded a message that the VIII Corps commander was 'most anxious to push forward as soon as possible.' But O'Connor was not at this time directing the battle from Corps headquarters. He had come forward to see for himself what was happening at the front. The Household Cavalry history recounts how

> *General O'Connor, coming forward to see for himself what was holding things up, jumped up on to a tank containing one of the* [Guards] *tank battalion commanders in the process of ordering forward his squadrons. On the back of this tank was also the Brigade Commander and beside him the Divisional Commander, Major-General Adair, all urgently ordering one another on in descending orders of seniority, the final version doubtless reaching (in wireless form) some harassed subaltern as he struggled through Cagny.* [This was overly optimistic, towards Cagny might have been more appropriate!] *A Household Cavalry trooper witness of this unusual party, turned aside to his companion,*
>
> *"Well, I thought that when I had the Colonel and two other bastards giving advice on the back of my Daimler at Linney Head it was bad enough, but three Generals is bloody murder!"*[29]

As the afternoon wore on, harsh realities became clear to Roberts. So long as there was a realistic chance of pushing further forward, unbridled optimism had been the order of the day. He reluctantly recognised that 'the armoured brigade was now held by strong and accurate fire along the whole front.' While O'Connor was limiting his perspective to that of a tank commander amid the smoke of battle, it was Roberts who took stock of the overall position of VIII Corps. At least he was soon to have the opportunity to bend the Corps Commander's ear.

> *Now, at two o'clock I met the corps commander, General O'Connor, and the commander of 7th Armoured, General Erskine, just behind le Mesnil Frémentel, and I explained the situation to them, and I explained too that all these small villages, all inter-supporting, were held by strong antitank guns, either from tanks or from the ground. And no real advance could be achieved unless they were all dealt with, or neutralized. At the same time, I said that as my objectives were over to the right, I couldn't do much more until*

the gap between ourselves and the Guards on our left was taken over by the 7th Armoured Division. General Erskine understood this and he said that he would get his division forward as soon as possible and fill that gap and take over their line of advance. So I had great hopes that during the afternoon we would see the arrival of the 7th Armoured Division and we would be able to continue the advance towards our objectives over on the right.[30]

Some time later, at 16.20 hours, following his meeting with Roberts, O'Connor had a personal message sent to 7th Armoured HQ: 'Tell me what is holding up things?' The diplomatic reply offered an excuse and a guarded promise: 'Answer: Traffic but Sunray BQT (Gds Armd Div) and own Sunray [i.e., Adair and Erskine] held conference and a plan has been arranged. Difficult to say how long before it would be put into effect but an estimate 30 mins.'

Roberts was quite unforgiving in his later assessment:

I cursed both my old division and my old brigade... I managed to get a word across to Bobbie Erskine that I was disappointed that "Looney" Hinde did not seem to want to get into the battle.

Apologists for 7th Armoured Division have suggested that deliberate delay would have required an improbable degree of collusion between the brigadier, his leading regiment, and his divisional commander. [31] However, for his part Hinde later admitted freely that he was fully aware of the situation and had advised Erskine 'that it did not appear sound to advance further.' Perhaps outright collusion was not necessary given a tacit agreement between Eskine and Hinde that the overall plan was unsound, and the apparent evidence before their eyes that it was already unravelling. The Desert Rats division had experienced a tactical calamity a month previously when ambushed column of march, and its leaders had no desire to see the disaster repeated on a grander scale. Apparently trying to cover his division's shortcomings, Erskine wrote to O'Connor on 21 July complaining of poor VIII Corps staff work, 'an odd, almost insubordinate, letter which can have done him little good.'[32] Nor did it.

21. PANZERDIVISION

From the point of view of Hans von Luck, the afternoon of 18 July brought a steady improvement in the overall situation. Since his morning discovery of a massed armoured breakthrough to his front which threatened to overrun his entire sector, the position had stabilized. Becker's mobile guns and Brandt's infantry had formed a stop line west of Frénouville. By *Hauptmann* Kurtz's initiative, the surviving elements of *II/125. Panzergrenadierregiment* had been pulled together into a screening force north of Cagny. The heart of the division, its tank regiment and accompanying heavy tank battalion, had achieved little more than temporary distraction of the enemy. But at least that distraction by a handful of surviving tanks had discomfited the enemy until afternoon, when reinforcements appeared in the form of a *LXXXVI Korps* antitank battalion.

Thrown into the line north of Cagny on its arrival, *Artillerie-Pak-Abteilung 1039* brought into play twenty seven of the most effective antitank guns in

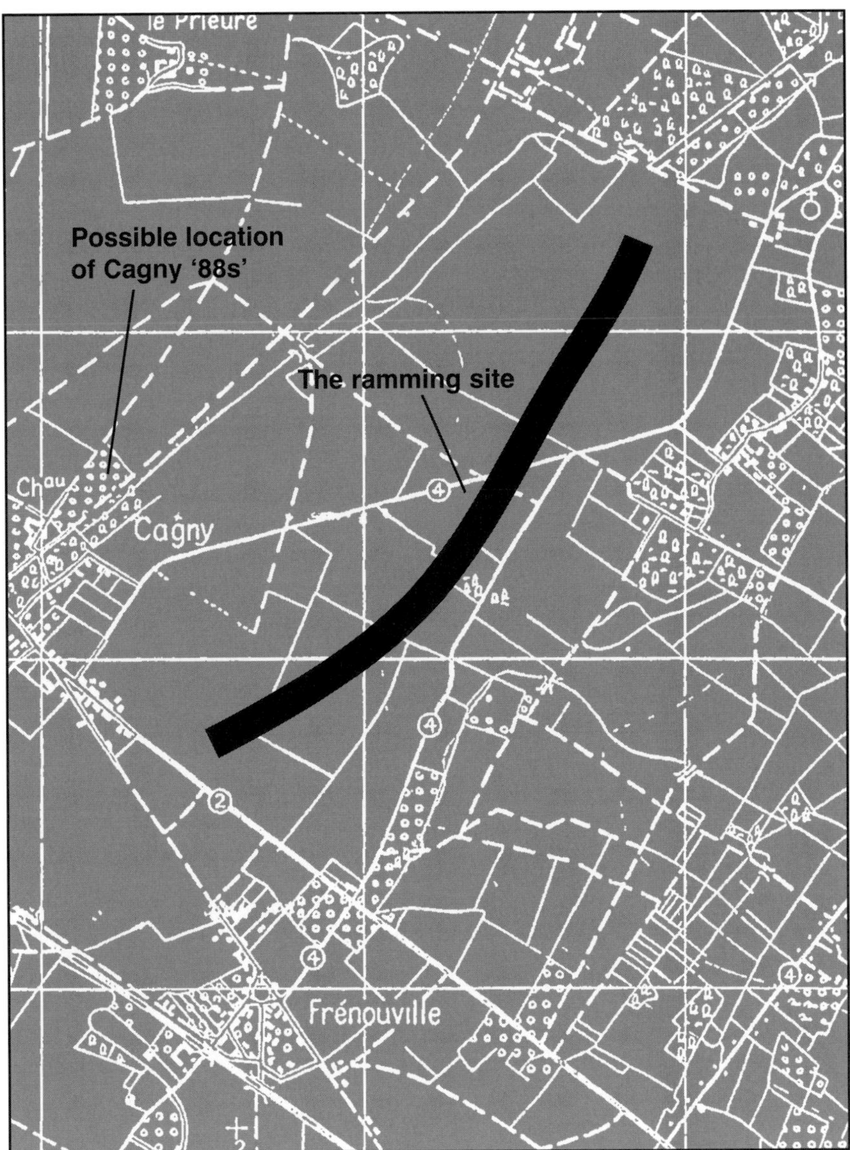

The hastely formed German 'Pakfront' east of Cagny.

existence: the 8.8cm Pak 43. The rushed deployment of these fine weapons limited their potential. Ideally emplaced where they could enjoy lines of sight to match their awesome killing range, these guns were instead hastily unlimbered behind any convenient hedgerow, ready for immediate action. With no time to prepare concealment of the guns or slit trenches for the crews, half the battalion was lost within twenty-four hours of combat. But for the loss of thirteen guns (and the battalion commander), *1039. Abteilung* was credited with the destruction of thirty-five enemy tanks. What is more, the

Thrown into action: the guns of *1037. Abteilung*. Some did not even have time to unlimber. Note the power lines north of Cagny.

Right: *Tiger 213* immobilized in the Manneville haras. (See page 60)

battalion made a major contribution to the sense of hopelessness which afflicted their opponents.

As well as the praise of his commander, von Luck's stand was rewarded by the promise of still more substantial assistance. *Oberkommando West* (OKW) had finally acceded to Eberbach's pleas and at 15.00 hours *12. SS-Panzerdivision* was released to his control. The division was immediately turned from its redeployment north and, after a circuitous approach (made necessary by the destruction of the Dives river crossings) would begin to arrive from the south by the evening of 18 July. From 05.30 hours on 19 July, the *Hitlerjugend* began to relieve *21. Panzerdivision* from the front it had held without respite for six long and costly weeks.

References

(1) 'The Leibstandarte IV/I', Lehmann & Tiemann, 1993, 0-921991-16-9, p 147
(2) This appears to have occurred *before* Roscoe Harvey's move west to the vulnerable position by the railway embankment. Quite possibly the FCP was located by efficient German radio interception since the immediacy of its role required signals to be received and sent uncoded, 'in clear'.
(3) Gooderson, p 32; 8 Corps Operational Instruction 'Op GOODWOOD'
(4) Lehmann & Tiemann, p 148
(5) This is well covered in 'Panzertruppen, vol 2' Thomas L Jentz, 1996, ISBN 0-7643-0080-6, p 182-190
(6) 'Operations of Eighth Corps', G S Jackson, 1948, p 99
(7) 'Fields of Fire: The Canadians in Normandy', Terry Copp, 2003, ISBN 0-8020-3730-5, p 157: '*What ought to have been forbidden was the practice of launching immediate local counterattacks.*' There is hindsight at work in this comment. Whatever its merits or demerits on 18 July, the practice of immediate local counterattack had long worked well for the German army. It was a basic tactical tenet whose abandonment was not lightly to be countenanced by any field commander.
(8) Much later, 3rd Division sappers' delight at discovering 'undestroyed' *Tiger* tanks in the haras quickly turned to respect for the German salvage crews as they realised the enormity of shifting a fifty-eight ton dead weight. (27th Armoured Brigade signals log)
(9) This issue is discussed in 'Operation GOODWOOD – The Caen Carve Up', Martin Samuels, British Army Review, December 1990.
(10) Roberts, p 176
(11) 'GOODWOOD', A G Heywood, Household Brigade Magazine, Winter 1956-57, p 171-177.
(12) '153rd Leicester Yeomanry, 1939-1945', Winslow & Brassey, 1945, p 14; Rosse & Hill, p 41. Unlike Germans and Americans, British artillery commanders accompanied the troops their guns were supporting; the system led to enhanced responsiveness but the price was often high.
(13) Boscawen, p 31
(14) Boscawen, p 33
(15) 'The Coldstream Guards 1920 – 1946', Michael Howard & John Sparrow, 1951, p 268
(16) Graham, p 133
(17) 'The Times of My Life', Sir John Gorman, 2002, ISBN 0 0 85052 906 9, p 38.
(18) Personal correspondence with Richard Freiherr von Rosen.
(19) Rubbel, p 243. Thaysen maintains that this was a 7.5cm German round from a *Pak 40*, presumably aimed at Ballyraggett; this is not at all unlikely, as there were German antitank guns emplaced nearby. At some later time, the abandoned Ballyraggett was holed in its turret from the same direction as this shot.
(20) Graham, p 170
(21) All this from 29th Brigade War Diary.
(22) Major Anthony Kershaw, quoted in 'The Pendulum of Battle', Christopher Dunphie, 2004, ISBN 1-84415-010-0, p 128-129.
(23) 11th Armoured Division signals log.
(24) 'From the Beaches to the Baltic', Noel Bell, 1947, p 28
(25) Bishop, 23rd Hussars, p 75
(26) 11th Armoured Division War Diary; 7th Armoured Division 18 July signals logs
(27) 7th Armoured signals logs, abbreviations as in original
(28) Roberts, p 177. Roberts relates the events of 18 July somewhat haphazardly. While it is understandable that some of his timings might be imprecise, even the sequence of some events as related by him is questionable.
(29) 'The Household Cavalry at War: Second Household Cavalry Regiment', Roden Orde, 1953, p 72
(30) Roberts, interview at Staff College, Camberley, 1979
(31) 'Steel Inferno', Michael Reynolds, 1997, ISBN 1-873376-90-1, p 178, see also Roberts, p 175-176
(32) 'The Forgotten Victor', John Baynes, 1989, ISBN 0-08-036269-9, p 209

Chapter 9

19 & 20 JULY: THE END AND THE RECKONING

Since the close of GOODWOOD, debate has continued as to whether the operation was a success or a failure. Without the achievements of 19 July, there could have been little debate.

THE SCORE CARD

The great armoured assault of 18 July had pushed out the British bridgehead east of the Orne River by five miles in the direction of the Bourguébus ridge and the Falaise road. The ruins of Cuverville and Démouville were in British hands. The village of Grentheville was secured, likewise the farm complexes of le Mesnil Frémentel and le Prieuré, and around these three positions the new British front coalesced overnight.

On the flanks of VIII Corps, the ground gained was screened by moderate gains made by neighbouring formations. On the I Corps front, 3rd Division's 18 July advance had been impeded by the struggle for Touffréville and the total devastation of Sannerville. At length, Touffréville had been cleared as a firm anchor for the push into the Bois de Bavent, threatening Troarn and the Dives valley. On the Canadian II Corps front to the west, 3rd Canadian Division had been slowed by determined resistance in the chateau and village of Colombelles, and stopped dead in the Caen metalworks (by the defenders of Colombelles who escaped the worst of the bombing and subsequently occupied the factory debris). The straggling village of Giberville had been taken and held against determined counter attacks. South of Caen a small Canadian bridgehead had been pushed across the Orne River, guided by

A new pair of Class 9 bridges completed north of Colombelles.

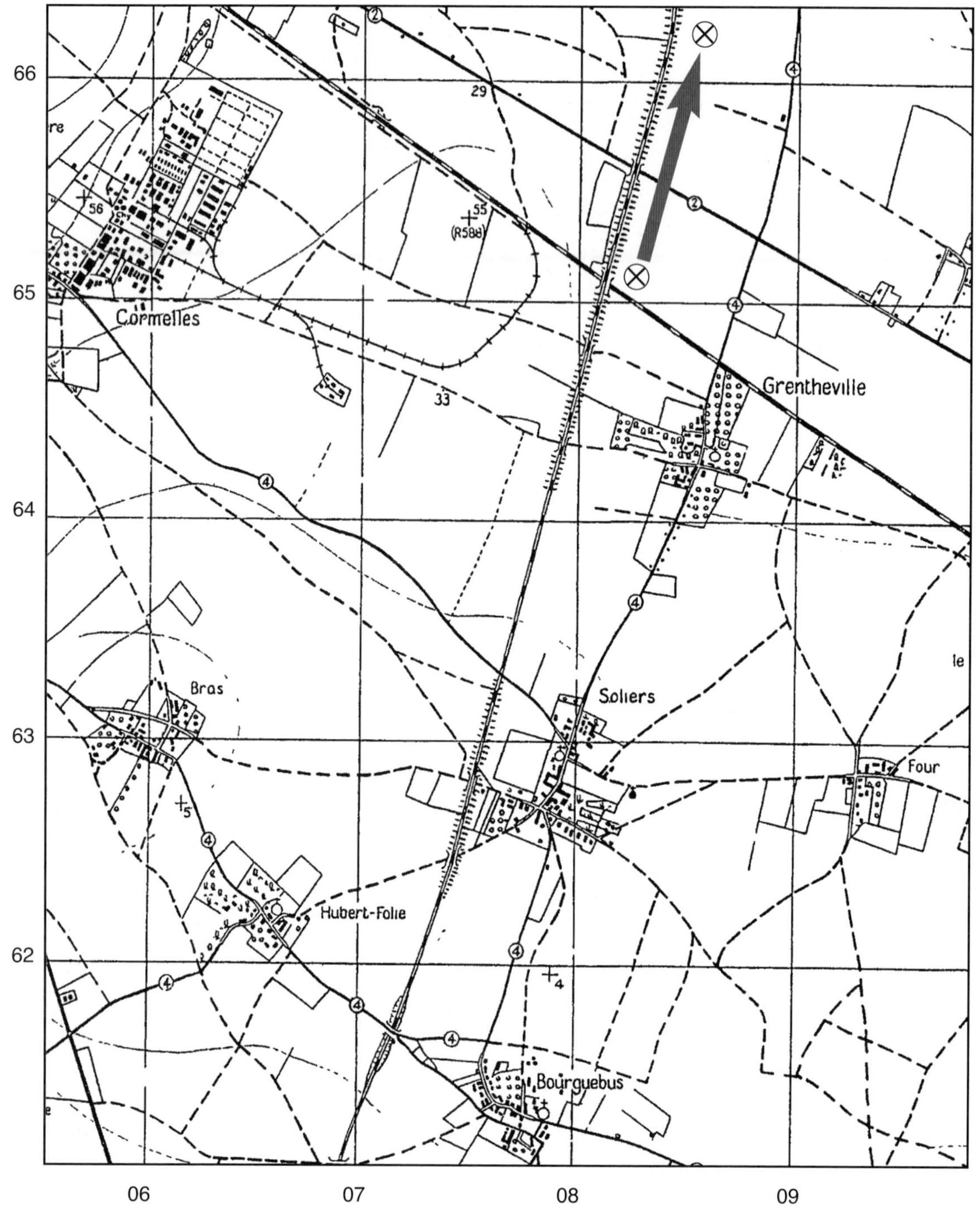

Arrow marks 29 Brigade Tac HQ move. (See page 195 and Appendix II for map coordinates)

resistance fighters into the ruins of Vaucelles. Construction of new bridges had been interrupted by continuing fire from Mondeville and the metalworks. But by the end of the day, a new pair of Class 9 bridges ('TAY' Bridge) and a DUKW crossing (ramps for amphibious trucks) were nearing completion north of Colombelles, while work had commenced on the first of several bridges intended to restore road links between Caen and Vaucelles.

So far, no gain of great strategic value could be set in the balance against a huge investment in logistics and air support, to say nothing of the previous day's losses in men and (especially) materials.

On the German side, the key ground had been held. The Bourguébus ridge was reinforced. So long as it remained in German hands the loss of its lower slopes, from Vaucelles and Cormelles to Grentheville, could be tolerated. Events to the east were a lesser concern: the close terrain between Banneville and Troarn would exact a high price from any attackers, and still further eastwards the soggy Dives valley with its broken bridges offered no easy route for armoured breakout. Many of the defenders of 18 July had already been relieved, with the greater part of *1.SS-Panzerdivision* (the *'Leibstandarte Adolf Hitler'*) holding the line from Ifs to Frénouville, and *12. SS 'Hitlerjugend'* moving up to relieve *21. Panzerdivision* to the east.

Nevertheless, the damage done to the Germans was considerable. Being forced to move the SS armour out of reserve and back into the line was a defeat in itself. Already in the course of 18 July, the *Leibstandarte* had suffered heavily. The vehicle strengths of its *Panther* and *Sturmgeschütz Abteilungen* fell sharply after 18 July; many a damaged *Panther* was retrieved and repaired but few new replacements were forthcoming. Already below establishment at the beginning of July, the *Leibstandarte* experienced heavy losses during the month: the tank regiment ten percent of its manpower, the assault gun battalion over fifty percent. Much of this loss occurred on the Bourguébus ridge.[1] While some new formations, mainly infantry, were arriving to shore-up the Normandy defences, most of the units already there continued to suffer losses of men and materials considerably exceeding the meagre issue of reinforcements. And less visible but no less acute was the impact on morale. From inexperienced units to veterans of the Russian front; from *Oberbefehlshaber West* von Kluge, keeping up the pretence of possible victory, to the *Landser* focused merely on surviving from day to day in his foxhole: confidence ebbed. Rommel had predicted in mid June that the Normandy front could hold only a month more. By 18 July the field marshal was gone but his prediction remained prophetic.

The bombing was an important psychological blow. Troops who had (almost) become accustomed to the day-to-day reality of enemy air superiority were taken aback by this awesome display of overwhelming power. The sheer material extravagance contrasted markedly with German supply shortcomings. And few things sap the morale of the front line soldier more readily than attacks against which he can make no effective reply. Neither those who suffered under the mind-numbing bombardment of 18 July nor those who arrived later could predict when a similar ordeal might again be visited on them. The apprehension was ever present. It bred caution. A senior officer of the relieving *Hitlerjugend* recalled,

> *The devastating effects of the carpet bombing in the morning of 18 July on the front line positions made it appear reasonable to only establish individual positions forward, i.e., battle front positions, and to set up the main line of defence markedly separate and to the rear. The operational reserves would be held as far as possible to the rear.*[2]

For the individual soldier, a new terror was added to the experience of life at the front. From now on, at every dawn, wary eyes scanned the lightening sky for danger signals.

PREPARATIONS AND PLANS

While German troops anxiously anticipated a resumption of the previous day's bombing, the British set about urgent reorganization. Having spent the night in the field at his Tac HQ by le Mesnil Frémentel, one of Pip Roberts' first tasks of the day was to inform his nearest neighbours of the state of his division.

> *Having established the situation in 29th Armoured Brigade, I sent a message over to Bobbie Erskine in 7th Armoured Division that the reorganisation required in 29th Armoured Brigade was such that we could not do much in the way of offensive action for the first few hours of daylight.*[3]

That a unit as seriously mauled as 29 Brigade might even be contemplating offensive action seems remarkable. For 18 July, 29 Brigade reported 126 tanks lost from its 'sabre' squadrons. Such figures always require further explanation. In this case, the total excludes many other armour losses: reconnaissance and antiaircraft tanks, plus scout cars, carriers, and half-tracks; it includes a proportion of tanks subsequently repaired.

3rd RTR had continued losing tanks throughout the previous day: as late as 22.15 hours, six further Shermans were recorded as knocked out by enemy fire from the ridge. By the end of the day, the regiment had lost forty-one of its Shermans (including eight Fireflies). Only twelve tanks remained when the regiment finally leaguered at 22.30 hours. Fortunately, many tank crews had survived, and replacement tanks permitted the formation of two squadrons: A under Major Close; B under Major Watts; C Squadron survivors were allocated to A and B. The Fife & Forfar Yeomanry had lost forty-three Shermans, including eight Fireflies. They too consolidated their remaining strength into two squadrons: A under Major Powell with twelve tanks, and C under Captain Millar with eleven, with a regimental headquarters of just two Shermans. 23rd Hussars had lost so many officers that the regiment was to remain in reserve throughout the day.

To imagine the division spending the morning hours of 19 July in peaceful rest and repair would be quite wrong. For all its losses of tanks and personnel, 11th Armoured remained in the front line. No one was under any illusions about the German will to fight. The divisional intelligence assessment promulgated at 08.00 hours, 19 July began,

> *Tuesday's fighting has... provided convincing proof, if this were not already at hand, that the enemy will relinquish no ground without being driven from it by very hard*

> *fighting. Whatever their long term feelings, the Germans, particularly SS tps are determined to take advantage of any advantage in ground and the undoubtedly efficient weapons which they possess… It is unlikely that he will be content with static defence, and a counter attack is to be expected.*

Signs of German aggression were not slow in coming. As Pip Roberts rose from his tent, a burst of shellfire spilled his morning tea. As early as 06.15 hours, the M10 tank destroyers of 119 Battery around Grentheville rebuffed an advance by three Panther, led by a captured Sherman. At 07.15 hours, German infantry attacked north out of Hubert-Folie: these were stopped by 8th Rifle Brigade and broken up by artillery concentrations. Meanwhile, enemy infantry and tanks were observed strengthening positions the length of the line from Bras to Four, while German artillery sporadically lashed out at the positions their own troops had so recently occupied. 3rd RTR reported 'intermittent shelling'. Roscoe Harvey's Tac HQ, still west of the rail embankment at 083652, was caught by a severe burst in the early afternoon. The Protection Troop commander, Lieutenant Gordon, was badly wounded and the Brigade Major, Anthony Kershaw, received a shoulder wound which he endured for four hours before being evacuated. Even the fearless brigadier recognised the need to move the Tac HQ a mile north up the embankment (to 086664), though as he stipulated, 'to an equally good point of vantage'! All this time, the Cromwells of 2nd Northants Yeomanry and the armoured cars of the Inns of Court probed aggressively to the division's front as well as its flanks, testing for points of weakness and alert for the first signs of the expected counter-attack.

About 10.30 hours, Roberts received word that his task for the day was to take Bras, in order to 'dominate' the main Falaise highway. Shortly after, the three divisional commanders met for a conference, significantly at Roberts' own Tac HQ. Roberts, Erskine, and Adair between them agreed a plan for the day. The plan was aggressive: Operation GOODWOOD was by no means

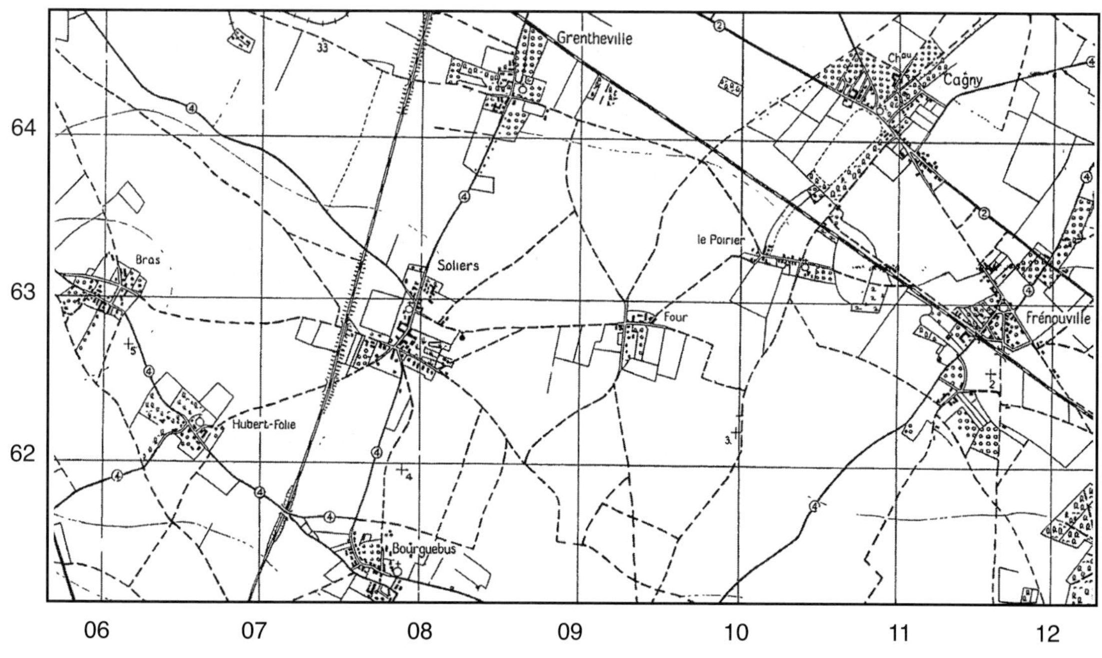

over. Each division established a primary and a secondary objective. 11th Armoured would attack Bras then carry on to Hubert-Folie; 7th Armoured would attack Four then Bourguébus; the Guards would take le Poirier with a view to carrying on towards Frénouville. O'Connor's role in this decision making process remains unclear. He subsequently arrived at 11th Armoured Tac HQ and gave his approval to the divisional commanders' plan. For a senior commander urgently striving to rehabilitate his reputation, the battle so far must have been a keen disappointment, the limited goals set for the second day unlikely to excite Montgomery or Dempsey, even if achieved in their entirety. One commentator has likened the 19 July plan to Third Ypres of 1917, in which O'Connor commanded an infantry battalion.[4] More likely, the corps commander now recognised that a strategic breakthrough was unlikely and now (at last) delegated tactical management to his division commanders. Many years later, O'Connor chose not to dwell on the subject:

'I do not look upon GOODWOOD as one of my more successful battles, and I would like to leave it at that.'[5]

BRAS

For all its losses, 11th Armoured Division now enjoyed one supreme advantage. For the first time, the division was to go into a major battle as a single unit, its tactical plan directed solely by its own leader. The three infantry regiments of Churcher's 159 Brigade were now available to support the division; so too the towed 25 pounders of the Ayrshire Yeomanry, its twenty four guns and the Sextons of 13th RHA giving Roberts two full field regiments of dedicated fire support. The Cromwell tanks of 2nd Northants Yeomanry were released to rejoin 29 Brigade. And freed of the rigid requirement to apportion its rifle companies to regimental battle groups, the 8th Rifle Brigade could be employed more flexibly.

The planned attack on Bras and Hubert-Folie involved all arms of the division, working in coordination as they had so long trained. The tanks would lead over the open ground, supported by the division's own artillery and closely followed up by the motor infantry, racing across the open fields to get to grips with the defenders of the village. Once taken, the place would be secured by the infantry battalions of 159 Brigade, and the armoured elements quickly reorganized for the next task. But even a plan devised and executed by the division's own commanders could go wrong.

All indications from the morning's reconnaissance were that the enemy line was weakest in the west. After a morning spent venturing far and wide, from Frénouville to the outskirts of Caen, the armoured cars of the Inns of Court reported at 10.55 hours 'Have a small party almost into CORMELLES. Does not appear to be strongly held.' Added credence came from Corps intelligence who claimed Vaucelles 'practically clear'. No longer tied to giving close support to the infantry brigade, the Northants Yeomanry reverted to its 'official' reconnaissance role. C Squadron probed westward into Cormelles: first a reconnaissance of the area around the 'blockhouse' at 068647 (actually, a former powder magazine, served by its own narrow-gauge railway), and by

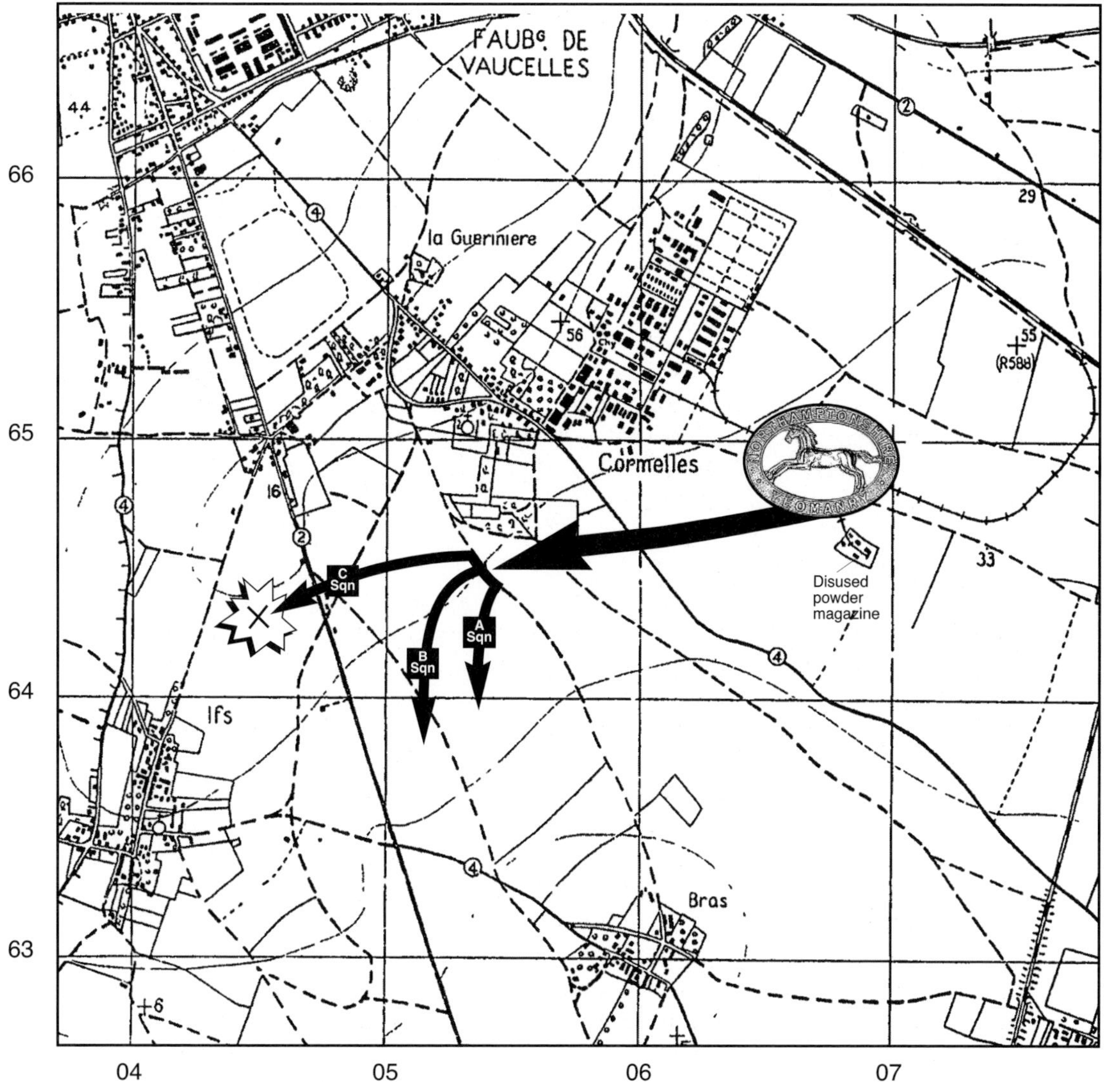

The Northants Yeomanry advance.

about 12.30 hours the orchard south of Cormelles was reported clear. The regiment was told off at 15.10 hours to 'be certain of getting the Eastern part of BRAS so that they can sp 3 R Tks attack on HUBERT FOLIE which was to follow up immediately.' Clearly, there could be no better spot than C Squadron's orchard from which to begin the battle, and the rest of the regiment assembled there by 16.00. Pip Roberts later claimed that,

> *'I was able to warn the CO of 2nd Northants Yeomanry personally and said he would have to support the Rifle Brigade into the village from the north-east – he must not get due north of the village or he would be shot at.'*[6]

But since their starting position was to the north-west of Bras, the Yeomanry could hardly be blamed for missing the target.

The Northants Yeomanry history recounts that:

'At about 17.15 hrs the Regiment set off with "C" Squadron Right, "A" Squadron Left, "B" Squadron in reserve. The main road from Caen to Falaise was the Right boundary and the Canadians were reported to be attacking Ifs in the valley beyond it. From the Start Line to the Objective was only about 1,000 yards, but across completely open ground covered with high crops to the ridge beyond. Heavy mortar fire greeted the advance, a smoke screen put down on the right flank blew back making visibility very poor; while the crops were studded with foxholes filled with snipers and bazookas. The enemy fired until in danger of being run down… long range AP shells kept on knocking out tanks… one of the A/Tk guns , previously reported destroyed, suddenly came to life again and brewed-up 3 tanks at point-blank range… Two complete troops returned on their feet after losing their tanks.[7]

A destroyed Cromwell IV/CS (Close Support) with its short 95mm howitzer. The Cromwell was one of the fastest tanks of the Second World War.

The picture painted in this regimental history is vivid but at fault in some details, not least in that it fails to disentangle the two separate actions fought by the 2NY that afternoon. The account is clearly drawn from the 2NY war diary, itself usually a model of accuracy but in this instance lacking precision, due to the original being later lost in action along with the officer who had written it. In fact, the advance began about 16.00 hours. Churning through the tall crop, their vision obscured by the smoke helpfully laid down by 13th RHA, C Squadron's route led them to become hull-down to the objective. Lacking a visual reference they strayed westwards. This path took them towards German guns which were poised to defend the Falaise highway against all comers.

A personal reminiscence fills in some of the detail. With C Squadron locked in its close-range struggle for survival, B Squadron to their left received the order:

> *You will not close with the objective. Halt well clear of the perimeter. Make feint attack by maintaining fire into area until ordered to stop. Real attack will be made from other side by friends on left.*[8]

So it was that the Yeomanry Cromwells' assault on Bras was first delayed, then abandoned, replaced by the task of shooting a regiment of Shermans onto the objective.

> *Along the line the bell muzzles of the forward troops' 75mms were recoiling as projectiles spurted on their way, then smoking blue until the next round followed. The sun shone brightly down on us all... the whole area was becoming a Hades of flame and smoke, tree splinters and other debris. I had seen nothing human there, even from my very first view... and yet it was illusory because the enemy was there, no doubt making use of the available cover. We continued firing into the smoke.*[9]

The village of Bras.

Earlier that day, Colonel David Silvertop had warned his surviving 3rd RTR officers to be ready to follow through after the Northants Yeomanry took Bras; meanwhile they should 'try not to get involved.' Most knew better than to take his warning at face value. Silvertop had every intention of 'getting involved' if the need arose. Seeing the Northants' Cromwells advance stalled, Silvertop lost no time proposing to Roscoe Harvey that his own regiment immediately take on the role of supporting the Rifle Brigade into Bras. This was agreed, with roles being reversed and the Yeomanry told to prepare for an assault on Hubert-Folie as soon as they had reorganized.

The engagement that ensued was a good example of a combined-arms assault on a strongly entrenched enemy in a superior position. With two field regiments laying down smoke around the objective, enemy artillery was blinded and the village effectively isolated from the rest of the battlefield. About 16.25, while B Squadron of the Northants Yeomanry fired into the western side of the village, 3rd RTR began their advance. The ground was familiar. Just as the day before, the approach to the village stretched for a mile, upwards across the open fields, the heading this time due south from a start position by Cormelles. The tanks suffered losses but carrying on regardless. Within fifteen minutes the leading troops reached the outer buildings. 'Some a tk and Bazooka fire. Odd snipers.' Some paused to fire as others plunged on. By 16.50 hours, 'Fwd tps enter village. Progress slow because of rubble etc in streets. Some tks had to break walls by firing 75mm. Prisoners surrendering in twos and threes.' The few remaining tanks used shock tactics to suppress the defenders, but only infantry could secure the objective. Keeping up abreast of the tanks, two 8th Rifle Brigade scout platoons in their fast carriers had swept forward, guns blazing, 'thrashing through the corn like destroyers'. For a brief period, the tanks remained exposed, with only the dismounted carrier crews for infantry support. With one depleted squadron passing through Bras and another working around its eastern side (and the Northants' Cromwells still firing from the west), there was a risk that the overrun SS *Panzergrenadiere* might recover their composure. Then, urged on

The view north from the German gun positions above Bras.

by 29th Brigade, the half-tracks of H and F Companies' motor platoons sped through the crops, flushing out as-yet undetected German positions, halting just short of the village. Their riflemen dismounted and moving in bounds covered the short distance into the builidings, F Company to the east and H to the west. Further still to the west, from the watching Yeomanry tanks,

> *through gaps in the smoke and flames we could see a company of the armoured brigade's motor battalion, operating in small groups, covering each other forward, fire and movement at the double, clearing ruins, dug-outs and other posts of the surviving SS garrison.*[10]

Bras had been held by the third battalion of the *1. SS-Panzergrenadier-Regiment*, closely supported by elements of the *Leibstandarte Sturmgeschütz Abteilung*, whose thirty five assault guns had taken up positions on the ridge the previous evening. German accounts of the engagement are understandably confused, as the whole affair was conducted with great speed using shock as well as firepower. Tanks confident of their following infantry entered narrow lanes, temporarily trusting in buildings and rubble to protect their vulnerable flanks while their fire suppressed the defenders; the infantry in their turn found many Germans pinned in their entrenchments by the tanks' very presence. By 17.20 hours, one F Company platoon led by Philip Sedgwick had fought its way to the far side of the village. Now the open country played against the *Panzergrenadiere*, as their avenue of retreat was swept by fire. While the three remaining tanks of Bill Close's A Squadron...

> *had an excellent shoot at some fleeing Germans… B and C Squadrons, also depleted, and down to two or three tanks each, entered the village at the same time. We were able to knock down the walls of houses from where cowering Germans emerged with their hands raised. Antitank guns were knocked out at point blank range.*[11]

By 17.40 hours the village was effectively clear. The German defenders were mopped up: to sixty or so dead were added three hundred prisoners, greatly outnumbering their Rifle Brigade guards. The cost had been heavy. An 8th RB rifleman found,

> *We had lost an awful lot more men… All the sections were short handed and some no longer existed. Many of our own vehicles, particularly bren carriers, had been lost.*[12]

Even as 3rd RTR prepared to pull its handful of tanks out of the village, Lieutenant Maurice Thompson, one of the last surviving officers, was killed by a single shell falling amidst an O Group. Nevertheless, an entire battalion of *1.SS-Panzergrenadier-Regiment* had been eliminated in about an hour.

VIII Corps' history records, 'This little action is not only of text-book perfection, but the prize thereby won was of the utmost importance to the Corps.'[13] The Corps commander took an immediate interest in the victory, declaring that no effort must be spared to preserve the precious gain from counter-attack. At 18.05 hours, VIII Corps signalled 11th Armoured: 'Super Sunray [i.e., O'Connor] directs BRAS will be firmly held. Cdns will take over as soon as Super Sunray can arrange.' To complete the picture of an armoured division working as an integrated, multi-arm force, Churcher's 159th Brigade was already standing ready to reinforce any success on the ridge. Shortly after Bras was taken, the 3rd Monmouths were ordered forward. Soon after 18.00 hours, the 'Mons' were in Bras. Already, 29th Brigade had its sights set on the next objective.

HUBERT-FOLIE, BOURGUEBUS, FRENOUVILLE

Even before 8th Rifle Brigade's H and F Companies had handed over Bras to the infantry of 3/Monmouths, E (Support) and G Companies were preparing for the attack on Hubert-Folie. This was now to be led by the tanks of 2nd Northants Yeomanry, who were put on immediate notice by Brigade at 17.03 hours and at 17.33 given the direct order to move on Hubert-Folie. But once again the Northants were thrown into confusion, this time by an unconfirmed (and inaccurate) report that the place had already been entered by elements of 7th Armoured Division's 22nd Armoured Brigade.[14] The delay caused confusion to the Northants Yeomanry at a time when they were shaking out into attack formation, under enemy fire. By 18.30 they were reported to be taking heavy losses in their vulnerable, fire-swept position. At length reduced to a single squadron, they were simply unable to continue forward. At 18.40, it was decided that the Fife and Forfar should do the job. This was not the only source of confusion. As the Rifle Brigade companies in Bras waited to give fire support to the advance on Hubert-Folie, the intermittent shelling from the south was supplemented by an intense British concentration, intended for Hubert-Folie, falling on Bras. There followed 'a very unpleasant ten minutes.'[15]

The Fifes' tanks moved up to a position north east of Hubert-Folie, mortared and shelled all the way. At 20.00 hours they attacked: C Squadron leading, followed by A. This time the advance went relatively smoothly. By 20.35 hours, to Roberts' evident relief, he was able to report to Corps '2 FFY going in now. Little opposition.' Meanwhile, G Company of 8th RB advanced from the direction of Bras. With 10 and 11 Platoon up and 12 Platoon in support, the first infantry reached Hubert-Folie at 20.35. G Company commander Noel Bell recalled,

> *The village had been previously shelled and the tanks were pumping stuff into it too. As the motor platoons moved in I called over the air for the tanks to stop firing but one went*

on firing and nothing could be done to stop it. It later transpired that this was a tank knocked out the day before and a German was manning its machine gun. The carriers who were acting as flank protection ahead of the motor platoons came under fire from this machine gun, and Cpl. Isard, a very old and popular member of the Company, was killed. We later had the satisfaction of this German "brewed up" in no uncertain manner at very close range.[16]

E Company followed G into the village and by 21.15 hours Hubert-Folie was reported occupied – occupied, but not necessarily cleared. Once again, it fell to the division's infantry brigade to secure the valuable prize.

The 4th King's Shropshire Light Infantry marched three hundred yards up open slopes to Hubert-Folie. This was a classic infantry action. Lieutenant Mike Sayer was a C Company platoon commander:

The advance on Hubert-Folie was an infantryman's nightmare. There we were in a huge open field of corn dominated by high ground ahead and a railway embankment on the [left] *flank, from which the enemy machine gunners and artillery FOOs had us in full view. At first we were encouraged by the sight of a squadron of tanks, in battle formation, ahead of us but to our astonishment and discomfiture it became apparent that they had all been knocked out on the previous day.*

The KSLI Carrier Platoon moved ahead around the eastern flank to give covering fire. By 21.15 hours, 4th KSLI were in possession of Hubert-Folie, and frantically digging-in around the place. Company commander Ned Thornburn '*did not normally dig my own slit-trench*' but now dug frantically in the soft sandy soil as mortar bombs descended.

I don't think I have ever been in such a flat spin as I was for the first few minutes at Hubert-Folie. However, by 22.00 hours the company was adequately dug in and prepared for any eventuality.[17]

All the afternoon and evening of 19 July, Guards Armoured Division kept up the pressure on the eastern side of the battlefield. But the defence line hastily thrown up behind Cagny held. With no repeat of the previous day's bombing, the antitank screen in the hedges and orchards from Frénouville to Emiéville was able to stop the tanks of the Coldstream and the Irish Guards from breaking through towards Vimont. Even the small farm complex of le Poirier succeeded in putting up a stiff fight until its defenders were finally thrown out around 17.00 hours by 1st Welsh Guards. By last light on 19 July, the infantry battalions of 32 Guards Brigade were firmly in charge of Cagny and le Poirier, and poised to assault Frénouville the next morning, following air support planned at first light.

Meanwhile, far from threatening Hubert-Folie, 7th Armoured was still struggling forward along the eastern side of the Minier railway. Only in the early hours of 19 July had the last fighting elements of the division cleared the monumental traffic jams around the Orne crossings. Only as the infantry battalions of 131 Brigade arrived in the course of the afternoon would the division be able to tighten its grip on Four and push forward with confidence towards Bourguébus. And confidence ebbed as stern resistance was encountered around Soliers, with long-range fire taking its toll of the tanks moving south to Bourguébus. As afternoon turned to evening, 22nd

Armoured Brigade had repeatedly to report the objective of Bourguébus still untaken. By 19.25 hours Hinde's Tac HQ was calling for air strikes on La Hogue and the ridge behind, 'first top priority and must be done this evening and sooner the better'. Amid the smoke and confusion, tanks of both sides infiltrated north and south. Even the village of Four, believed to be clear, came to life again. Around 18.45 hours an exasperated General Erskine had to report to Corps,

> *Our chaps attacking BOURGUEBUS, SOLIERS and FOUR – lost 3 tks in FOUR after the place had been reported clear by Inns of Court.' (It is interesting to note how widely the Inns were operating.) At last light, Bourguébus could not be claimed as taken, and even around Soliers the situation remained uncertain, with 11th Armoured complaining as late as 22.50 of fire on Hubert-Folie from that area: 'Tracer and MG coming from SOLIERS.' 131st Brigade's response was 'tell 29 Armd Bde that SOLIERS is definitely ours', though the 11th Hussars were less certain, 'We are not shooting but some shells may be coming from houses east of PEKINESE (BOURGUEBUS) not yet cleared.*

Once again, German infiltration and *Panzerkampftrupptaktik* had sowed confusion amongst the British attackers. The day ended without a clearly defined front line east of the Chemin de Fer Minier. Nevertheless, to the west of the railway embankment the ridge was held. The prongs driven into the German line the previous day had by the end of 19 July become stakes firmly implanted in the Bourguébus ridge.

RAIN AND RECRIMINATION

O'Connor had promised that 'Cdns will take over as soon as Super Sunray can arrange', and the corps commander was as good as his word. Through the morning of 20 July, though interrupted by yet further German counter attacks, the relief of 11th Armoured Division in Hubert-Folie and Bras was completed by 3rd Canadian Division. Meanwhile, the Guards' renewed their advance on Frénouville. The promised air support was laid on and at 05.45 hours 1st Battalion Welsh Guards and 5th (Armoured) Coldstream Guards charged in unopposed. The place had been evacuated the previous night. In 7th Armoured Division's central part of the battlefield, B Squadron of 5th RTR attacked Bourguébus at first light, destroying one German tank. There was no further opposition. The division established its part of the Bourguébus ridge line and turned to support the Canadians' left flank as they prepared to advance further south, in the direction Verrières.

Suddenly the weather changed. About 16.00 hours there began a violent thunderstorm. All Allied air was grounded. Within a short time, entrenchments began to flood and soon all tracks except metalled roads became impassable. Wheeled vehicles in open ground became immobilized and had to be towed onto roads by tracked tanks. At 10.00 hours on 21 July, VIII Corps ceased to have responsibility for any section of the front, and Operation GOODWOOD was officially terminated.

The storm of protest that followed the GOODWOOD battle is beyond the scope of a history focusing on the details of the battle itself. Suffice to record that Montgomery's enemies took every opportunity to criticize his failure to

The village of Hubert-Folie.

achieve a clean breakout. Eisenhower had been allowed to form the impression that GOODWOOD was to be a decisive breakthrough battle. His aide later recalled the staff being 'completely disgusted with the lack of progress'. Tedder encouraged his superior to sack Montgomery, and Eisenhower might well have taken this step had it been politically feasible. Bomber Command felt let down. On the face of it, an advance of five miles seemed small reward for their support, let alone the loss on the ground of three hundred tanks and fifteen hundred men. It was said with some bitterness that at the rate of one thousand tons of bombs for each mile advanced, it would be 'six hundred thousand tons to Berlin'.

Ever one for the dramatic claim that would make headlines, Montgomery had gone a step too far in his 18 July announcement that 'Early this morning British and Canadian troops… attacked and broke through into the area east of the Orne and south-east of Caen.' Fleet Street seized on the words 'break through'. On 19 July, the *Times* headlines trumpeted 'Second Army breaks through – armoured forces reach open country'; as late as 24 July the *Manchester Evening News* front page still carried news of 'Montgomery's Break

Through in Normandy'. A breakthrough GOODWOOD was not. Montgomery himself later admitted that he had been 'too exultant' at the 18 July press conference.

But, as has been shown, the battle had made a deep impression on the German defenders of Normandy. The day after the battle ended, barely a month before his sacking and suicide, von Kluge wrote to Hitler of his conviction that the struggle was hopeless:

> *In the face of the enemy's complete command of the air, there is no possibility of our finding a strategy which will counter-balance its truly annihilating effect, unless we give up the field of battle.*

Strategically, GOODWOOD had contributed to the matériel and morale weakening of the German army in Normandy. Tactically, it had shown up British weaknesses and (a few at least) strengths. To varying degrees from division to division, British and Canadian units took important lessons from GOODWOOD which would influence later operations such as BLUECOAT and TOTALIZE. To this extent at least, GOODWOOD was a step in the honing of operational and tactical skills which would take the British Liberation Army to the Baltic, and make some parts of it worthy heirs to the victors of 1918.

References

(1) Zetterling, p 307-8; 'Waffen SS Panzer Units in Normandy', M Wood & J Dugdale, 2000, ISBN 0 9528867 0 7

(2) Meyer, 'Hitlerjugend', p 159

(3) Roberts p 180-181

(4) 'Panzer Bait', William Moore, 1991, ISBN 0 85052 3281, p 155

(5) O'Connor quoted in Dunphie, Pendulum of Battle', p 187

(6) Roberts, p 182

(7) 'The 1st and 2nd Northamptonshire Yeomanry', D G Bevan, p 121

(8) 'Sixty-Four Days of a Normandy Summer', Keith Jones, 1990, ISBN 0 7090 4240 X, p 104; the 29th Brigade war diary confirms that the 2NY was ordered at 16.20 hours '*to get up on the West side of the village.*'

(9) Jones, p105-7

(10) Jones, p 108

(11) Close, p 129

(12) 'Soldiering at the Sharp End', R W Jefferson diary

(13) Jackson, 'Eighth Corps', p 106

(14) Communication in mid-battle between the armoured division headquarters was not a precise science. After an ambiguous signal about 16.50 hours ('*Tell 11 Armd Div... another regt* [of 22 Armoured Brigade] *will be on later – task GRIFFON (HUBERT FOLIE) and BRAS*') there followed misunderstandings and an increasingly urgent exchange of communications between 11th and 7th Armoured HQs which can be followed in the 7th Armoured signals log.

(15) BAOR Battlefield Tour, 1947

(16) Jefferson diary

(17) This and preceding quote from 'The 4th KSLI in Normandy', Major Ned Thornburn, 1990, p 77-78

APPENDIX I

THE GOODWOOD BATTLEGROUND

Each of the three Allied corps taking part in the GOODWOOD battle was destined to fight over distinctly different terrain. The main thrust on 18 July was to run southwards across a flat plain interspersed with small villages and orchards. Meanwhile, on either flank, more-or-less separate battles were to be fought over contrasting landscape. To the east lay wooded hills; to the west a built-up area characterized by factories, railways, rubbled town and suburbs, and crossed by a deep river.

MISCONCEPTIONS

This author was first moved to write about GOODWOOD upon visiting the battlefield and realising that his mental picture of the battleground, based on published accounts, was far from accurate. Even after reading a great many studies of the battle, the reality still held surprises.

Just as familiarity with the terrain assists understanding the battle, so can ignorance of it lead to wrong deductions. One account of GOODWOOD written soon after the war mistakenly blamed the Normandy 'bocage' for stopping the British: 'It was the hedgerow country that lost Montgomery the battle... The hedgerows won over the individual courage and brilliance of soldiers who had survived Africa... but who did not understand the terrain in which they now fought.'[1] The writer may be entitled to his opinion that Montgomery 'lost' the battle; some would disagree. But his comments betray a lack of knowledge of both the soldiers and the terrain. As far as GOODWOOD is concerned, only a small percentage of VIII Corps' tank crews were desert veterans, and the ground was largely open. Ironically, and rarely mentioned, there were indeed some stretches of substantial hedgerow crossing the GOODWOOD battlefield; far from hindering, these served to offer the advancing British very welcome protection from German fire.

Even apparently authoritative documents have promulgated similar misconceptions. The *BAOR Battlefield Tour* document[2] and the authorized history of *Operations of Eighth Corps*[3] both state: 'Between the villages the ground is completely open with no banks or hedges and very few fences.' (The two documents are virtually contemporary, with no indication which came first.) Little wonder that old soldiers relying on memory might omit mention of such, officially non-existent, features in their memoirs; nor that later writers unfamiliar with the actual terrain have accepted such statements without question.

THE ARMOURED CORRIDOR

The main thrust of Operation GOODWOOD was to run southward, down an open corridor between the industry and suburbs of Caen and the foot of the Bois de Bavent. Most of this was, and remains, rich arable farmland, dotted with substantial, prosperous farm complexes and the occasional small village clustered around a Norman stone church. Today the villages are larger, but the overall feel of the countryside is little changed.

Standing near the 18 July Start Line, the overall impression remains one of wide-open country. In the direction of the armoured advance, flat fields extend as far as the eye can see. Only as one moves further south does it become evident that the distant southern horizon lies on an elevated ridge. Indeed, from the Start Line near Escoville the Bourguébus ridge lies all of eleven kilometres distant, yet barely forty metres higher. This open aspect of the land east of the Orne contrasted with the dense 'bocage' country to the west, which had caused so many unexpected difficulties in the first six weeks of the Normandy campaign.

Apart from the industrial estates of Caen which nowadays spread across the western flank of the armoured corridor, the most conspicuous change from 1944 to be noted on a summer's day is the appearance of the modern crops. Today's much-modified strains are designed to direct more of their energy into the edible crop rather than the stem; in 1944 the ripening corn stood much taller. One point which the Battlefield Tour states entirely correctly is that 'during the battle, the crops were shoulder high and it was hard to locate such field defences as were sited in the intervening ground.'[4] Then, as in all previous summertime battles of European history, wheat grew to the height of a man's shoulder or higher. On a largely flat battleground, this was important.

The ground is well drained. Once the two parallel waterways of the Caen Canal and the Orne River had been crossed, the armoured corridor presented no significant water obstacles. The GOODWOOD planners hoped that the two railways running across the path of the advance would similarly present little problem. This hope was to be disappointed.

The first railway, the single-track line from Caen to Troarn, no longer exists, though most of its path along the northern side of the N175 highway from Mondeville to Banneville is still clearly visible. Aerial photographs and pre-war maps failed to show that much of the length of this railway lay on a small embankment, between one and two metres, and in parts borded by ditches and hedges.[5] This was to prove utterly impassable to wheeled vehicles, and a stiff challenge for half-tracks and the light, tracked carriers. Even tanks occasionally had their tracks damaged by crossing the metal rails, until Royal Engineers could come forward and bulldoze earth over the lines. In itself this obstacle was only a minor hindrance, but encountered at an early stage of the advance it caused hold-ups and bunching as vehicles queued for the few level crossings.

Ironically, the dual-track Caen to Paris railway (sometimes referred to as Caen to Vimont) encountered further south caused fewer problems, since by the time it was reached units had deployed onto a wider front and were not so narrowly constrained to following-the-leader. Indeed, as the day and the battle wore on, the shelter offered by its alternating embankments and cuttings was later to prove a welcome haven, the railway itself a rallying line against German counter-attacks. Note that the distortions in several narratives of GOODWOOD are caused by mis-identification of the three railways crossing the battlefield. The 1947 Battlefield Tour document refers to the Caen to Paris railway as having embankments and cuttings with steep banks 'up to ten feet high'. The statement is true but potentially misleading. There were few points along the railway in question at which the elevation of the permanent way differed by so much from the surrounding ground level, and fewer still where vehicles could not negotiate the crossing. The alternating cuttings and embankments of the Paris railway were generally wide enough that their slopes presented relatively little obstacle to vehicles. Exaggeration of this feature has led to some confusion. A major history of recent years claims, 'The two railway embankments were also natural barriers... breached only through small tunnels.'[6] This is entirely wrong, mistakenly likening the short elevated stretches of the Paris railway to the very different embankments and underpasses of the third, the 'Chemin de Fer Minier'.

This third railway deserves special attention. Running roughly north to south, the Chemin de Fer Minier passed over the former two railways and the main Caen to Paris highway at right angles. This railway supplied the massive factory complex of the Société Métallurgique de Normandie between Colombelles and Mondeville. To achieve an even gradient for the heavily laden trains, the line ran for most of its length from west of Giberville to Soliers on a very high and steeply-sloped embankment. The military significance of the embankment was that for six kilometres it effectively blocked lines of sight, and was virtually impassible to vehicles save via a dozen stone-lined underpasses. (Even on foot the ascent of the steep embankment remains today a tough challenge except where established footpaths run diagonally up the side.) Only along a short stretch of slightly raised ground 500 metres due north of Soliers was the bank slightly less steep. Here alone might fully-tracked tanks attempt the crossing, with great care, and of course with the attendant risk that any enemy guns on the other side would be given a brief but attractive glimpse of the tank's thinly-armoured floor! Southbound, abeam Soliers, the embankment resumes, before meeting the rising ground west of Bourguébus, where the rail line enters a cutting, passes under the road bridge linking Bourguébus and Hubert-Folie, and continues south to the mines.

Two further points of vital importance were missed – or ignored – by the planners. The first of these, covered extensively in histories of the battle, concerns the regular spacing of farm complexes and small hamlets. Giberville and Démouville; le Mesnil Frémentel and le Prieuré; Grentheville and Cagny; Soliers, Four and le Poirier: evenly spaced farms and villages, each a potential mini-fortress, and all arranged checker-board fashion approximately a thousand metres apart, ideal killing range for German antitank artillery.

By contrast, the second point has rarely been mentioned in accounts of the battle though its importance is no less. While the GOODWOOD battlefield was characterized by wide vistas and open space, there were some substantial and lengthy stretches of sturdy hedgerow, running generally east to west and offering considerable shelter to the attacking force. Much of this hedgerow has now been thinned out or completely grubbed-up, and the most important reaches disappeared altogether with the construction of the modern Autoroute de Normandie, which nowadays cuts a swathe across the armoured corridor. One of the few accounts of GOODWOOD to admit the presence of hedgerows does so wholly inaccurately, claiming that 'hedgerow country… beat the men who had learned their trade on the flat desert' and that a young American colonel had 'predicted what would happen to armour in hedgerow country' in the GOODWOOD battle.[7] This nonsense presumably reflected the writer's unfamiliarity with the actual terrain. In fact, the few stretches of dense hedgerow encountered on the central part of the battlefield provided Heaven-sent refuge to the attacking forces at key stages of the battle.

THE EASTERN BATTLEFIELD: WOODED HILLS

On the Allied left, I Corps was to advance into woodland. The Bois de Bavent is wooded country atop a low, north-south crestline. This line of rolling hills separates the lower reaches of the Orne River to the west from the extensive marshland to the east, the valley of the River Dives, flooded by the Germans as a pre-invasion precaution. Eastwards from Amfreville and Escoville, the ground rises gently upwards and open fields give way to orchards. More or less along the top of the low ridge runs the D37 road, running north west out of Troarn then angling due north on its way to Bréville. The road marks the start of the Bois de Bavent proper, dense woods covering the spine of the ridge and its eastern slopes. These woods remain almost as dense to this day, preserved as a popular area for rural holidays, its campsites and caravan parks interspersed with reserves where French hunters satisfy their passion for shooting wildlife.

On 6 June, 6th Airborne Division was tasked to establish a firm bridgehead to the east of the dual waterways running north from Caen to the sea: the Canal de Caen and the Orne River. For all the glorious capture, intact, of the actual bridges over river and canal ('Pegasus Bridge'), the remainder of the day's achievements were disappointing. The Dives River bridges were all blown, but then abandoned with the result that they were quickly rebuilt; the battery at Merville was secured at great cost but then abandoned since no one was equipped to destroy the guns, and the position was back in German hands at day's end. Also at great cost, the extreme northern tip of the ridge was seized and the village of Amfréville held, but the key vantage point of Bréville remained in German hands. Further advances were to prove more costly still. In the weeks leading up to GOODWOOD, both 6th Airborne and 51st Highland Divisions struggled to make further inroads into the woodland, pushing south and east from the now heavily entrenched landing grounds up into the woods.

For weeks after the 6th Airborne Division landings of 6 June, these woods had harboured tenacious German defenders who opposed all attempts to enlarge the airborne bridgehead. Following 6 June, the Airborne dug themselves into the open ground east of Ranville; the German infantry held the woods above; between them lay an open no man's land dotted with the hulks of British gliders. Conditions within this 'airborne bridgehead' east of the Orne were appalling. Not only were positions routinely shelled by German artillery on the eastern slopes of the woods, but as bad or worse were the persistent mosquitoes that infested the area. One Scot recalled, 'Battledress was no bar: if a mosquito decided it would dine off your knees, then dine it did, battledress or no battledress; and as it sucked, its friends would be wriggling happily inside your gaiters to nibble your ankles while others clamped down in hordes upon your wrists and face.'[8] Some accounts disguise the seriousness of the affliction with humour. But this was a very real and morale-sapping hardship: men were genuinely denied their eyesight or the use of their weapons by swollen faces and hands.

Between Bavent village and the small town of Troarn, the woods are thick. Even after suffering weeks of 'airburst', artillery shells detonating in their branches, sufficient foliage remained over much of the area to limit lines of sight, and lines of fire, to short ranges. Only a few straight roads crossed the woods; most of the tracks were narrow paths or fire breaks. Vehicles were limited in their manoeuvrability: even tanks were largely restricted to the few roads, and this was no place for unarmoured vehicles.

This dense terrain might favour either side on the defence. On the evening of 18 June a *21. Panzerdivision* counter-attack had been raging for twelve hours. *II./Pz.Gr.Rgt. 125* had already forced the 5/7 Gordon Highlanders to concede some ground, when an armoured column threatened to slip behind the right flank of the Scots' east-facing line. Due east of Escoville, two *Panzer IV* charged north up the Bréville road (modern D37b).

A Royal Artillery 17 pounder took a shot, narrowly missed, and in return was smashed by a High Explosive round from the lead tank. Emplaced (and heavily camouflaged) beside the straight road, the crew of a 6 pounder antitank gun (of the Gordons' own antitank platoon) watched with dismay as the enemy roared closer. At 500 yards, the gun commander Lance-Sergeant Fraser gave the order to open fire. The first round stopped the first *Panzer IV*; the following shot destroyed the second tank. Any following vehicles disappeared from view. Taking no chances, the gun crew kept firing, expending thirty rounds until both *Panzer IV* had convincingly blown up, the lead tank's turret flying from its hull.[9]

Over this area, Operation GOODWOOD was not going to introduce any new form of fighting, simply 'more of the same', albeit conducted by British troops who had not yet been worn down by the dispiriting woodland struggle.

THE WESTERN BATTLEFIELD: RUBBLE AND RIVER

In total contrast, II Canadian Corps was to fight in a variety of urban terrain. The city of Caen covered far less ground in 1944 than today, but nevertheless was a substantial centre, surrounded by considerable industrial development.

North and west of the Orne River, the city centre itself had been pulverized on the evening of 7 July by the Royal Air Force: 467 heavy bombers diverted from Air Marshall Harris' strategic campaign against German industry. The sight of this massive airstrike was a tonic to the ground forces due to commence Operation CHARNWOOD the following morning. And though grudging in their support of the Army, the RAF was enthused. By all normal measures, the raid was a tremendous success, with the target being bombed extremely accurately and only one bomber failing to return.[10] Sadly, the military impact of the bombing was counter-productive. As a safety margin, the RAF demanded a bomb line 6,000 yards ahead of Allied ground forces. This target area proved too far behind German defences to weaken their resistance; if anything, the rubbling of their rear areas would have hampered any attempts to retreat. And the military failure proved a civilian disaster. Quite apart from the damage done to a fine city (including sites identified before D Day as being of special cultural significance), civilian casualties were substantial.[11] It was believed that up to a third of the 60,000 population had remained in the city in the month following invasion. Now the devastation prevented recovery or even numbering of the dead and survivors led a troglodyte existence in the cellars of the city.

Some of the first Allied troops to enter Caen found, '...just a waste of brick and stone... The people gazed at us without emotion of any kind; we could hardly look them in the face, knowing who had done this. These were the people we came to free, and this is the price that freedom cost.'[12] Others had a more uplifting experience. On 9 July, Canadian skirmishers infiltrated the ruins, edging forward with guns levelled, hugging the walls, to find the streets suddenly full of celebrating townspeople. 'No Canadian unit,' states their Official History, 'recorded any complaint of the warmth of the welcome.' The welcome was all the warmer when it was found that some of the liberators were French Canadians.[13] For the 1st KOSB, on the left flank of 1st Division's advance on 9 July, 'Inside Caen, the people who had been under cover since the R.A.F. bombing on Friday night came out of their shell buildings and their cellars to cheer their liberators, tears of joy trickling down their grimy faces. It was the first large-scale spontaneous welcome the

British had received in Normandy… made all the more touching by the fact that it was given by people who had seen half their city crumble under the devastating blast of bomb and shell.'[14]

Ever since 12 June, local authorities and resistance workers alike had been passing messages to the invaders about the numbers of displaced and homeless people gathering in and around the great edifice of the Abbaye aux Hommes and the adjacent Église St-Étienne. The information was noted, and this whole south western corner was largely spared the devastation visited on the rest of the city. Elsewhere the destruction was severe, especially around the university and castle hill in the north and the area around the Vaucelles bridges and the main railway station in the south. While the city centre was largely rubbled, these particular areas were almost entirely razed and deeply cratered.

OPERATION ATLANTIC

By 18 July, II Canadian Corps held Caen and the left bank of the Orne Rive from its junction with the Odon to the Allied bridges around Bénouville. Though completely co-ordinated with GOODWOOD the Canadians' part in the operation was given its own title. Since all the objectives of Operation ATLANTIC lay on the right (eastern) bank of the Orne, the river necessarily had to be crossed.

8 Canadian Infantry Brigade led the way, its regiments crossing the southernmost pair of bridges over the Caen Canal and Odon River to reach their Start Line 600 yards south east of le Bas de Ranville. With the Queen's Own Regiment of Canada on the left and the Régiment de la Chaudière on the right, the initial advance was over open fields. This soon changed. The Queen's Own, the easternmost regiment of the corps, became embroiled in the ruins of Giberville, and the Chaudière likewise in the château and village of Colombelles. Both places are today immeasurably bigger. In 1944 they were separate villages; now they have been overwhelmed by industrial development and the eastward sprawl of the city of Caen. Some imagination and ideally 1944 maps are required to understand the actions fought there. And still further south, yet another different landscape awaited the remainder of II Canadian Corps.

South of Colombelles, on a plateau above the right bank of the Orne River, with its own port facilities on the Caen Canal, and girt by the sweeping curves of several railway lines, stood the massive steelworks of the Société Métallurgique de Normandie. Of this huge industrial complex little remains today except a very distinctive cooling tower (which was not even constructed in 1944) and two original water towers. Previous attempts by the British 51st Highland Division to capture the steelworks – at least long enough for demolition parties to destroy its tall chimneys – had ended in failure. Throughout the weeks since the invasion, spotters in the chimney tops and the water towers continued to overlook every move the Allies made in the sector. South of the steelworks were extensive railway marshalling yards. Further south still, in the area known as le Plateau, stood row upon row of long wooden huts, resembling military barracks but in fact accommodating the migrant workers serving the steelworks. Many of these were eastern European: Poles and many Russians (the northernmost building in nearby Giberville, its attic used as an observation post by a German battery and its courtyard a park for the battery armoured command vehicle, was actually a Russian family bakery). Beyond these civilian barracks were the homes and amenities provided by the steelworks for the more senior supervisory and management members of this self-contained industrial community.

Further south and west, around a bend in the Orne River, the ground dropped down to the riverside suburb of Vaucelles, the main residential area south of the city, already in 1944 covering an area equal in size to the city centre. In its midst stood the Caen railway station, an important nexus of several lines. Here the Orne River flowed from west to east, dividing Vaucelles from Caen and bordered by wide roads and stone-lined banks. The river itself was here fifty metres wide and three deep, precluding wading. Three road and one rail bridges crossed this stretch. Even before the tragic bombing of 7 July, much of Vaucelles had been devastated by bombs and artillery directed at the area around the main railway station and its extensive marshalling yards. Late on 9 July, the first Allied troops to push through the city as far as the river bank were elements of the Inns of Court and, under their command, two squadrons of 7th Canadian Reconnaissance Regiment. The armoured car patrols struggled forward hoping to find the Orne bridges still standing unblown by the retreating Germans. They arrived to find that the rail bridge had disappeared and two others were down, with some rubble remaining above water. The third bridge was impassible, covered with rubble and mined.[15] Only on 18 July, after assault teams had crossed the rubbled bridges to suppress direct enemy fire from the southern side of the river, could the engineers set to work on new crossings. Bridges were hastily thrown across the river to support a bridgehead in the ruins of Vaucelles.

And beyond Vaucelles ran the main highway: straight as a die, slowly gaining height as it ascended the Bourguébus ridge, towards Falaise.

References

(1) 'Top Secret', Ralph Ingersoll, 1946, p. 162-163
(2) BAOR BFT, 1947, Section II
(3) Jackson, 'Operations of Eighth Corps', p 78
(4) BAOR BFT, Section II
(5) Various accounts mention a 'six foot embankment' (e.g., Jackson, p 78), and though the obstacle may have reached this height at certain points it is misleading to suggest this as the average.
(6) 'Decision in Normandy', Carlo D'Este, 1983, p 359-360
(7) Ingersoll, p 163
(8) 'Battalion', Alastair Borthwick, 1994, ISBN 1-898573-35-2, p 150
(9) 'The Life of a Regiment: The Gordon Highlanders' vol 5, Wilfrid Miles, 1961, ISBN 0 7232 2785 3, p 259
(10) 'RAF Bomber Command', Denis Richards, 2001, p 237; McKee, 'Caen: Anvil of Victory', p 225-230; Stacey, 'Victory Campaign', p 157-159
(11) Casualties were between 300 and 400 according to Stacey (p 160) and others.
(12) Anon, quoted by McKee, 'Caen: Anvil of Victory', p 388
(13) Stacey, p 163
(14) 'Borderers In Battle', Hugh Gunning, 1948, p 106
(15) Stacey, p 162; 'The Devil's Own: A History of the Inns of Court Regiment', D M Hatton, ISBN 0-85131-550-X, p 117

APPENDIX II

ARMY MAPS AND MAP REFERENCES

The Germans conducted the Normandy campaign using maps developed from pre-war French examples, which used hachure (shading) to give an impression of elevations. The British used much better, contour maps of France. These were prepared using a combination of earlier French cartography and aerial photographs interpreted with stereoscopic viewers. This was quite a remarkable achievement, considering that the first contour maps of the land were produced without access to the enemy-held territory being mapped; the British Army Geographical Section coyly printed on their maps of enemy-occupied Normandy, 'not been checked on the ground'.

All map references given in this text refer to the standard British Army 1:25,000 tactical map. British map references were generally given in six figures, to indicate a precise location, or in four figures indicating a map square (measuring 4cm, representing a square kilometre).

In a four-figure reference, the first two digits indicate the longitude, and so correspond with the matching pair of digits on the south edge of the map. The third and fourth digits are latitude, matched with a pair on the west map edge. Tracing the indicated lines of longitude and latitude to their intersection, the crossing point is the south-west corner of the indicated map square. Thus, '1064' indicates the map square containing the town of Cagny.

In a six-figure reference, the first two digits similarly indicate the line of longitude (as numbered along the horizontal edges of the map). The third digit indicates the precise 'easting', the distance in hundreds of metres to the east ('right') of the ruled line. Likewise, the fourth and fifth digits indicate the line of latitude (as numbered along the vertical edges of the map), and the sixth digit the precise 'northing' in hundreds of metres to the north ('above') the ruled line. Having plotted the coordinates, the point at which they intersect is the map reference. So, '109643' approximates the location of Cagny church. Estimating hundreds of metres (or tenths of a kilometre 'box') comes quite easily with a little practice: until familiar with the system, it may help to start by using the master four digits to locate the map square, then work out which quarter of the square the reference falls into, remembering that a third digit of '5' indicates half way along a side of the square.

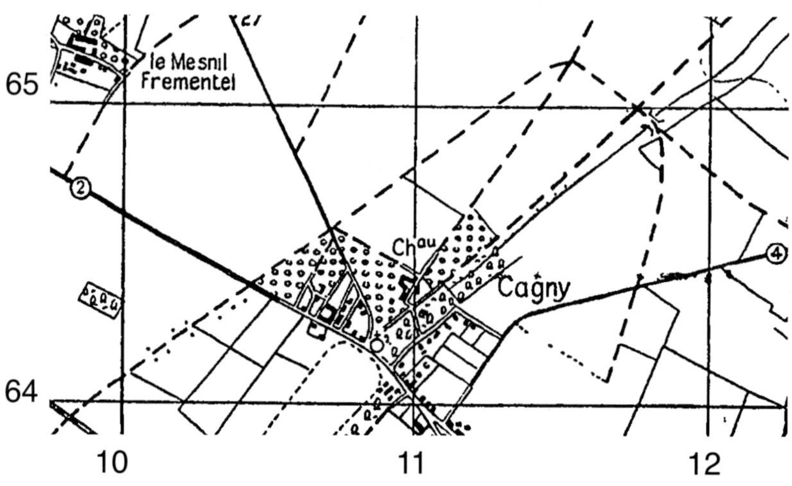

APPENDIX III

TELLING THE TIME

In the course of researching the Normandy campaign, the author encountered some differing views on the time being used by the various combatants. After extended study, and with help from many quarters, the following discoveries were made.

SUMMERTIME

The idea of changing the clocks in summer was first seriously raised in 1907 when William Willett, a member of the Royal Astronomical Society, circulated a pamphlet 'The Waste of Daylight', proposing that clocks be advanced by twenty minutes on each of four Sundays in April, and retarded by the same amount on four Sundays in September. British time is regulated by Parliament, where this and further attempts to introduce such schemes met with ridicule and opposition, especially from farming interests. However, the pressure of modern war eventually tipped the scale, leading to the introduction of British Summer Time. In the summer of 1916 the clocks were advanced by one hour.

Following the outbreak of the Second World War, a further change to the British clocks was legislated, to take effect in May, 1941. To Greenwich Mean Time and British Summer Time (GMT plus one hour) was introduced the novelty of GMT plus two hours. On 18 April of that year, Sir Stephen Tallents of the British Broadcasting Company was moved to write to Sir Alexander Maxwell at the Home Office asking whether there was any official designation for what the BBC had informally been announcing as 'Double British Summer Time'. In his reply of 21 April, Sir Alexander informed Sir Stephen that he knew of no official designation; nevertheless, 'I cannot think of anything better than "Double British Summer Time", which could not be said to run counter to any official description.'

1944

By 1944, the British had become accustomed to wartime daylight saving. 'DBST' began that year on Sunday, 2 April, with clocks advanced to two hours ahead of GMT. The British Army and the Allies in Europe used this time, as broadcast hourly by the BBC on 6195 kilocycles: Operational Orders for GOODWOOD as for other Normandy operations specify synchronization by 'BBC time'.

Germany in 1944 based its clocks on Central European Time, 'CET' (*Mitteleuropäische Zeit*, 'MEZ') which was GMT plus one hour. Like Britain, Germany adopted daylight saving from 02.00 hours on 3 April: *Mitteleuropäische Sommerzeit* (MESZ) was GMT plus two hours. Unsurprisingly, occupied France fell in line with this change, the clocks there also going officially to GMT +2 on 3 April.[1]

To confuse the issue slightly, Paris and other areas did not necessarily conform to the time standard, and there is evidence that 'official' time was not universally observed in France. Some rural and farming communities appear to have worked to sunlight time instead of clock-regulated hours. There is the famous example of the Gondrée café alongside Pegasus Bridge, whose plaque proudly claims it to be the first house in France to be liberated (which is true enough) 'dans la dernière heure du 5 Juin'. While John Howard's gliders timed their landing at a quarter-hour after midnight on the morning of Tuesday, 6 June, the Gondrées still thought it was Monday night.

ARMY SOURCES

In the majority of personal accounts of Operation GOODWOOD, apparently precise timings must be regarded with great circumspection. For a great many participants, the experience of 18 July began at dawn after a largely sleepless night and did not end until well after the end of a long summer day. In between there was little opportunity to consult a wristwatch and less to note the precise timing of events. Not surprisingly, a number of those timings in Allied and German accounts of the battle which are capable of being checked are discovered to be wild estimates – sometimes out by hours. Some war diaries have significant gaps at times of intense activity when no one was free to record events.[2]

However, it is useful to know that when dealing with reliable timings, British and Germans alike are working to the same clock hours. This is of particular importance when dealing with signals logs or with war diaries which have been composed using such logs as a guide. Where available, such documents can provide valuable frameworks around which less accurately timed accounts can be positioned.

16 SQUADRON

Some events not otherwise timed can be precisely placed by virtue of their being captured by aerial photography in the course of reconnaissance missions whose timings were accurately recorded. In the specific case of Flying Officer Wetz's sequence of 18 July photographs, his times of departure from and return to Northolt are definitively logged. Combined with his precisely recorded route and estimated speed we can construct a reasonably accurate assessment of the timing of each of his nine photographic 'passes' over the battlefield. In terms of his log, there can be little doubt that he was present over the battlefield between 11.40 and 12.25 hours.

But even this record is problematic. Aircraft and shipping the world over nowadays use a common clock setting. This is a necessity both to avoid confusion of schedules and to avoid constant re-setting of clocks as time zones are crossed. This setting is variously known as 'GMT' (Greenwich Mean Time), 'UTC' (Universel Temps Coordonné), or simply 'Zulu' (indicating the letter 'Z' using the modern phonetic alphabet: 'Z' for the 'zero' meridian). In 1944, this convention was observed by the Royal Navy, and also widely by the Royal Air Force. But not universally. Many aircrews operating out of the United Kingdom logged their flight times using local time.

This realisation led the author to investigate whether 16 Squadron pilots operating from Northolt in the summer of 1944 used GMT ('Zebra', using the 1944 phonetic alphabet) or local time (DBST, two hours different). If the latter, then Mike Wetz was over the battlefield either side of midday, Army time; if the former, his pictures record events two hours later. After expert study of Mike Wetz's photography, it was concluded that he must have logged his sortie using local time. Thus, his pictures reveal the stage the battle had reached either side of midday, Army time.

The conclusion is based on multiple clues on the ground. At Caen on 18 July, 1944, the sun rose at approximately 04.19 hours and set at 19.56, with zenith about 12.07 (all times GMT). Note that 'daylight' is widely assumed to commence thirty minutes before sunrise and end thirty minutes after sunset, giving a total of just under 17 hours 'daytime' on the first day of GOODWOOD. Shadows in Mike Wetz's photographs consistently reveal the sun at least 30 degrees east of south. Therefore the recorded 'mean time' of the photography of 11.55 hours cannot be GMT, as GMT noon would put the sun almost due south. The earth rotates relative to the sun at 15 degrees per hour, so 30 degrees east of south would equate to two hours before noon. Therefore it is concluded that Mike Wetz was clearly over Caen two hours earlier than GMT noon, and that his flight was logged using local time, BDST.[3]

In other words, Mike Wetz's aerial photography records the period either side of noon, as measured by all the combatants on the ground below. The author apologizes to readers for the complexity of the above. However, given the premise of this work that most written records of the battle contain ambiguities and errors, the value of hard, photographic evidence is paramount.

References

(1) Physikalisch-Technische Bundesanstalt (PTB) department of time; Ephémérides Astronomiques from Bureau des Longitudes.

(2) Examples are very common and easily found. The War Diary of 3rd Royal Tank Regiment for 18 July begins to cause concern with an inexplicable entry as early as 08.00 hours. Following the 10.00 entry, the diary has no further entries until 14.00. Far from indicating a lack of activity, this absence of entries actually covers four hours of heavy fighting. On a wider scale, General Wolfgang Pickert, recording the story of his III. Flakkorps in Normandy, consistently records the GOODWOOD battle as beginning on 19 July.

(3) For this and other discoveries related to aerial photography, the author remains indebted to Geoffrey Stone, who in July 1944 was an officer in 11th Armoured Division's small but invaluable Aerial Photography Interpretation Section

APPENDIX IV

ARMOUR IN COMBAT DURING GOODWOOD

The following is intended to serve as a simplified guide to a complex subject: the mechanics of armoured combat in 1944 Normandy.

EVOLUTION AND EXPERIMENT

In 1944, the tank had existed for barely a single generation. Through the 1920s and 1930s, tank tactics and design were still evolving, and in the absence of a major war they evolved slowly. The upkeep, manning, and transport of tanks is expensive; their loss even more so. Many British generals doubted the need for heavy tanks (and many a British politician questioned their cost) in an army still very much oriented to policing the Empire.

As the Second World War developed, Britain continued to experiment with tanks of all varieties: light and heavy, fast and slow; all had their supporters and detractors. The fighting in North Africa taught some lessons and reinforced some prejudices. In particular, it was in the latter stages of that campaign that Montgomery adopted the principles which were to inform his direction of tank warfare in North West Europe. Essentially, Montgomery rejected the widespread belief that two sorts of tank were necessary. According to the accepted wisdom, tanks were needed to fulfil two distinct roles: heavy tanks for infantry support, land battleships which could afford to sacrifice speed for heavy armour since they would only be required to move at an infantry pace; and faster, lighter 'cruiser' tanks for reconnaissance and exploitation. Montgomery's tidy mind rebelled against this diversity. His ideal was to be a 'capital' (or later, 'universal') tank which could do both jobs.[1] The idea had some merit. British tank design in the early war years lacked focus and the consequent volume production of useless models was highly wasteful of resources. Had there been a truly 'universal' tank available to Montgomery, the policy might have borne fruit. But there was not. For all its success, even the Comet of late 1944 was still a linear descendant of the 'cruiser' tank line; only later did a British 'universal tank' take shape, first in the form of the post-war Centurion and later the Chieftain, a design which suffered from many faults but nevertheless became the first true 'main battle tank' of the British Army. In mid-1944, the Allies were committed to invading Normandy with the tanks available. For the armoured divisions, this meant 'cruisers': Shermans and Cromwells. And even with his dislike of the dedicated 'infantry tank' concept, Montgomery could not ignore the existence in England of over 500 forty-ton Churchill tanks, grouped in three brigades trained in infantry co-operation. Which, given the close country that awaited in Normandy, was just as well.

During the Normandy campaign, the British and American armoured divisions were primarily equipped with the American Sherman tank. It was this model (and its British cousin the Cromwell, of which more later) which General Montgomery had in mind when he famously expressed total confidence in the tanks he commanded. 'We have no difficulty in dealing with German armour, once we have grasped the problem.' Lacking any realistic chance of re-equipping his armoured forces in the short term, Montgomery could not afford to allow morale to be undermined, and struck back at his critics. 'In cases where adverse comment is made on British equipment such reports are likely to cause a lowering of morale... It will generally be found that when the equipment is used properly and the tactics are good, we have no difficulty in defeating the Germans.' He dismissed reports from the battlefield as 'alarmist' and the work of 'officers with no responsibility and little battle experience'. (The American General Bradley could afford to appear more conciliatory, recognizing that the 'willingness to expend Shermans offered little comfort to the crews who were forced to expend themselves as well.')

Monty's critics would not be silenced. They argued that Allied armour in the Normandy campaign was hopelessly outclassed; in particular they demanded more heavy tanks, suggesting that even the Churchill was not heavy enough.[2] Among other experiments, 'The Old Gang' of First World War tank designers had earlier been commissioned to develop a fortress on tracks, endearingly christened 'TOG'. Some have argued that this 80 ton monster, equipped with 100mm armour and a 17 pounder gun, would have been ideal for Normandy. Others have dismissed it as a ridiculous throwback to a past era. Ultimately, TOG's fate was determined by neither argument: she was consigned to Bovington as a museum piece largely due to the perceived impracticality of transporting her, by rail and ship, from England to any European battleground, let alone the deserts of North Africa where her bulk and snail's pace (under eight miles per hour) would have been less than ideal.[3] Replacements for the Sherman or Churchill would not be available for Normandy.

THE PROBLEM OF STATISTICS

Accounts of tank fighting in Normandy frequently give details of different tanks' armour thickness and gun calibre. Some go further, relating such statistics as muzzle velocities and degrees of armour slope. These are all well and good (when accurately reported, which is often not the case), but they still do not tell the whole story. Even today, attempts to model accurately the effects of antitank fire against tanks require massive computer power and still may not provide conclusive answers.

One major problem lies with the raw data. Surviving Second World War weapons data are often unreliable. Different armies' records of weapons effectiveness are found to be based on different assumptions: differences in armour quality, slope, projectile velocity, impact angles, and other variables. Official test firings may have been carried out using high quality rounds unrepresentative of ammunition in the field: it is true of most Second World War armies that wartime-produced ammunition was of more variable (and generally lower) quality than pre-war stockpiles. Also, different criteria were applied. Some nations defined 'successful' armour penetration as fifty per cent of rounds 'defeating' a given thickness (and even definitions of 'defeating' varied). For Soviet analysts, a statistical 'kill' required an eighty per cent probability of penetration. And when the benefits of sloped armour were debated by the British, some experts stoutly maintained that the issue was impossible to resolve since rounds fired against tanks' armour could be expected to impact from so wide a range of angles and elevations.

The test environment rarely reflected battlefield reality. One well documented example of test firing was carried out by the British to assess the effect of air-launched rockets on German tanks. A captured Panther tank was drained of fuel and parked on an exposed hilltop, with huge crosses painted on it to ease identification. Then, two successive flights of four Typhoon fighter-bombers took their time to launch salvoes of rockets, untroubled by antiaircraft fire (or the fear of any). Three of the sixty-four rockets fired hit the tank, and the strike rate was solemnly recorded as somewhat under five per cent. But even that low rate was hardly representative of combat against camouflaged and protected tanks in the close Normandy hedgerows.[4]

In addition to all these reservations, sometimes the data are simply inaccurate. Over the years, errors arising from misprint or anecdote have been repeated in accounts of the Normandy campaign, gaining credibility in the re-telling. One German source, widely consulted and respected for its authority, nevertheless eventually turned out to be based on little more than British intelligence estimates. (Hence, a German weapon's effective range given as the suspiciously precise '457 metres' may be found to have originated from a rough guess that it was 'about 500 yards'!)

Fortunately, so far as the GOODWOOD operation is concerned, much of this statistical complexity can be set aside. In armoured combat, the human factor (though barely measurable) remains vital. The men fighting in tanks in Normandy were not for the most part physicists or mathematicians. Their battlefield tactics were shaped by experience rather than laboratory analysis or predictive models. If the following summaries contain generalizations rather than tables of precise data, this is intentional. Tank combat in the swirling smoke and dust of the GOODWOOD battlefield was not an exact science. Nevertheless, most of those involved eventually had a fair idea of their chances. It is a tribute to them that so many carried on fighting in spite of that knowledge.

GERMAN GUNS: KILL, MISSION KILL, AND OVERKILL

Of the GOODWOOD battleground, it is fair to say that almost any Allied armoured vehicle squarely hit by a dedicated armour-piercing round would be put out of action. Tank crews knew this. Indeed, a report by the armoured brigade of Guards Armoured Division even complained that their own Browning machine guns were capable of penetrating deep into the armour of Sherman tank turrets: 0.30 calibre to a half inch, 0.50 calibre guns to an inch and a half.[5]

Setting aside a handful of Royal Engineers' Churchill 'AVRE' tanks, not intended for tank-to-tank combat, there was no Allied armour on the GOODWOOD battlefield stronger than the front of a Sherman tank. Of the main German classes of antitank gun found here, the most numerous was the high velocity 7.5 cm Kw.K.40 in its two varieties: the L/43, largely phased-out by July, and the longer-barrelled L/48[6]. Whether firing from a tank turret, a self-propelled mount, or from a concealed ground position, this gun's crews could be moderately confident that a solid hit would incapacitate a Sherman tank out to one thousand metres. As a broad generalization, German projectiles tended to be harder and achieve better penetration than Allied rounds of similar calibre; having penetrated, their effectiveness was further enhanced by a High Explosive bursting charge contained in all standard German APCBC rounds (Armour Piercing Capped, Ballistic Capped). A hit might still fail to achieve an outright kill. The round might ricochet off or it might shatter, causing only superficial damage. But in either of these cases, the target was usually neutralized: a 'mission kill' in terms of short-term removal from the action.

There were few British tank crews at GOODWOOD who would remain in their tanks once hit by even a glancing blow. Though strictly contrary to standing orders, most would commence evacuation without waiting for the order to 'bale out' (and it should be remembered that most of the Sherman tanks at GOODWOOD had only a single turret hatch: when the three-man turret crew evacuated it was the commander himself who was necessarily the first to leave, disconnecting his intercom microphone in the process). It was generally recognized that the good fortune of surviving a hit or a near miss was unlikely to be repeated. Few crews were as stoical as the Churchill tank commander of 6th Guards Tank Brigade, overheard on another battlefield calmly transmitting, 'Hello, Able 2. Have been hit by 88. Permission to bale out. Able 2. Over.' After a ten second pause, the calm, monotonous voice was heard again. 'Hello Able 2. I say again. Have been hit by 88. Am baling out… Out.'[7] The transmission was memorable as an exception to the rule. And of course, a stricken Churchill was reckoned to allow substantially more time than a Sherman 'Tommy cooker' before it brewed – as much as ten seconds, some believed. It should also be remarked that by this time '88' had become a standard expression covering any German antitank fire. Operations Research dryly noted that 'Estimates by fighting soldiers were found to be unreliable since many reported they had been knocked out by 88mm, when in fact it had been 75mm shot, while the reverse has not yet been discovered.'[8]

More common was the experience of Stephen Dyson (B Squadron, 107 Regiment, R.A.C.) when his Churchill was hit: 'I've never reacted to anything as fast as I did on that occasion… We were drilled to wait for the tank commander's order before abandoning the tank, but in action that's a joke... Countless numbers of tank crews owe their lives to the speed in which they reacted... My tank commander didn't utter a word before the frantic exit from the turret.'[9] Similarly, in the experience of Keith Jones, 2nd Northamptonshire Yeomanry (in Cromwell tanks): 'For all concerned, entrance and exit were something they were used to, so long as they stayed alive and athletic. For a wounded crew member, getting out was another matter… we could expect to find, like all other crews, that when a tank is hit, the motivation to bale out is a reflex action, like the corks in five bottles simultaneously drawn.'[10]

Training aside, such behaviour made good sense. Generally in antitank warfare, a gun that has acquired a target will not shift its fire until the original target is demonstrably knocked out (which at GOODWOOD usually meant burning). As a general rule, a British tank crew surviving a first hit would anticipate imminent destruction by a second. They were not wrong.

Analysis of a sample of knocked-out Sherman tanks up to 10 July by 21st Army Group Operational Research showed that about 63% of losses had been caused by just one hit, and nearly all the rest by a second.[11] Most hits penetrated: virtually all 8.8cm rounds and about 95% of 7.5cm rounds hitting a Sherman would go through the armour, quite regardless of which aspect of the tank was hit, from what angle, or whether any form of extra (*'appliqué'*) armour stood in the way. It therefore mattered little that armour quality varied, nor that some Sherman tanks on the GOODWOOD battlefield had been reconditioned from previously knocked-out wrecks, with consequent but unmeasured weakening of their armour plate. Operations Research concluded that up-armouring the Sherman tank was pointless, but the authorities wisely turned a blind eye to battlefield expedients which might, after all, raise the morale of the men asked to fight encased in the armour. It is sad to relate that, at a time when tank crews were busily welding on extra armour plate, lengths of track, and other metalwork to supplement their tanks' armour, the overall performance of their Sherman tanks might have been improved by reducing their weight. A reduction in the Sherman's armour would not greatly have diminished the crews' chances of survival and might even have conferred some slight benefit in manoeuvrability.

So, a 7.5cm round which did succeed in hitting a Sherman would usually penetrate. If it hit in the engine, a fire was likely to ensue and once started would take as little as three seconds to spread to the crew compartment. By 1944, the statistics were similar for diesel or petrol Shermans: the popular myth that petrol-fuelled Shermans caught fire more readily was largely unfounded.[12] If the crew compartment was penetrated, then fragments of armour plate along with the detonating warhead would ricochet around the internal walls. Added to whatever damage these inflicted was the high risk of detonation of the tank's own ammunition, again leading to fire. At the time of GOODWOOD, most British tank ammunition was still stored in open racks; often extra ammunition was carried loose. Only later was it recognized that burning ammunition, rather than fuel, was responsible for initiating most 'brew ups', and steps were taken retard its spread. In a Sherman, 'You were in a "Ronson", and if you were hit it was best to bale out PDQ.' ["pretty damned quick!"] Later, crews learned to cope with the inconvenience of storing rounds in steel containers, some of these even jacketed with water. 'The Comets that we had later were different. Their ammunition was in heavy metal bins – awkward to get at but safer. Then, if hit, it was better to stay in. You just calculated your chances.'[13]

The larger German guns were designed to cope with much sturdier armour than the western Allies possessed. The natural prey of the Panther and Tiger was the sturdy T34 of the Russian front, later the even more heavily armoured Klimenti Vorishilov and Ioseph Stalin models. A round from the Panther tank's Kw.K.42 L/70 gun could hardly fail to destroy any Sherman tank it hit squarely. If the Panther was deadly, 8.8cm rounds from the Tiger tank variants and the 8.8cm antiaircraft and purpose-built antitank guns present were devastating. Turrets were dislodged, sometimes bodily ripped off and hurled clear.

HITTING THE TARGET

Killing was one thing. Hitting was another matter. As a general rule, German antitank guns had longer range, flatter trajectories, and gunsights with superior optics (though by 1944 this superiority was gradually reducing). GOODWOOD was fought over ground more open than most earlier Normandy battlefields, often allowing the more vulnerable towed antitank guns and thinly armoured 'sp's to engage at greater range. (Becker's improvised batteries depended on long range fire, siting firing positions from which they might 'shoot and scoot' before the Allied tanks closed to within effective range of return fire.)

But even on this relatively 'open' battlefield there were limits to visibility, which helped restore some balance to the conflict. Uncut grain, mostly wheat and rye, stood on the 1944 GOODWOOD battleground much higher than modern, modified strains: four feet high and more, shoulder height for the infantry. Combined with minor undulations of terrain this could create blind areas where tanks might seek shelter or at least remain 'hull down'. When advancing through grain, tank drivers often found their vision totally obscured. Even in the biggest tank engaged in the battle, the *Königstiger*, it proved possible for a driver lacking direction from a busy tank commander to incapacitate his vehicle by plunging it into an unseen bomb crater. Farmers had begun an early harvest just before the battle, with the result that some fields were lined with hay ricks. These provided a degree of concealment, if not hard cover; as the fighting wore on numbers of them caught fire, further diminishing visibility.

For much of the first day of GOODWOOD a breeze blew from the north east. This spread the smoke of the aerial bombardment and the dust of the advancing army without entirely dissipating the haze. The summer sun broke through from above, but along the ground visibility remained poor. And of course, many of the forward German guns, especially the towed pieces relying on concealment rather than armour for protection, were caught in the initial bombardment and their crews stunned if not entirely neutralized. Conversely, the Sherman tank was a particularly tall target. Since conspicuous target height is a major factor in range finding, especially in achieving a first-shot hit, and since the Allied Shermans were often caught advancing with minimal cover, this mattered. (A lower profile was one of the advantages the Cromwell tank enjoyed over its American cousin.)

The M5 Stuart light tanks (especially those still retaining turrets) and the Crusader antiaircraft tanks might be mistaken in the heat of battle for standard gun tanks, and were targeted accordingly, suffering alongside the Shermans and Cromwells. As to the other Allied armoured vehicles on the battlefield, the tracked Universal (or 'Bren') Carriers, half-track vehicles, wheeled scout cars and armoured cars all had relatively thin armour, generally proof against small arms fire, but extremely vulnerable to anything heavier. For these, size, speed, and concealment counted for more than armour thickness. Open-topped vehicles could be taken on with High Explosive rather than Armour Piercing rounds, most effectively when the former was fired into treetops for 'airburst' or delay-fuzed and bounced off hard ground for a 'scattergun' effect.

OTHER GERMAN ANTITANK WEAPONS

The German artillery arm should be mentioned. Apart from the dedicated antitank guns, the role of most of the artillery was indirect supportive or suppressive fire. True, many German artillery pieces were furnished with Armour Piercing rounds for emergency use; some on the GOODWOOD battlefield almost certainly possessed specialist 'HEAT' ammunition (High Explosive Anti Tank: better suited to large calibre, low velocity guns since the rounds relied on chemical rather than kinetic energy to penetrate armour). As a rule, these guns were less accurate by virtue of their less flat trajectories, their crews' lack of specialist training, and (crucially) the higher priority normally given to their primary role of area fire. The many *Nebelwerfer* rocket batteries present on the battlefield were conspicuously inappropriate weapons for use against tanks; on more than one occasion on 18 July charging Allied tanks rolled right over their positions. As to the many heavy antiaircraft guns in the area, most of these were under *Generalkommando III.Flakkorps*. Divided into three *Flaksturmregimenter* under the command of *Generalleutnant* Wolfgang Pickert, these were *Luftwaffe* units whose primary task emphatically remained antiaircraft fire. Indirect fire support for the army was a second priority, and antitank defence against deep penetrations was a last resort. Apart from a battery of four 8.8cm guns supposedly sited forward near to the village of Cagny, the bulk of the *Flakartillerie* – as many as eighty six tubes – was sited well back from the battlefield, many in emplacements purposely selected to shield them from ground line-of-sight using hedgerows and other terrain features. It is unlikely that many of these (except perhaps the aforementioned Cagny detachment) engaged Allied tanks with direct fire during 18 July.

While GOODWOOD is characterized by tank vs. tank combat, nevertheless it should be remembered that the German infantry had its own inherent antitank capability. The hand-held *Panzerfaust* now allowed a lone infantryman to deal a death blow to a tank. The fact that we come across few records of *Panzerfaust* use at GOODWOOD is easily explained. This revolutionary single-shot, recoilless weapon was the original ancestor of today's ubiquitous RPG (rocket-propelled grenade). The *Panzerfaust* had enormous armour penetration capability but lacked accuracy and range. It required close proximity to its target. Throughout the campaign in North West Europe, and even after versions with a theoretically longer range became available, most *Panzerfaust* shots were taken at ranges of less than 60 yards. Above 40 yards accuracy diminished rapidly; even at ranges of 20 yards or less about half the shots still missed. Firing a *Panzerfaust* required a degree of bravery. Not only were many users 'frankly terrified' of firing it [14] but surviving after the attempt required luck. In combat, few men ever tried a second shot at the same target. After firing, most either surrendered or tried to escape. Barely a third survived after hitting their target, usually succumbing to the revenge of other Allied tanks, while perhaps half of those whose shot missed succeeded in escaping.[15] British accounts of the time rarely distinguish between the one-man, disposable *Panzerfaust* and its cousin, the bazooka-like *Racketenpanzerbüchse* (or *Panzerschreck*, 'tank terror'). This 8.8cm rocket launcher was usually manned by specialist infantry antitank teams. More cumbersome yet more reliable and longer ranged than the *Panzerfaust*, its lower penetration was academic: it could penetrate any British tank with ease.

For all its shortcomings, the *Panzerfaust* was ideally suited to the close terrain of so many Normandy battlegrounds, where a man might creep along a hedgerow or through rubble, take a close-range shot, and still retain some chance of escape. The open GOODWOOD battleground was less forgiving. While a man might use the tall grain to hide, there was less chance of escape once revealed. Pip Roberts, commanding 11th Armoured Division, observed that his opposite number, *'Alan Adair, commanding Guards Armoured Division, arrived and I had a few words with him and he went off to do a recce of the area, but within a few minutes I saw his tank doing a sharp retreat with the GSO2 firing smoke over the rear of his tank. Apparently a couple of Germans in a slit trench … thought the time had come to take some action, so fired a bazooka* [in other words, a *Panzerfaust*] *at the General's tank. They failed to score a hit and were soon dealt with by some Grenadiers nearby.'* No doubt the aggrieved Guardsmen exacted a price for the attempt on their general. Significantly, Roberts reflected, *'I had been in the same spot a few minutes before, but I suppose the bazooka party had not worked up sufficient courage to disclose themselves.'*[16] 11th Armoured Division's intelligence summary prepared on the morning of 20 July noted *'a certain amount of trouble by sniping at our tks with "bazookas". As soon as our own inf. appeared, however, they appeared very much more willing to come out and give themselves up without any trouble.'* Armour and infantry were learning the necessity of close cooperation.

And finally, mines. To the surprise of some British, including VIII Corps commander O'Connor, German antitank mines were not an important factor in the GOODWOOD battle. Most British losses to mines were caused by minefields laid by the British defenders of the sector and not lifted in time for the advance. After the fighting had moved on, it was to take three field companies of Royal Engineers a full five days to clear the remaining British minefields, which prior to the battle had only been hastily 'gapped'. Why the Germans did not employ mines remains open to conjecture. Von Luck categorically stated that he did not want minefields limiting his free tactical movement. Roberts remained unconvinced by this logic. Far more likely, he argued, that the Germans simply did not have the mines available for what would seem a sensible defence of an important position.

BRITISH GUNS AND GERMAN ARMOUR

It is harder to generalize about the chances of a British gun firing at a German tank at GOODWOOD. Broadly speaking: large numbers of British tanks on the GOODWOOD battlefield carried a medium-velocity 75mm gun whose antitank performance was outdated for tank combat; smaller numbers had a high-velocity 76mm gun whose armour-piercing performance was very good. Both these guns had a chance of destroying or at least immobilizing any German tank which they could hit in the flank or rear. Against the Germans' frontal armour the story was different.

For battle-experienced British tank crews of 1944, taking the field at a qualitative disadvantage to the enemy was nothing new. Through the desert campaigns, where so much depended on mechanized forces, the British tanks' guns, armour, and tactics proved generally inferior to the Germans'. In 1941, 3rd Royal Tank Regiment was pleased to take over obsolescent captured Italian tanks in place of British models. By 1942, the British tanks' 2 pounder gun would not penetrate German armour except at close range, but the British crews frequently opened fire regardless. Since there was little chance of penetration, accuracy hardly mattered. One tank commander recalls, *'I knew what it was to experience the sound of solid shots screaming and tearing past one's head… with 'rapid fire', as soon as he* [the gunner] *got near the target I just slammed shells in as fast as I could* [in the Valentine's two-man turret, the commander was also the loader] *as he continued firing with little or no correction…'*[17] By this device, a troop of three tanks (normal in the desert campaign) could loose as many as forty-five rounds a minute, and create the impression of much greater numbers. Only in May, 1942 did the British acquire in the American M3 Grant a tank with a gun capable of firing 75mm High Explosive rounds. Now they could reach out to the German antitank guns that had tried them so sorely. Later, the M4 Sherman with its dual-purpose (AP and HE), turreted and fully-traversing 75mm gun appeared even more promising. That promise was sadly dashed as long-barrelled *Panzer IV* 'specials' appeared on the scene in increasing numbers. In firepower, the early models of the *Tiger* appearing in Tunisia were simply beyond meaningful comparison.

By the time of GOODWOOD, several successive stages of Second World War British tank designs had been abandoned: some after failure in the field, others – mercifully – recognized as unbattleworthy even before men were asked to die in them. The only descendant of these to take the field at GOODWOOD was the Cromwell, equipping 7th Armoured Division's tank regiments as well as one so-called 'reconnaissance tank regiment' in each of the three British armoured divisions. These Cromwells carried a 75mm gun similar to that of the Sherman tanks used by the British. The Cromwell's fire control systems were marginally superior, but for purposes of tank killing they could be considered roughly equivalent.

The Sherman had been designed to the established American theory that the job of the 'medium' tank did not include the destruction of enemy tanks. That was supposed to be left to specialist 'tank destroyer' artillery, either towed or self-propelled. Instead, the Sherman's envisaged role recalled General Sherman of the American Civil War, whose destructive raids ravaged the hinterlands of the Confederacy. The tank that bore his name was to be a weapon of exploitation. Like the cavalry of old, Sherman tanks would sweep around and behind the enemy, harrying his lines of communication and supply. To which end, the Sherman was well equipped with a gun whose High Explosive round could deal very effectively with 'soft' targets.

Most British Shermans were equipped with an American 75mm gun whose Armour Piercing capability was adequate (just about) to deal with an enemy whose armour was no better than Sherman's own. And some of the German tanks encountered at GOODWOOD fell (just about) into this category. The tank regiment of *21. Panzerdivision* was equipped with the *Panzer IV*, mostly later models with flank armour protection somewhat weaker than the Sherman or Cromwell and (in later models at least) frontal armour somewhat superior. (Though as noted above, the disparity in armament was far greater, the German long 7.5cm gun much superior to the Sherman's in hitting and killing power.) All things being equal, a Sherman 75mm could often destroy a *Panzer IV* with a single side or rear hit, and could expect something close to a 'fifty-fifty' chance of a penetration after achieving a solid hit on the front from 500 yards or less. Against the *Tiger* tanks attached to *21. Panzerdivision*, the *503. schwere Panzerabteilung*, or the *Panther* tanks appearing on the field later on 18 July, the 75mm Sherman's chances of a frontal penetration were virtually nil. Analysing German tank losses between 8 and 31 August, Operational Research could only confirm one *Panzer VI* (Tiger) whose front armour was defeated by any calibre of Allied armour-piercing shot (in fact by a 57mm, 6-pounder gun firing APCBC, which happened to hit the *Tiger's* front hull machine gun aperture). As to the *Panther*, Ops Research concluded, *'The small success of our A.P. projectiles against the sloping glacis plate of the Pz Kw Mk V is outstanding… and in many cases a gunner will not fire against a head-on Panther.'*[18] The report concurred that not firing (in the hopes of remaining unnoticed) was indeed the best tactic.

This grim state of affairs was relieved by one British innovation conceived in the latter part of 1943. In a classic confrontation between imaginative engineering and official scepticism, imagination won. With the support of the Royal Armoured Corps and the Ministry of Supply, a scheme was devised to fit the British 17 pounder gun into a Sherman tank turret. In time for the Normandy invasion, 17 pounder-armed 'Firefly' Sherman tanks were available in sufficient numbers to allow most regiments a ratio of one Firefly per four-tank troop. In addition, 17 pounder antitank guns were provided to the Royal Artillery antitank regiments, in both towed and self-propelled batteries.

Advances in tank armour during the Second World War were accompanied by the parallel development required of antitank guns. In 1940, the British 2 pounder antitank gun performed very well. By 1942 it was obsolescent, its replacement by the 6 pounder long overdue. By mid-1944 the 6 pounder was itself approaching obsolescence. True, with the 'APCBC' (Armour Piercing Capped, Ballistic Capped) round its armour penetrating capability was somewhat greater than the 75mm gun. A new 'APDS' (Discarding Sabot) round further boosted this penetration, though at a cost of diminished effective range and greatly reduced accuracy. Also, the 'sabot' round was in short supply; it caused increased bore-wear; and before July there was little opportunity for crews to discover the range settings needed to compensate for its unusual trajectory. Many crews fired their first 'sabot' round when facing a real enemy (urged by superiors to save the precious rounds for 'special' occasions, many a gun commander determined that the approach of any German tank was quite special enough!). Though an excellent weapon in its time, which continued to soldier-on in many post-war conflicts, the 6 pounder's usefulness against modern tanks fell away rapidly after mid-1944.

In its turn, the 17 pounder went a long way towards restoring the balance in tank combat. It could cleanly penetrate any German tank from the side, and the *Panzer IV* from any angle. Out to a thousand yards, it could take on an early model *Tiger I* from the front with something approaching a fifty percent chance of a hit penetrating, and a *Panther* with somewhat less, perhaps one-in-three, with a better chance against the turret front than the sloped glacis plate. Against the *Königstiger*, first met in combat during GOODWOOD, the seventeen pounder enjoyed a statistical possibility of a frontal penetration if it hit the turret (the early, Posche-turreted models assigned to *schwere Panzerabteilung 503* had turret front armour of 'only' 10cm, as opposed to the 18cm of later, Henschel turrets). In the event, no *King Tiger* tank suffered a frontal penetration by British fire in this battle (nor, so far as this writer is aware, in any later combat).

The picture was not as one-sided as is often portrayed. Though outranging the British tanks and virtually impenetrable through their frontal armour, at closer ranges the *Panther* tanks of the *Leibstandarte* lost their invulnerability. While the aspect of hits on a Sherman was almost an irrelevance, the case was very different with the *Panther*. On the defensive, it was easier to keep the strongest armour facing the enemy. When they descended from the Bourguébus ridge into the smoke-filled 'cauldron' of low ground around Four, the *Panther* tanks too suffered losses in the close fighting. Fewer losses than their opponents, it must be said, but nevertheless a *Panther* penetrated through its side or rear would blow up almost as readily as a Sherman 'tommy cooker' would burn. As a broad generalization, Operations Research concluded that knocked-out *Panther* tanks had on average succumbed to 2.55 hits (vs. Shermans 1.63), and 63% of them burned (vs. Shermans 82%).[19] At the close of play on 18 July, a major of the 23rd Hussars noted, 'We had suffered a very "bloody nose"... But all those Shermans were not blazing in the cornfields for nothing. Many a *Panther* blazed there too.'[20]

Bombing apart, it appears that the only early-model *Tiger I* tanks knocked out by antitank fire at GOODWOOD were two which apparently had the misfortune to be accidentally engaged by German 8.8cm guns. And while the front armour of a *Königstiger* remained proof against most antitank guns in the Allied arsenal, few of these seventy-ton monsters were deployed in the Normandy campaign; most of those involved were lost to breakdown during the retreat to the Seine rather than to enemy fire. Only fourteen were present at GOODWOOD and not all of those took part in the action. As previously noted, one was immobilized in a bomb crater. Shortly after, in the same location, two more succumbed to flanking fire, probably by multiple tanks including at least one Guards Firefly. (At the time unsung, this was the first occasion on which any *Königstiger* was destroyed by ground fire.) Elsewhere, another was abandoned after being rammed by a Sherman (while reportedly also penetrated by 'friendly fire').

In one respect, the odds on 18 July were stacked against the *Panzertruppen*. GOODWOOD was one of the two recorded instances during the Normandy campaign of heavy bombers catching concentrations of German armour. (The other being 25 July when prior to the COBRA breakout Bayerlein's *Panzer Lehr Division* was caught by carpet bombing as its armour concentrated to repel the expected ground attack.) These events were exceptional. Allied airpower was directly responsible for destroying relatively few tanks. We now know that throughout the Normandy campaign barely one hundred German tanks were actually destroyed by the Allied 2nd Tactical Air Force, for the loss of upwards of 1,600 aircraft.[21] But this was not how the German tank crews saw things. The dread of air attack led to the abandonment and loss of many more tanks than were ever destroyed from the air, to say nothing of the interdiction of tactical movement of tanks and their vital supplies during long daylight hours of summer as German vehicles remained static under camouflage.

THE HUMAN ELEMENT

Once again, combat between tanks is hard to reduce to statistics. The German *Panzertruppen* invading France in 1940 and Russia in June 1941 frequently came up against tanks bigger and more heavily armoured than their own. Yet what they lacked in hardware might be made up by ingenuity and tactics. French tank units were relatively poorly co-ordinated; individual French tanks, for all their heavy armour, had poor guns and worse fire control.[22] Tanks encountered in Russia were in theory more formidable still. Yet even pitted against enemy tanks whose armour was virtually impenetrable, the *Panzertruppen* found ways to prevail. After six months in combat on the Russian front, after-action reports from *Panzerregiment 203* recorded the destruction of 115 enemy tanks for the loss of fifteen. Enemy armoured forces superior in both numbers and quality were overcome by superior German tactics. 'Success has always resulted when our *Panzer* unit builds a fire front and overwhelms the enemy with fire. Even when no penetrations can be achieved, the enemy, impressed by the accuracy and rate of fire of the German *Panzer*, almost always breaks off the action.'[23] When Russian armour proved impenetrable, the Germans fired High Explosive and even smoke rounds, disorienting inexperienced Russian tank crews and causing them to withdraw (some appear to have succumbed to rumours that the Germans were firing poison gas). On other occasions, German armour incapable of penetrating Russian tanks are documented as having rammed vehicles, stunning their crews and dragging them out literally by the scruff of the neck.[24]

In Normandy, it was not uncommon for British tanks to fire High Explosive rounds at German heavy tanks. This apparently pointless practice would at least encourage the German crews to 'button up', greatly reducing their situational awareness, and might achieve more. Examples are recorded of HE rounds failing to penetrate German tanks yet detonating their ammunition stores. And even *Tiger* tank crews dreaded being subject to large-calibre artillery fire, which in the Normandy campaign included massive shells hurled from ships at sea. When 'buttoned up', crews could not readily identify the calibre of the incoming fire and were often observed to retire from combat rather than risk being bracketed.

Whatever the statistics, the psychology of the armoured forces should be considered. German armour engaged at GOODWOOD included large numbers of highly experienced tank men who had been victorious in combat on many occasions and had high confidence in their vehicles. Some leaders maintained their units' cohesion throughout the bombardment and prepared to repel the subsequent massed tank attack. But others who had not previously harboured doubts about their equipment became depressed by the shattering experiences of aerial bombardment and armoured assault on such unprecedented scale.

The human element in armoured warfare must never be forgotten. Hardware is not everything. Sometimes this is just as well. As the historian of British tank forces records, 'On the design and production side, much of what occurred was little short of a scandal,' yet many of the Sherman tank crews, 'knew the odds and did not flinch, even when it meant stalking a tank of twice the size and power in order to ensure victory.'[25] During GOODWOOD, most of the British crews leading the VIII Corps charge at the heart of the battle were comparatively inexperienced. 'We learned as we went along.'[26] They learned very quickly the shortcomings of their tanks. Armoured regiments arriving in Normandy conducted their own trial shoots against wrecked *Panther* and *Tiger* tanks. The results were not encouraging. Yet the knowledge that their tanks were inferior in one-to-one combat did not deter the regiments of 11th Armoured Division from a bold assault on the German lines. In the first day of battle they experienced losses as unpleasant in their nature as in their numbers. Yet the regiments of VIII Corps returned to the fray on 19 July. And a mere ten days later, its complement restored with replacement personnel and with Sherman and Cromwell tanks no better than those lost in such numbers at GOODWOOD, VIII Corps embarked on Operation BLUECOAT, its crowning achievement in Normandy.

References

(1) This subject is treated in depth in 'The Universal Tank', David Fletcher, 1993, ISBN 0 11 290534 X, see also Harrison Place, 'Military Training', p 89-92; and French, 'Raising Churchill's Army', p 102.
(2) In heated debates in Parliament, the Honourable Member for Ipswich, Richard Stokes loudly criticised British tank policy, culminating in a challenge to single combat outside the palace of Westminster: Stokes in a *Tiger*, versus the Prime Minister in an (eponymous!) Churchill tank.
(3) Though not always reliable on points of detail, a good source for this story is 'Rude Mechanicals', A J Smithers, 1989, ISBN 0-586-20305-2, p 98-99.
(4) Gooderson, 'Air Power', p 103-4
(5) No 2 Operational Research Section: 21st Army Group: Report no 2
(6) That is, a gun with a barrel 48 times its calibre: 48 x 7.5 cm giving a barrel of 3.6 metres.
(7) '6th Guards Tank Brigade, The Story of Guardsmen in Churchill Tanks', Patrick Forbes, 1946, p 33.
(8) ORS Report no 12
(9) 'Tank Twins', Stephen Dyson, 1994, ISBN 0 85052 274 9, p 59.
(10) 'Sixty-Four Days of a Normandy Summer', Keith Jones, 1990, ISBN 0 7090 4240 X, p 64
(11) ORS Report no 12
(12) The issue of combustibility, its causes and preventive measures, is well covered in 'British Armour in the Normandy Campaign', John Buckley, 2004, ISBN 0-7146-5323-3, p 127-128
(13) This and preceding, Steel Brownlie diary.
(14) 'Men Against Tanks', John Weeks, 1975, ISBN 0 7153 6909 1, p 70
(15) ORS Report no 33
(16) Roberts, p 176
(17) 'Armoured Odyssey', Stuart Hamilton, 1995, ISBN 1-871085-30-6, p 44
(18) ORS Report no 17
(19) ORS Report no 17
(20) Bishop, '23rd Hussars', p 76
(21) 'Normandy 1944', Niklas Zetterling, 2000, ISBN 0-921991-56-8, p 38
(22) 'L'Arme Blindée Française, vol 1, Mai – Juin 1940', Gérard Saint-Martin, 1998, ISBN 2-7178-3617-9, p 113-120 gives an honest and authoritative précis of the shortcomings of the French armoured forces.
(23) Quoted in 'Panzer Truppen' vol 1, Thomas L Jentz, 1996, ISBN 0-88740915-6, p 232
(24) One photographic record of such an event is found in '7,000 Kilometers in a Sturmgeschütz', Heinrich Engel, 2001, ISBN 0-921991-65-7, p 97-99.
(25) Fletcher, 'Universal Tank', p 22
(26) Steel Brownlie diary

APPENDIX V

LESSONS LEARNED FROM GOODWOOD

Interest in the Normandy campaign of 1944 continued in the post-war years. First to visit were the combatants revisiting their battlefields and the relatives of the fallen. Then came the old soldiers lecturing Staff College students. And at length Normandy came under serious scrutiny from military theorists seeking a model for the defence of Cold War Europe against the threat from the east.

GOODWOOD AND THE COLD WAR

In fact, it was not so much the Normandy campaign as a whole that excited the military, but specifically Operation GOODWOOD. NATO generals charged with maintaining the Central Front as a bulwark of the free world faced a complex problem. For much of the latter half of the twentieth century, it was considered possible that the Soviet Union might decide to attain its political objectives in Western Europe by military might. The armoured forces of the Warsaw Pact massively outnumbered the two-dozen divisions which could be mustered by NATO. The NATO force was a coalition of six national armies, with 'no uniform binding operational concept'.[1] Their flexibility in defence would be severely restricted by the reluctance of the (then) West German government to allow withdrawal. Voluntarily abandoning swathes of the homeland to the invader was altogether too bitter to contemplate. And the terrain over which the envisaged battle would be fought presented its own challenges. Never before had mechanized forces fought over such heavily urbanized areas, well provided with good quality roads, the intervening open country dotted with substantial villages rarely more than three kilometres apart.

In the words of the British General Scotter, 'We searched the history of modern armoured warfare for a parallel... We finally arrived at a classic operation in Normandy in 1944 in which a weak German regimental group held the assault of three British armoured divisions concentrated on an eight mile front... We know the operation as Goodwood.'[2] The German conduct of GOODWOOD was a very attractive model for NATO to consider. Here was a small but well coordinated force, surviving massive aerial and artillery bombardment prior to stopping a charge of massed armour. More attractive still, much of the impact of the Allied assault appeared to have been absorbed by lightly armoured antitank assets protected by small numbers of 'leg' infantry (i.e., unarmoured and unmechanized). This had appeal to governments keen to economize on defence expenditure.

The argument attracted critics. By the mid-1980s, the Warsaw Pact armoured divisions had much higher proportions of infantry (and mechanized, armoured infantry at that) than 11th Armoured Division enjoyed in July, 1944. One commentator accused Scotter of forcing the facts to fit his argument, asserting that his 'diligent scouring of the pages of history has discovered the all-but-unique example of primarily infantry formations checking an armoured assault enjoying total air superiority in open country.'[3] In spite of the critics, necessity remained the mother of invention, and with the infantry arm being keen to retain its pre-eminent battlefield role, the idea took hold.

LESSONS LEARNED AND HALF-LEARNED

During GOODWOOD, the British tank forces began to realise that open country was not of itself necessarily 'good tank country'. But after the battle, criticism of the British tactical plan tended to focus not so much on the risks of open ground covered by antitank assets, as on the role of the villages and hamlets interspersed across the GOODWOOD battleground. These provided a chequerboard of defensive strongpoints with potentially overlapping fields of fire. It was argued that if mobile infantry had accompanied the leading tank squadrons, such bastions of the defence as le Mesnil Frémentel, Grentheville, and Cagny might have been speedily secured, leaving the tanks to forge on ahead untroubled. That argument has strengths and weaknesses.

On the positive side, thinking became more focused on what modern infantry required in order to remain 'mobile'. After GOODWOOD Pip Roberts freely confessed that, even though his infantry brigade was left far behind on 18 July, 'I do not think you could have had them trundling along in three-ton lorries in this very open country.'[4] An immediate consequence of the GOODWOOD experience was the Canadian General Simonds' request that he be equipped for Operation TOTALIZE with armoured infantry vehicles. Between 3 and 6 August, an ad hoc Advanced Workshop Detachment plated-over the gun embrasures of seventy six American 'Priest' self-propelled guns to convert them into infantry-carrying 'Kangaroos'.[5] Consequently, though the idea of armoured 'battle taxis' for transporting infantry through fire zones goes back to the British Mark IX tank of 1917, August 1944 is often seen as the inception of the 'Armoured Personnel Carrier', leading in turn to the modern 'Infantry Fighting Vehicle'.

On the other hand, over-concern for the GOODWOOD villages blinded critics to some of the facts. In the early stages of the battle, the villages on the flanks of the battlefield were largely neutralized. Had a battery of guns truly been emplaced in the centre of Cagny before the battle, it would have been destroyed in the aerial bombardment. Though limited, the infantry assets of 29th Armoured Brigade proved adequate to clear le Mesnil Frémentel, and would without doubt have achieved the same in Cagny had Pip Roberts allowed Alec Scott's planned attack to go in. Neither the performance nor the equipment of the Rifle Brigade companies accompanying the leading tank squadrons should be disparaged.

GOODWOOD attempted to reverse the accepted wisdom of the day that infantry (with artillery support) opened gaps in defences and armour exploited them. On 18 July it was the armoured brigades that were thrust forward to break the enemy lines, each with only its one motor infantry battalion. Tanks alone were far too vulnerable to enter woods or villages unaccompanied. The motor battalions with their high proportion of specialists (drivers, gunners, etc.) were mobile but always suffered from insufficient rifles on the ground. Yet together, using the right tactics, the tank regiments and motor companies of 11th Armoured Division proved that they could take Grentheville, Bras, and Hubert-Folie. (Admittedly, taking was one thing; holding was a matter for the infantry brigades; nevertheless this was eventually achieved.) 7th Armoured similarly – eventually – took Soliers. The fight for Bourguébus was an armour battle of attrition, raging rather more around the village than within it, through 18 and 19 July; when the place was abandoned by the Germans on 20 July it was the motor infantry who first took possession.

Even long after the battle it was not realised in many quarters how vital had been the contribution of German antitank units operating around the fixed defences of the GOODWOOD villages. In the early stages of the battle, lightly armoured yet powerfully armed mobile batteries proved highly effective. These conducted a mobile defence, falling back in controlled stages, using carefully prepared and camouflaged firing positions which were invariably sited outside the villages. Even von Luck, who set so much store in his tale of the Cagny '88s', confessed in interview that, on his return to his headquarters after supposedly giving his orders to the young Luftwaffe officer, he believed the line between Colombelles and Cagny to have burst open and that, 'From this moment on, the sp [i.e., self propelled] battalion of Major Becker was the only unit with antitank to help us.'[6] When opposing commanders met after the war, Pip Roberts noted that he had been aware of the lack of deep minefields in the German defences. He clearly did not believe the Germans' assertions that this lack was intentional, referring with some justification to the Germans' logistical inability to ship enough mines north from the huge stores at Verdun. Nevertheless, von Luck and von Rosen continued to argue that the absence of mines was a vital part of their plan – a plan highly dependent on mobile defences. And lastly in this context, for all the achievements of the village outposts of *Kampfgruppe* Luck, the timely arrival of an élite *SS-Panzerdivision* in the form of the *Leibstandarte* had a material impact on the outcome.

A final comment on mobility: in the later stages of 18 and 19 July, it was a hastily assembled 'stop line' of specialist German antitank guns in fields north of Cagny that prevented the collapse of the eastern sector. These were *Pak 43*, at the time among the best (towed antitank guns) in the world. But their great range was negated by the closer country north of Cagny and Frénouville. Lacking armour and dependent on heavy tractors for mobility, they were unsuitable for being inserted into an essentially mobile engagement. Their awesome killing power took a toll of Guards Armoured Division tanks, but their lack of mobility left them unable rapidly to redeploy, condemning many to being overwhelmed and overrun.

THE WAR THE ALLIES WON

Fortunately, the Warsaw Pact divisions never ventured into West Germany and the theories arising from these studies were never put to the test. But the British Army in particular developed a fascination with Operation GOODWOOD, generations of post-war officers being encouraged to study the German conduct of the battle. This left a mark. The German army of the Second World War continued to be upheld as providing examples of supreme military skill, an attitude typified by post-war British soldiers whose writings continue to liken the fighting prowess of the best of the German army (and the *Waffen SS* in particular) to Caesar's finest legions, Napoleon's Garde Impériale, and Robert E Lee's lean greycoats.

It is ironic that so much attention was paid to the German conduct of GOODWOOD to the detriment of the Allies' performance, particularly that of the British armour. Whatever may be argued about Montgomery's true objectives, GOODWOOD was an essential step on the road to Falaise, and for the Germans a severe if not unexpected blow which shattered their generals' confidence and took them a step closer to eventual defeat in Normandy.

GOODWOOD was a key step in the forging, by Britain's youngest general, of one of the most effective British units of the Second World War. 11th Armoured Division crossed the Orne River on 17 July confident in having performed creditably in its first battle a fortnight before. Returning across those bridges after GOODWOOD, through mud and drenching rain, the division had taken a severe battering. Many were resentful. Some were mutinous.[7] It was easy to think in terms of comrades lost and objectives not achieved. But this was not all the story. In the short period of rest before the division was committed to the BLUECOAT offensive, morale strengthened and confidence remained high; lessons learned from GOODWOOD were absorbed and tactics perfected. The divisional commander was later to record his feelings, 'It was not until our third battle in Normandy that we got it right.'[8]

Let it never be forgotten that late on the second day of GOODWOOD a tired and heavily depleted combined-arms force in battalion strength advanced over open ground against prepared positions and within a half hour defeated an entire battalion of the *1.SS-Panzerdivision*, Hitler's 'lifeguards'. In short order, three hundred *Panzergrenadiere* of the *Leibstandarte* were taken prisoner and the village of Bras was secured. By taking Bras, and later Hubert-Folie, 11th Armoured Division established a grip on the Bourguébus ridgeline, an essential anchor for securing the gains of GOODWOOD, and a potential springboard from which Canadian forces might further extend the bridgehead south of Caen preparatory to further advances along the Falaise road.

In his first battle, Operation EPSOM, and in both the planning and the first day of GOODWOOD, Pip Roberts did not enjoy full control over his division. On both occasions the infantry brigade under his command was prevented from acting in co-ordination with the tanks. On 19 July that co-ordination was permitted, the result was a striking tactical victory, and the lesson learned was quickly implemented.

On 24 July, 1944, a post-battle conference was held within 11th Armoured Division and its attached units. After considering and recording all the factors which prevented greater success on 18 July, the conference turned to the lessons learned in assaulting a strongpoint. The conclusions formed a blueprint for future actions. Their relevance went beyond the specific instance, introducing a whole new philosophy of co-operation between armour, and infantry, and artillery. The closing days of July would see this co-operation rewarded in the tremendous successes enjoyed by 11th Armoured in its third major battle, Operation BLUECOAT. And the confidence arising from this success would carry the division onward to the Baltic.

References

(1) Brigadier General G Brugmann, Hamburg symposium, April 1980

(2) General Sir William Scotter, Hamburg symposium, April 1980

(3) Charles J Dick, 'Situating the Appreciation', Royal United Services Institute, March 1982

(4) Roberts, interview at Staff College, Camberley, 1979

(5) 'The Victory Campaign, vol III', C P Stacey, 1960, p 209-210

(6) Von Luck, interview at Staff College, Camberley, 1979

(7) Buckley, p 36. Buckley cites increases in desertion and AWOL following GOODWOOD.

(7) Roberts, p 159

APPENDIX VI

11TH ARMOURED DIVISION GOODWOOD ORDER OF BATTLE 18 JULY, 1944

OVERALL DIVISIONAL STRUCTURE:

'Tac' (or forward) Headquarters: Major General G B P 'Pip' Roberts

Main Headquarters

Divisional troops

- 2nd Northamptonshire Yeomanry (2 NY) (reconnaissance regiment)
- 13th Regiment, Royal Horse Artillery (13 RHA)
- 151st Field Regiment, Royal Artillery, 'Ayrshire Yeomanry' (151 RA)
- 75th Anti-Tank Regiment, Royal Artillery (75 AT)
- 58th Light Anti-Aircraft Regiment, Royal Artillery (58 LAA)
- The Inns of Court (reconnaissance) armoured car regiment (attachment from mid-July to last for much of the NW Europe campaign)

29th Armoured Brigade: Brigadier C B C 'Roscoe' Harvey

- 23rd Hussars (23 H)
- 2nd Fife & Forfarshire Yeomanry (2 FF Yeo)
- 3rd Battalion Royal Tank Regiment (3 R Tks)
- 8th Battalion The Rifle Brigade (8 RB)

159th Infantry Brigade: Brigadier J B 'Jack' Churcher

- 3rd Battalion The Monmouthshire Regiment (3 MON)
- 4th Battalion The King's Shropshire Light Infantry (4 KSLI)
- 1st Battalion The Herefordshire Regiment (1 HEREFORD)

plus detachments including:

- One squadron of Sherman 'Crab' flails of 22nd Dragoons (approximately 15 x 75mm gun tanks with minesweeping flails)
- 10 Armoured Vehicles Royal Engineers of 26 Assault Squadron (Churchill AVRE tanks mounting 290mm spigot mortars manned by sappers equipped with demolitions)
- One troop 612 Field Squadron, Royal Engineers with sappers mounted in half-tracks and 2 armoured bulldozers to deal with unforeseen obstacles

Notes:

1. After GOODWOOD the division's two brigades operated with sub-units intermingled; up to and including GOODWOOD the brigades fought largely independently of each other. Thus at the start of GOODWOOD the only infantry in direct support of the tank regiments was 29th Brigade's single motor battalion, 8 RB, with one motor company initially assigned to each tank regiment.
2. 13 RHA (armoured, self-propelled) generally supported 29th Armoured Brigade and the 151 RA (towed guns) 159th Infantry Brigade.
3. Lacking the firepower to engage in a tank battle, the role of the Inns of Court was to act independently, probing for gaps in the enemy line and penetrating the rear areas wherever possible.
4. The flail tanks were pressed on Pip Roberts against his wishes. As he expected, they were not needed to clear enemy minefields, but served usefully as gun tanks in support of 8 RB storming le

Mesnil Frémentel. Numbers engaged are approximate as some had difficulty getting forward past obstacles in their path.

11th ARMOURED DIVISION

Detailed Order of Battle
18 July, 1944
(HQ and armoured units, excluding the infantry brigade which fought separately throughout the day, and much soft-skinned transport)

Tank Tac HQ

General Officer Commanding	1 x Cromwell command tank
General's ADC (Aide-de-Camp)	1 x spare Cromwell command tank
CRA (Commander Royal Artillery)	1 x Cromwell command tank
Defence (or 'Protection') Troop	4 x Sherman gun tanks
	2 x Crusader AA tanks

Notes:

1. Command tanks had map tables and multiple radios (the GOC's and his spare tank each had one radio set for contacting brigades and Main HQ, and a second for talking back to VIII Corps). Cromwell tanks were selected for their greater speed and lower profile. Some but not all of these had no main armament, simply a wooden dummy gun, differing from the normal 75mm in various ways including lack of a muzzle brake.
2. Depending on circumstances, the divisional commander personally allocated vehicles between his Tac and Main HQs. For the likely close fighting at GOODWOOD, Roberts decided to form his TAC HQ with tanks only. During 18 July, TAC HQ frequently used terrain and movement to avoid enemy fire. On the evening of 18 July, Roberts had his personal ACV brought forward for him to bivouac at the back of the vehicle rather than leave the field to return to Main HQ.

MAIN HQ

Staff: CRE (Commander Royal Engineers)
CRASC (Commander Royal Army Service Corps)
CREME (Commander Royal Corps of Electrical and Mechanical Engineers)
Field Security Section & APIS (Intelligence Corps)
Discipline & Traffic (Corps of Military Police)

Vehicles:

ACV 1 Command
ACV 2 Intelligence
ACV 3 Operations
ACV 4 Rear Link (to Main HQ)
ACV 5 Rear Link (to VIII Corps)
ACV 6 Signals
ACV 7 RAF Liaison

Liaison Troop 10 x Humber scout cars

Notes:

1. Only a selection of Main HQ's hundred-plus vehicles is indicated.
2. Armoured Command Vehicles were generally windowless AEC 4x4, tailored to their specialist functions.

ARMOURED CAR REGIMENT (Inns of Court)

This regiment underwent several reorganizations as it gained experience in Normandy. In mid-July, its 'sabre' squadrons had been revised to make them lighter and more flexible.

Sabre Squadron (four, designated A, B, C, & D)

Light Troop	(6 per squadron)	2 x Daimler 'Dingo' scout cars
Heavy Troop	(3 per squadron)	2 x Daimler Armoured Cars 1 x 'SOD'
'Blitz' Troop	(1 per squadron)	1 x Daimler Armoured Car 3 x half-tracks

Notes:

1. Although one of the most successful armoured cars of the war, the Daimler proved somewhat bulky for use in Normandy. The unorthodox solution adopted by the Inns was to remove the turret and forward mudguards, in an improvised workshop in Ver-sur-Mer. The resulting 'Sawn Off Daimler' (or 'SOD') was lighter and faster, reportedly capable of 70 miles per hour. With experience, its single Bren gun might be augmented with a .50 cal Browning or even a pair of Vickers 'K' guns, though of course its primary 'weapon' remained its Number 19 Wireless set, relocated to the hull when the turret was removed. Other armoured car regiments, notably the Guards' Second Household Cavalry Regiment, scorned such wanton desecration of His Majesty's property.
2. One armoured car in each Heavy Troop would normally have a 'Littlejohn Adaptor', a barrel extension designed to enhance the velocity and penetration of its 2 pounder gun.
3. The 'Blitz' (or 'Assault') Troop contained three infantry sections whose dismounted role was to support the recce troops against moderate enemy resistance and to defend to the squadron in 'harbour'.

ARMOURED RECONNAISSANCE REGIMENT (2NH)

HQ	1 x Daimler scout car
HQ Squadron	4 x Cromwell gun tanks 2 x jeeps 2 x half-tracks 1 x carrier
Reconnaissance Troop	12 x Daimler scout cars
Communications Troop	9 x scout cars
AA Troop	5 x Crusader AA tanks

Armoured Reconnaissance Squadron (3 per Regiment)

HQ Troop	2 x Cromwell CS (95mm) 2 x Cromwell gun tank (75mm) 1 x Jeep 1 x Cromwell ARV1 (Armoured Recovery Vehicle) 2 x half-track ambulances

Armoured Reconnaissance Troop (5 per Squadron)

3 x Cromwell 75mm

Notes:
1. No Sherman Firefly tanks were assigned to the regiment; the first 17 pounder-armed 'Challenger' tanks arrived on 10 August, just one week before the regiment's last action prior to being disbanded.
2. Cromwell ARV1 was a turretless tank capable of towing only (no winch or lifting gear).

29th ARMOURED BRIGADE HQ

HQ vehicle	ACV
Command Group	4 x command tanks 6 x defence tanks 2 x half-tracks 9 x scout cars 3 x bridging tanks
Air Support Signals Unit	1 x turretless Marmon Herrington armoured car

Notes:
1. The bridging tanks were turretless Valentines which could place and recover a hydraulically-activated scissors bridge capable of spanning a 30 foot gap. There is no known record of their employment by 11th Armoured Division during GOODWOOD though at least one is identifiable in aerial photographs of the armoured advance.
2. The attachment of an ASSU (formerly, a 'tentacle') at brigade (or even divisional) level was at this time an exceptional experiment. The car was to function as a Visual Control Post, manned by a Royal Signals Corps operator, and an Air Liaison Officer. The latter was an experienced Flight Lieutenant able to 'speak the language' of the fighter pilots assigned to support the advance. The ALO was wounded early on 18 June and the inexperienced operator was consequently not able to 'call in' fighter support as effectively as planned.
3. In April, 1944, the Brigade received ten 'bulldozer attachments' which were fitted to Sherman tanks and gave 'satisfactory results'. It is assumed that these were assigned to Regimental HQs.

ARMOURED REGIMENT (3 per division: 23 H, 2 FF Yeo, 3 R Tks)

HQ	1 x scout car
HQ Squadron	2 x Sherman gun tanks 2 x Sherman command tanks 2 x half-tracks
Reconnaissance Troop	11 x Stuart tanks ('Honeys')
Communications Troop	9 x scout cars
AA Troop	6 x Crusader AA tanks

Notes:
1. Earlier in the war, when tank 2 or 6 pounder guns had no HE capability, the HQ Squadron's tanks included two gun tanks (usually AP-capable only) and 2 'CS' (Close Support) tanks with howitzers capable of firing smoke and (usually) High Explosive. In Cromwell-equipped regiments (also in Churchill Infantry tank regiments) this arrangement was retained, the 1944 CS tanks having short 95mm howitzers.
2. The turret of the Stuart light tank was cramped and its 37mm gun very little use against German tanks. For reconnaissance purposes the tank's height was a disadvantage. 29th Armoured Brigade War Diary for 6 July states: 'It was decided to remove turrets from all Stuart tks in the light of experience in the recent battle.' By the time of GOODWOOD, 23rd Hussars had already removed

the turrets from half their Stuarts and by the end of the year all their turreted Stuarts had gone. After GOODWOOD, they disbanded the AA Troop. The Fifes went further prior to GOODWOOD, removing all their Stuarts' turrets, and training the underutilized Crusader AA tanks in recce work. (Sellar 165) 3rd RTR's recce troop had removed some, possibly all of their Stuart turrets. Other formations did not follow suit – once again Guards Armoured Division proved less willing to abuse the property of the King.

Armoured Squadron (3 per Regiment)

HQ Troop	4 x Sherman (75mm or some Fireflies)
	1 x Jeep
	1 x Sherman ARV1
(Armoured Recovery Vehicle)	
1 x half-track ambulance	
Armoured Troop (4 per Squadron, designated 'A', 'B', 'C', & 'D')	
	3 x Sherman V (75mm)
	1 x Sherman VC (17 pounder Firefly)

Notes:

1. Sherman ARV1 was a turretless tank capable of towing only (no winch or lifting gear).
2. The earlier arrangement of five troops with three tanks each was altered as Firefly tanks became available in February, 1944. Allocated fifteen Fireflies per regiment, 29th Brigade decided to allocate five per squadron: one per four-tank troop and one to squadron HQ. (Other brigades sometimes decided to form whole troops of Fireflies; in some some situations, Fireflies with their longer effective range acted as rearguards covering withdrawing 75mm Shermans.) As numbers of Fireflies increased later in the NW Europe campaign, troops increasingly contained 2 x Fireflies and 2 x 75mm gun tanks.

MOTOR BATTALION (8 RB)

HQ	1 x Humber scout car
HQ Company	1 x carrier
	1 x command half-track
	1 x ambulance half-track
	20+ soft-skin lorries
Signals Platoon	3 x half-tracks
Support Company (In 8 RB designated 'E')	1 x command half-track
Antitank Platoon (3 per battalion)	
4 x Loyd carriers	
	2 x 6 pounder antitank guns
Machine Gun Platoon (2 per battalion)	
	4 x carriers with Vickers MG (mounted on engine cover)
Motor Company (3 per battalion, in 8 RB designated 'F', 'G', & 'H')	
HQ Platoon	1 x Universal carrier
	2 x half-tracks
	2 x Universal carriers with 3" mortars (for dismounted fire)
	2 x Humber scout cars

Carrier (or Scout) Platoon (1 per company)	
	11 x Universal carriers (section 2 i/c with 2" mortars mounted in fighting compartment)
Motor Platoon (3 per company)	4 x half-track

Notes:
1.Though confusingly referred to as '8th Rifle Brigade', this was shorthand for 8th Battalion, the Rifle Brigade.
2. Though armoured and more heavily armed than lorried or 'leg' infantry, motor battalions suffered greatly from the low proportion of riflemen in the unit, the rest being specialists such as drivers, weapons crews, and technicians.
3. Early in the Normandy campaign (indeed, before their first battle) 8 RB had already begun to acquire and fit extra weapons to their vehicles, in particular 0.5 calibre Browning machine guns discarded by tank squadrons.

SELF-PROPELLED FIELD REGIMENT RA (13 RHA)

HQ

Command Troop	2 to 4 x Sherman tanks
	1 x half-track
	1 x 15cwt office
Survey Troop	4 x jeeps
Admin Troop	soft skins and 15cwt water bowser

Battery (3 per regiment: in 13 RHA these were 'G', 'H', & 'I' Btty, RA)

Command Troop	1 x 75mm Sherman tank
	1 x jeep
Signal Troop	5 x half-track
Ammunition Troop	3 x 3 ton lorry

Troop (2 per Battery: in 13 RHA 'A' & 'B' = G Btty; 'C' & 'D' = H; 'E' & 'F' = I)

	1 x jeep
	1 x 75mm Sherman tank
	1 x half-track
	1 X carrier
Section (2 per Troop)	2 x Sexton 25 pounder sp

Notes:
1. In Normandy, the colonel's Sherman tank (only) had a dummy gun, with a wooden barrel, leaving internal space for maps and radios. The regimental commander usually accompanied the armoured brigade Tac Headquarters, in contact with the brigade commander.
2. Three battery officers (the battery major and two troop captains) would usually be forward, in their 75mm gun tanks, with the tank regiment commander and the squadrons being supported. In theory the third (i.e., junior) captain was in charge of the gun positions, though in practice this was often rotated, all captains sharing the experience (and danger) of the Forward Observation Officer

role. Note that in a towed Field Regiment, battery commanders in Normandy typically had half-tracks, not tanks, putting them at some disadvantage when they had to perform a FOO role.
3. After Normandy, FOOs and tanks were increased by one captain/tank per battery. FOOs' Sherman tanks were increasingly involved in actual combat as the north-western Europe campaign progressed. (11th Armoured Division's towed regiment, the Ayrshire Yeomanry, later had their Shermans replaced by Cromwells from tank regiments reequipped with the new Comet tank; they also received tanks for their battery majors).
4. Battery half-tracks usually had pulpit-mounted .50 cal machine guns.
5. Other vehicles varied constantly due to breakdown and 'acquisition'.

ANTITANK REGIMENT, RA (75 AT)

HQ	8 x jeeps
Self-Propelled Battery (x 2: 117 & 119 Btty, RA)	6 x jeeps
Troop (3 per Battery: 'A','B',& 'C' = 117 Btty and 'G','H',& 'I' = 119)	1 x carrier / cmmnd tank
Section (2 per Troop)	2 x M10 tank destroyers
Towed Battery (x 2: 118 & 338 Btty, RA)	6 x jeeps
Troop (3 per Battery: 'D','E', & 'F' = 118 Btty and 'J','K',& 'L' = 338)	
Section (2 per Troop)	2 x 17 pounder a/tk gun

Notes:
1. By 1944 most antitank regiments had standardized on 48 guns divided between 4 batteries, but equipments varied widely. Some batteries retained 6 pounder guns, mainly those supporting infantry divisions.
2. SP troop commanders found carriers unsatisfactory as command vehicles. By July these were being replaced by tanks, usually turretless Crusaders or redundant Crusader AA tanks.
3. Although generally the SP batteries supported 29th Armoured Brigade and the towed guns 159 Infantry Brigade, nevertheless Batteries were assigned very flexibly, and sometimes outside the division. On 18 July, the SP batteries spent time accompanying companies of 8 RB, and covering 29th Brigade and Division TAC HQs.
4. The self-propelled batteries of 75 AT Rgt. were exclusively M10 'Achilles' (17 pounder main armament and externally mounted Browning .50 calibre antiaircraft machine gun). (Some other regiments had batteries of M10 'Wolverine' with a somewhat inferior American three inch naval gun.) The towed batteries found their wheeled tractors generally unsatisfactory for towing heavy 17 pounder guns. Troops improvised half-tracks and even redundant Crusaders as towing vehicles, and some eventually received purpose-built Crusader Gun Tractors.

APPENDIX VII

21. PANZERDIVISION
GOODWOOD ORDER OF BATTLE
18 JULY, 1944

OVERALL DIVISIONAL STRUCTURE

Headquarters
Commander: Generalmajor Edgar Feuchtinger
Ia (Operations): Oberstleutnant von Berlichingen
Ib (Logistics): Major Scharnhorst
Ic (Communications): Hauptmann Vorster

22. Panzerregiment: Oberst Hermann von Oppeln-Bronikowski
- **I./Pz-Rgt 22: Hauptmann von Gottberg**
- **II./Pz-Rgt 22: Major Vierzig**

+ attached
503. schwere Panzer-Abteilung: Hauptmann Fromme (Hptm. Scherf deputizing)
- **1. Kompanie: Oberleutnant Oemler**
- **2. Kompanie: Hauptmann von Eichel-Streiber**
- **3. Kompanie: Hauptmann Scherf (Ltn. von Rosen deputizing)**

125. Panzergrenadierregiment: Major von Luck
- **I./Pz-Gr-Rgt 125: Hauptmann Schenk zu Schweinsburg**
- **II./Pz-Gr-Rgt 125: Hauptmann Kurz**

192. Panzergrenadierregiment: Oberstleutnant Rauch
- **I./Pz-Gr-Rgt 192: Hauptmann Rätzer**
- **II./Pz-Gr-Rgt 192: Hauptmann Zippe**

21. Panzer-Aufklärungsabteilung: Major Brandt
200. Panzer-Jäger-Abteilung: Hauptmann von Lynker
200. Sturmgeschütz-Abteilung: Major Becker
155. Panzer-Artillerie-Regiment: Oberst Huhne
305. Heeres-Flak-Artillerie-Abteilung: Hauptmann Ohlendorf
220. Panzer-Pioneer-Bataillon: Hauptmann Hoegl

plus various signals, workshop, supply train, medical, post, etc. elements

Notes:
1. In theory, the structure of 21. Panzerdivision broadly reflected the standard 'Type 1944' ('freie Gliederung') pattern: with its two-battalion Panzer regiment; two Panzergrenadier regiments, each of two four-company battalions. In practice, things could be very different. The actual strength and structure of German combat units in Normandy frequently differed from the theoretical tables of organization and equipment (TOE). The routine German TOE report, the Kriegstärkenachweisung (or KStN), can be misleading if taken at face value. Apparently detailing precise numbers of men and vehicles, this chart is intended mainly to depict an ideal organization. Its date shows the time that organization became official, not its actual implementation, if indeed the ideal was ever achieved. By 1944, even newly-raised units might fall far short of the officially sanctioned complement, having to beg or scrounge equipment on their officers' initiative in order to approach the official TOE.
2. The original intent of equipping the armoured units of 21. Panzerdivision entirely from captured matériel (including at least one Churchill tank taken at Dieppe!) proved impractical. By mid July the divisional tank regiment retained few (probably only one) of the more or less converted French tanks previously on strength.

Nevertheless, even by mid July captured and converted French vehicles still represented an important part of most sub units' order of battle, from armoured personnel carriers and radio vehicles to the entire complement of the Sturmgeschütz battalion, not to mention a wide variety of extemporized artillery mounts and tractors.
3. The two tank battalions within a standard Panzerdivision typically belonged to a single, close-knit tank regiment, which in turn was closely integrated with the infantry and artillery regiments within the division. This contrasted with the British Army's emphasis on regimental identity. Within a British armoured brigade, tank 'regiments' (in battalion strength) had their own regimental traditions and training, and potentially changed brigade or division affiliation in the course of the war. Indeed, the majority of British 2nd Army's tanks fighting in Normandy were to be found in 'independent' brigades and not permanently attached to any particular division. And even within Commonwealth armoured divisions, tactical integration of the armour and infantry arms was not universally achieved during the Normandy campaign. As a broad generalization: German officers and men might identify more closely with their division than was the case within most Commonwealth formations.

21. PANZERDIVISION
Detailed Order of Battle
18 July, 1944

Introduction

11th Armoured Division had time to rest, refit, and absorb reinforcements before GOODWOOD. Consequently, its formal order of battle closely reflects its actual composition on 18 July. In contrast, 21. Panzerdivision had been in constant action since 6 June, and some aspects of its organization are harder to assess.

Although the division regularly returned highly detailed organization and strength reports, these require careful interpretation. As noted above, the monthly Kriegstärkenachweisung (KStN) depicted the division's organization down to individual vehicles and machine guns, but does not necessarily show what was actually available for use. The KStN should be read in conjunction with the monthly Meldung (strength report) which lists not only authorized strengths, but also numbers currently operational plus those undergoing short-term repair. (An important consideration, since German divisions retained many vehicles for repair which Allied divisions would have passed 'off their books' to external workshops, sometimes creating the misleading impression that Allied armoured units had many fewer vehicle breakdowns than was actually the case.)

22. Panzerregiment

The combat-ready strength of 21. Panzerdivision on 18 July, and its losses in the ensuing battle, can in part be deduced by interpolation between monthly returns for 1 July and 1 August. For example, 22. Panzerregiment enjoyed a theoretical permitted strength (Soll) of 139 Panzer IV. On the eve of invasion, on 1 June, the unit actually possessed 104 (of which 6 were undergoing repair expected to last up to two or three weeks). On 1 July, the total had reduced to 85 (of which 24 were in the divisional workshops), reflecting serious losses incurred in the post-invasion fighting. By 1 August, the total of just 58 included 16 under repair. The picture is further clouded by the departure of the regiment's II. Abteilung in late July to re-equip with Panther tanks, in order to bring the division into line with the usual pattern of one Panzer IV and one Panther battalion. Nevertheless, various pieces of evidence (including the daily strength report for 17 July) support the view that the regiment had approximately fifty Panzer IV combat-ready (einsatzbereit) on 18 July. Following GOODWOOD, and for the rest of the Normandy campaign, the regiment was reduced to a shadow of its former strength.

503. schwere Panzer-Abteilung

Following lengthy service on the Russian front, this unit was withdrawn and completely re-equipped before moving to Normandy. Companies two and three were given Tiger I to replace those left in the east. Company one found itself the first combat unit to receive the new Tiger II, Königstiger, issued with due ceremony on 16 June. The battalion's first action in Normandy occurred on 11 July, when 3. Kompanie under von Rosen supported a counter attack which stopped a British advance on Colombelles. A dozen British tanks were destroyed and two captured for only minor damage to the Tiger I tanks engaged. The first ground combat involving Königstiger (and that model's first ever loss to enemy fire) occurred at midday on 18 July.

At full strength, before the bombing on 18 July, the Abteilung was organized with fourteen tanks per company: three sections of four plus a two-tank headquarters. The 11th Armoured Division Intelligence Summary for 20 July mentions prisoners of the unit, claiming 'They give the org of the bns as three coys of three pls of five Tigers each with 2 Tigers at each coy HQ.' To this entirely accurate estimate, the writer adds, 'This seems too many and should be taken with reserve.' It was most fortunate for 11th Armoured that the prisoners' further comment that their unit 'had suffered cas in air attacks' was equally accurate.

Contrary to some British accounts, this was a strictly Wehrmacht battalion and had no SS members!

125. Panzergrenadierregiment & 192. Panzergrenadierregiment

The two infantry regiments of the division were similarly equipped, though the 125 appears to have been consistently better kept up to strength (partly due to the energy, charisma, and connections of its commander). At the beginning of July, the first battalion (I./Pz-Gr-Rgt 125) stood at 78% of its quota of manpower, while the second battalion and the entire 192. Pz-Gr-Rgt were close to 50%. Additionally, it must be remembered that these personnel had been in constant action for many weeks and were seriously overdue for relief. They (and their equipment) were worn out. Also, while these numbers were maintained (or rather, regained) by 1 August, this was only by virtue of reinforcement by inferior manpower (much of the later reinforcement coming from the breaking up of the 16. Luftwaffenfelddivision after GOODWOOD).

Each regiment had a central pool of artillery: typically six self-propelled 15cm howitzers mounted on diminutive French tracked chassis (Geschütz Pz. s.F.H.13 Lorraine); and a small number, typically three or four, of 'Reihenwerfer', French SOMUA half-tracks each carrying a rotating array of sixteen French 8.1cm Brandt mortar tubes.

Each regiment contained two infantry battalions each of four companies. The fourth company of each battalion (i.e., Kompanien 4 and 8) held the heavy weapons: typically three 7.5cm Pak 40 and three 2cm antiaircraft guns, all mounted on French half-track chassis.

Most unusually, both of the two regiments had an armoured infantry battalion; usually a Panzerdivision had only one such. At full strength, companies 1 to 3 of these battalions each enjoyed as many as eighteen lightly armoured SPW (Schützenpanzerwagen, French half-track troop carriers), three of which would be officers' mounts armed with 3.7cm Pak 38. A further twenty or so such SPW were shared between battalion and regimental headquarters, plus a similar number of armoured, half-tracked radio vehicles. Once again, there is some evidence that by July 125. Pz-Gr-Rgt enjoyed a disproportionate share of the remaining serviceable SPW.

21. Panzer-Aufklärungsabteilung

The reconnaissance battalion of a Panzerdivision typically had a complex structure, reflecting the wide variety of jobs it was designed to undertake. In July, 1944, 21. Pz.A.A. had five companies.

1. Kp. was mainly equipped with turreted half-tracks: about sixteen SdKfz 250/9.
2. Kp. had wheeled armoured cars, both eight-wheel SdKfz 231 and 233 and four-wheel SdKfz 221 and 222.
3. and 4. Kp. had half-tracks based on the French Unic P 107.
5. (schwere) Kp. was equipped with different models of the ubiquitous German SdKfz 251 half-track, variously mounting 3.7cm Pak 35/36, 8.1cm mortars, 7.5cm howitzers (le.I.G.18) and flamethrowers.

As noted in the text, as well as being equipped with highly mobile armoured vehicles, this unit was equally accustomed to holding the line as infantry, and it is primarily in the infantry role that we find it engaged during GOODWOOD.

200. Panzer-Jäger-Abteilung

This unit is believed to have been equipped with the 8.8cm Pak 43/41 L/71. This towed 8.8cm gun was a somewhat unsatisfactory improvization. Lacking enough specialized, cruciform Pak 43 carriages for the available barrels, guns were mounted with an improvised gunshield on the carriage of the obsolescent 10.5cm leichte Feldhaubitze 18. The resulting gun had a higher profile than the Pak 43, which earned it the name 'barn door'. It was nose-heavy and unwieldy. Nevertheless, properly emplaced, it was a potent weapon.

200. Sturmgeschütz-Abteilung

This unit was doubly unique. A Panzerdivision did not normally possess an assault gun battalion (1. SS 'Leibstandarte' was an exception, also in some e.g., 10. SS-Pz-Div, companies of assault guns might be found replacing tanks in the divisional Panzerregiment or alternatively replacing self-propelled antitank guns in the Jäger Abteilung). This unit was entirely composed of scratch vehicles designed and built by the battalion commander Major Alfred Becker in his Paris workshops. While the divisional KStN authorized four batteries of varying reported strengths, on 18 July Becker's battalion actually fielded five batteries, each with six 7.5cm Pak 40 and four 10.5cm leFH16 howitzers, all mounted on French Hotchkiss H39 tracked chassis. A sixth company under construction in Paris did not see service at the time of GOODWOOD. By 1944, the assault gun battalions had evolved from their original infantry close support role to place a greater emphasis on antitank defence. Becker's guns had much less armour protection than normal Sturmgeschütze and their tactical employment stressed long-range fire rather than risking close engagement.

APPENDIX VIII

BOMBING THE GOODWOOD BATTLEFIELD

Operation GOODWOOD was an unusual battle in many respects, especially in the use of massed strategic bombers to open a way for the Army through the German lines. Not surprisingly, most accounts of the battle have included assessments of the bombing. It is therefore disturbing to discover that many of these assessments have been contradictory and most of them more or less inaccurate.

CONTRADICTIONS

Some accounts maintain that RAF Bomber Command was simply unwilling to alter its accustomed bomb loads to suit a need different from the destruction of German industrial heartlands. Others however cite Harris as agreeing to aerial bombardment of the battlefield only after a change to impact-fuzed and fragmentation bombs was agreed.[1]

Cagny is a case in point. Even one of the latest and best-informed works on the subject of air power over the Normandy battlefield perpetuates the myth that Cagny was spared cratering: 'instantaneous-fused bombs, to avoid cratering were released on Cagny, the most strongly held village in the tank-run.'[2] A common explanation given for this argument is that, since Cagny was 'regarded as the toughest of the defended villages in the corridor' (and it was so regarded, albeit erroneously) it would be allocated '650 tons, the ration in a normal operation for a sizeable town target, but the bombs would be fused simultaneously to avoid cratering the tanks' avenue of advance.'[3] The argument defies logic. True, rubbling an area the size of Caen had created a serious obstacle in the path of the army. But a little town the size of Cagny was an ideal subject for total destruction. A tank-heavy force lacking infantry would not wish to enter such a place; once its defences were obliterated the tanks could simply bypass the rubble.

In fact, this is one of those cases where the 1947 Battlefield Tour document is entirely correct. It states clearly that 'The village of Cagny was to be destroyed and cratering was accepted.'[4] Also, since we are permitted the benefit of hindsight, let it be noted that Cagny was probably the least strongly garrisoned of all the villages.

Numerous histories have heeded von Luck's claim to have found a battery of Luftwaffe guns near Cagny church, intact and untroubled by bombs, and have seized on the idea of Cagny being spared cratering in order to make sense of the story. Some quite ingenious explanations have been offered to try to explain these contradictions. Wilmot agreed that 'Cagny, which stood at the parting of the ways of the 11th and the Guards, was to be obliterated by Bomber Command.' Yet he persevered with the belief that, 'In Cagny half a dozen "88s" and some *Tiger* tanks had miraculously survived amid the rubble of the ruined village.'[5] Again, the assumption that the place was strongly garrisoned was wrong. Given the lack of knowledge of German dispositions when Wilmot wrote in 1952, he can be forgiven for mistakenly locating *Tiger* tanks in Cagny. A more recent account posits that Cagny was 'ringed but not hit by bombs'.[6] This explanation is sadly the reverse of the actuality. Central Cagny was obliterated yet ringed by ground which was in large part untouched. Other writers have taken a cue from Wilmot's claim that 'All but one of these villages had been hit by fragmentation bombs, but by extraordinary chance a section of each village had been missed, and in every case it was the section which now faced towards the British line of advance that had escaped unscathed.'[7] It is unclear whether Wilmot intended these comments to apply to all the villages flanking the armoured corridor or only to those on the Bourguébus ridge: the context strongly implies the former. Either way, he was wrong. This 'extraordinary chance' is no more credible than the 'miraculous survival' in Cagny. The only target in the battle area to be partially levelled in this way was Démouville, where the bombers visited destruction only on the western end of the village. (The well known pictures showing the devastation of the eastern side, around the church, were taken later, after the medium artillery had worked over the place.)

ANSWERS

Hitherto, the most authoritative record of the GOODWOOD bombing has been understood to be the study undertaken by Operations Research ('Churchill's scientists') shortly after the battle. Some of the mistaken views mentioned above can be traced directly back to Report No. 6 of Number 2 Operations Research Section, documenting a survey initiated two weeks after the battle at the urgent request of 21st Army Group to analyze the effectiveness of the aerial bombardment.[8]

This was early days for ORS in Normandy. They did their best. Some of the findings of the project were remarkably apt, not least the conclusions that the aerial bombardment had probably yielded great morale effects, and that 'progressive' bombing rather than a 'one off' curtain raiser would have been more effective. But the Section confessed dissatisfaction with the outcome of their GOODWOOD study. They had simply too few resources and too much ground to cover. They lacked details of the precise targets, numbers of aircraft, and types of bombs used. The aerial photography made available to them was 'virtually impossible to interpret' since it was taken after sustained shell-fire had overlaid the effects of the bombing. And even on the ground, 'so much other fire power was used apart from bombing, [that] it is very difficult to assess the contribution made by the bombing.' With regard to the question of Cagny, the team had to record that 'The ground at Cagny where special instantaneous fuzes were used has not yet been studied.' Had they been granted access to the ground, they could hardly have missed the craters which belied that statement. As it was, they could only report anecdotal (and misleading) evidence that 'In spite of the bombing of Cagny, anti-tank guns and tanks were met there at 1200 hours.' Whoever fed ORS the information that 11th Armoured Division took 'about ten hours' to reach the Bourguébus ridge was misinformed; whoever told ORS that 'a further attack was made next day without success' was committing a grave calumny against that division.

The evidence that ORS sadly lacked is now available to us. The analyses that follow are based on aerial photographs taken within hours of the bombing. That is, after much of the dust had settled but before ground combat and especially medium artillery pulverized the key villages. All timings are those used by British Second Army's GOODWOOD plan and broadcast by the BBC. (See Appendix III)

THE BOMBING ANALYSED

RAF Bomber Command:
Areas A1 and A2
Colombelles (from 05.36 hours, approximately 220 aircraft, 1,300 tons HE)
& Mondeville (from 05.59 hours, approximately 230 aircraft, 1,200 tons HE)

A concentrated swathe of craters began from the high, open ground (40 metre ring contour) east of Colombelles village. The village itself was only relatively lightly affected. To the north of the village stood the château of Colombelles. In the château itself and further north in its woods alongside the banks of the Orne was established the first company of *Jägerregiment 32* (part of *16. Luftwaffenfelddivision*). The advancing Canadians would very soon find, to their cost, how little these infantry had suffered from the bombing.

South of Colombelles village, the great metalworks presented an obvious target and was heavily bombed. Thousand pound bombs wreaked havoc here. British Operations Research later found large numbers of damaged antitank guns and German dead. (This last was particularly unusual. German policy was whenever possible to remove their dead before abandoning a position; this policy was generally obeyed even when the impact on the morale of the troops carrying out the removal might be severe.) ORS concluded that, from the amount of debris it did not appear that anyone would have remained unhurt.' The first Canadian infantry on the scene recorded stiff opposition, especially from the northern extremity of the factory complex. However, it seems most probable that this was caused not by the factory garrison but by troops that had fallen back from the defence of Colombelles village.

The bombers ran almost due south, crossing the factory area and passing directly over the rows of factory workers' dormitory accommodation between Mondeville and Giberville. These wooden, barracks-style blocks would have offered little or no protection and any occupants must have suffered severely. The bombing was concentrated almost entirely within an area 3 kilometres long by little more than 500 metres across. Apart from the vast factory complex, whose superstructures were extensively damaged, much of this was open ground and railway. Some sticks of bombs fell as far east as the outskirts of Giberville, but clearly most of the damage done to that place was caused later by lighter fragmentation bombs. Had Target Area A1 been set even 500m further west, enemy opposition in Colombelles and along the right bank of the river might have been more effectively reduced.

RAF Bomber Command:
Areas H1 & H2
Sannerville (from 05.41 hours, approximately 230 aircraft, 1,200 tons HE)
& Manneville (from 05.59 hours, approximately 230 aircraft, 1,260 tons HE)

This area was targeted very precisely, with most heavy bombs falling within a north-south strip less than a half-mile wide (nowhere more than 750 metres), running from just south of Touffréville (purposely excluded by the RAF) to just south of Emiéville. Although the entire area was heavily cratered, the open ground between Sannerville and Guillerville received relatively fewer bombs. By contrast, the villages received an extremely heavy concentration. The road junction and rail line at Sannerville were devastated; the hamlets of Guillerville and Emiéville were virtually obliterated by overlapping craters, the outlines of buildings, the path of roads, and even the outlines of some fields became utterly indistinguishable. Within this area, even entrenched infantry must have been vulnerable to such devastation. Most of the *Panzer IV* remaining to *22. Panzerregiment* on the morning of 18 July were dispersed within this area, and nearly all of these were incapacitated. Greater still was the impact on the regiment's personnel and soft-skinned vehicles, with all communications lost and command and control above company level effectively neutralized. Additionally, the combat effectiveness of the *503. Abteilung* present in this area was reduced by delay and damage caused to the unit's personnel and *Tiger* tanks by the bombing. Overall, these losses were the most serious inflicted in a single bombing raid on a German armoured division in the course of the war. (Though *Panzer-Lehr-Division* was to suffer on 25 July a deluge of 4,000 tons of American bombs, it now appears that Bayerlein exaggerated his division's losses, and that relatively few of the division's tanks were directly destroyed by that bombing raid.)[9]

Amidst the debates over bomb lines, the RAF had unilaterally moved the target south to exclude the village of Touffréville from Target Area H. Strange as it may seem, it was generally the RAF who favoured increasing the distance from friendly troops to the bombers' targets. With the Army totally convinced that GOODWOOD could only go ahead with the support of strategic bombers, the RAF felt empowered to set conditions. Assurance was demanded that no troops would be within 2,000 yards of HE or within 2,500 yards of fragmentation bombing, and no troops at all unentrenched within 3,000 yards of any target area. In some cases, this meant withdrawal from FDLs (forward defence lines) prior to the bombing. On the ground, the infantry were understandably loath to give up ground so hard won and so long defended. Second Army grudgingly conceded that this was 'awkward but had to be accepted'. In return, equally grudgingly, the RAF accepted that leading elements of 11th Armoured Division needed to be on the Start Line for H Hour. Later, and without informing the Army, Touffréville was excluded from the target area, as 3rd Division would soon find to their cost.

RAF Bomber Command:

Area M

Cagny (from 06.15 hours, approximately 100 aircraft, 600+ tons HE)

The delivery on a point target of over 600 tons of High Explosive was predictably devastating. German accounts cite this example of the Allies' extravagant expenditure of matériel (*verschwenderischen Möglichkeit*). Much of Cagny was immediately reduced to ruin. (Many accounts claim that cratering of Cagny was not acceptable as this was to be an avenue of advance; like many another GOODWOOD myth, these claims are entirely unfounded.) The bombing was largely accurate and, as with the previous targets, most of the bombers did not stray far to east or west of their southbound track. Few bombs fell short of the small town; the town itself received the most dense coverage. The area south of Cagny as far as the Caen to Paris railway was carpeted, especially the obvious target of the thickly wooded avenue leading south to the railway station. A single bomber, inexplicably on an east to west track, dropped what appears to be a standard Lancaster load (ten 1,000 and four 500 pound bombs) in a single stick east of le Poirier.

Le Poirier itself was entirely untouched; likewise the gun emplacements between the le Poirier farm complex and the railway line. A kilometre to the east, Frénouville was untouched. On the western side of Cagny the chateau just north of the town centre was left blazing and the large church to the west reduced to ruins. Further west the devastation was much less. Structures barely two hundred metres west of the ruined church were left intact, and beyond this radius few RAF bombs had fallen.

Ninth United States Army Air Force:

Areas C, D, E, F, & G

(approx 318 medium bombers)

Area C: Cuverville

The impact of large quantities of fragmentation bombs on a tiny hamlet was nowhere greater than here. Many buildings in the village were extensively damaged. Elements of 3rd Monmouths were entering the ruins by H + 50 minutes and so were ideally placed to observe the suppression of the defenders. These were barely able to put up a fight. British ground troops found German infantrymen shaking uncontrollably, many prisoners incapable of walking back to the rear.

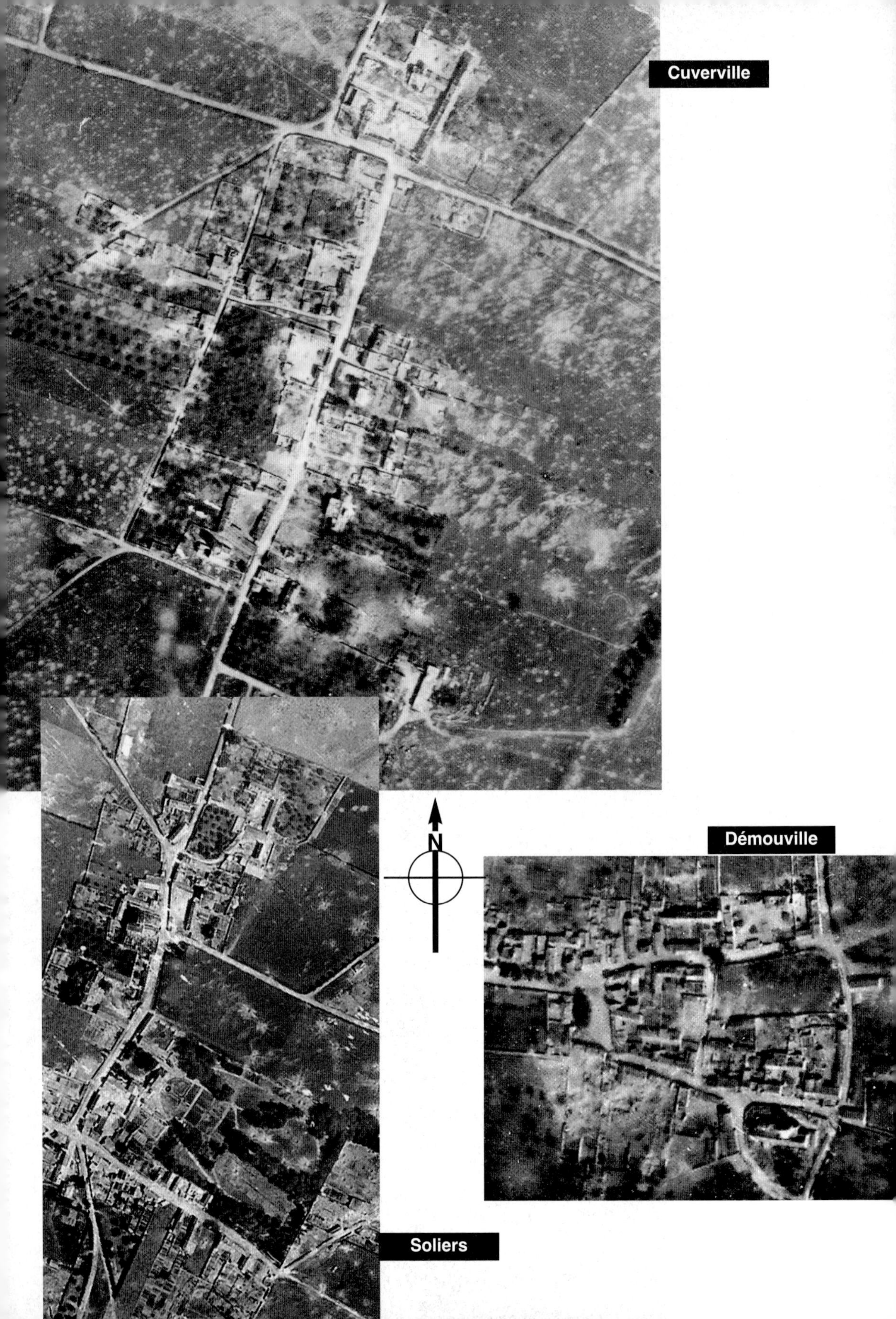
Cuverville
N
Démouville
Soliers

Four
N
Emiéville
N
Cagny Station
N
Frénouville

Area D: Butte de la Hogue

This largely open area of rising ground marked the beginning of the 'armoured corridor'. The leading tank squadrons set off through a heavy blanket of dust and smoke, tank commanders and drivers initially focusing on avoiding shellholes and entrenchments, and witnessing few of the enemy. Units following shortly after encountered enemy infantry still cowering in their slit-trenches, either surrendering willingly or else succumbing to grenades thrown into their entrenchments. ORS later found slit trenches hurriedly filled in by infantry to cover bodies so badly mutilated as to be unmovable. The three antitank guns discovered in this area after the battle had been knocked out not by bombs but later by high explosive rounds, though it was felt unlikely that their crews had recovered from the bombing in time to man them. More guns were found in the orchards to the west also apparently untouched by the bombing. From similar positions to the east of the corridor, guns were manned and commenced firing soon after the smoke and dust of the initial bombardment began to dissipate.

Area E: Démouville to Lirose & Area F: Démouville

To the north east of Démouville a unit of Becker's self-propelled guns (Eichhorn's *1. Batterie*) was caught in the bombing, its fate reported by Eichhorn himself, whose armoured command vehicle was located some distance away and survived. Photographs of some of the *1. Batterie* wrecks reveal shellholes through the armour, but it is most likely that the primary cause of these vehicles' loss was destruction or at least immobilization during the bombing. It does appear that in at least a few cases, the vehicles were attempting to change positions and were caught in the open, away from their customary, prepared positions.

All the area around Démouville received an even carpeting of fragmentation bombs. The village itself was an obvious target, and unsurprisingly appears to have been accurately hit by a particularly large concentration. However, aerial photographs taken some hours after the bombing reveal little physical damage to the buildings; most roofs remained intact. Defenders sheltering within would have suffered relatively little. While the stone buildings of the village and its imposing church were largely devastated during the course of the battle, it can be concluded that much of this damage was inflicted later by medium and heavy artillery. At the time of this photography, 3rd Monmouths were only approaching the westernmost part the village, 1st Herefords and 4th KSLI were still some distance away: respectively a thousand yards to the north and to the north-east; only in mid-afternoon and after further attention from the artillery was the place secured.

Area G: Giberville

Further west, the extended village of Giberville was a Canadian objective. Though today linked to Démouville by continuous suburban development, in

1944 Démouville and Giberville were separated by a half kilometre of open fields: alternating ripening hay and turnips. From a chateau just north of the railway line, a road ran north through orchards (today the D 230, amid modern housing and school) to reach an isolated group of buildings around a crossroads on rising ground between Démouville and Colombelles. This prominent position was heavily bombed. Contrary to Alfred Becker's claims that his only 'considerable' losses during the battle were in *1. Batterie*, it is now clear that other batteries suffered losses in the initial bombing. The five 7.5cm antitank guns of his *2. Batterie* were positioned between the buildings of Giberville on either side of the road. At least two of these were immobilized by the bombing and abandoned by their crews. But while open-topped vehicles had suffered, German infantry had survived in the buildings. Advancing on the place, the Queen's Own Rifles of Canada were shortly to suffer intense machine gun fire from the village. Officers and section leaders were lost; the fire was too intense to evacuate the wounded, and impromptu aid posts were set up in the first buildings taken. Only late on 18 July, after sustained artillery bombardment and energetic German counter-attacks, was the whole place secured.

Eighth United States Army Air Force:
Area I Troarn (from 07.30 hours, approximately 350 aircraft);
& Area P Soliers (from 09.00 hours, approximately 570 aircraft)
& Area Q Frénouville (from 09.00 hours, approximately 330 aircraft)

Areas I and Q can be quickly dealt with. Following the bombing, Frénouville remained untouched. For this we have not only clear photographic evidence, but also the fact that von Luck, arriving at his command post in the village after the bombers had departed, was not immediately aware of anything amiss. 'Shortly after nine, I arrived at my command post. I sensed that something was not right, for all the men at the command post seemed nervous.' In fairness, it may be considered that the Target Area entitled 'Frénouville' actually included a large area of open ground to the south of the village, and the fields in this area were indeed liberally plastered with bombs. It may be that some damage was inflicted, though later studies showed how difficult it was to damage emplaced artillery pieces with bombs, and how quickly entrenched gun crews could recover if not subject to ground assault immediately following the bombing.

Several miles away to the north east, the town of Troarn also escaped lightly. Though the surrounding fields were pockmarked with craters, and some damage had been done around the area of the railway station at the western end of the sprawling little town, most buildings remained intact. Given the weight of bombing intended, and given the destruction wrought around Sannerville, it is tempting to conjecture that many of the American bombers had mistakenly dropped their loads on the RAF target still smouldering two miles to the west.

Target Area P deserves special mention, since it was shortly to become the arena in which much of the day's armoured combat took place. This large area included names destined to become legendary after GOODWOOD: Grentheville, Soliers, Bourguébus. South of the Bourguébus ridge, an extensive area of open country was peppered with bomb blasts. Yet, on the ridge itself, the three vital villages suffered little. Bourguébus, Hubert-Folie, and Bras were left intact, their defenders hardly inconvenienced, at least one soft-skinned vehicle still parked in the street.

North of Bourguébus, Soliers itself escaped virtually untouched. By contrast the kilometre of open fields further still to the north was evenly carpeted by light bombs. And beyond these, the occupants of Grentheville and its surrounding orchards apparently suffered little. The area north of Grentheville and likewise the railway embankment and its underpasses to the west were much harder hit than the defended village. It is arguable that bombers unable to discern the point target of Grentheville, a small cluster of buildings screened on all sides by dense orchards, could nevertheless pick out a distinctive line feature such as the Chemin de Fer Minier, its railway embankment throwing a shadow in the early morning sun. Overall, one is driven to the conclusion that a proportion of the bombers allocated to this target area dropped inaccurately, short, or not at all. Hardly surprising, given the poor visibility as dust and smoke from earlier waves drifted south west on the breeze. The conclusion is reinforced by a German account which claims that as early as 07.00 hours 'many of their [i.e., the Americans'] targets were invisible under the dust clouds, and they left a few things undone.'[10]

References

(1) 'The Struggle for Europe', Chester Wilmot, 1952, p 394: 'His [Harris's] reluctance was overcome only when he learned that Dempsey wanted anti-personnel, not high-explosive, bombs dropped in the path of the main advance.'

(2) Gooderson, 'Air Power', p 143

(3) 'Six Armies in Normandy', John Keegan, 1982, ISBN 0 1400 5393 3, p 193

(4) BAOR Battlefield Tour, page 27, Section VIII AIR PLAN

(5) Wilmot, p 395-398

(6) Copp, 'Fields of Fire', p137

(7) Wilmot, p 398

(8) Gooderson p 11; Second Army ORS

(9) Zetterling,p 42-43 & 386-388

(10) Lehmann & Tiemann, 'Leibstandarte', p 149

APPENDIX IX

THE QUESTION OF THE CAGNY '88s'

Anyone with more than a passing interest in GOODWOOD will have come across the story of a battery of four Luftwaffe 8.8cm antiaircraft guns in Cagny, unwilling to engage ground targets until 'persuaded' at gunpoint by an army officer to change position and fire on the advancing British tanks. According to the story, these guns then commenced a wholesale destruction of British tanks (and in particular, wiped out most of C Squadron, the Fife & Forfar Yeomanry). However, the truth behind this intriguing anecdote is elusive.

QUESTIONS

On studying photographs of Cagny taken shortly after the supposed relocation of the battery, the author was surprised to find no obvious sign of its initial or final positions, nor any tracks indicating the movement of these heavy guns and their associated equipment. Further questions then arose.

Assuming the guns engaged the rear squadron of the Fife & Forfar between 09.30 and 09.45 hours, where were the guns when the Grenadier Guards came on the scene, and later when the Coldstream passed around Cagny? And if it was these guns which accounted for von Rosen's leading *Tiger* tanks towards 11.00 hours, what had they been doing in the meantime?

After some years of study, the author has as yet no conclusive proof as to the identity, movements, or firing positions of this battery. Rather than offering a speculative solution to the puzzle, the evidence so far gathered is presented here and you the reader are invited to form your conclusions.

THE EVIDENCE

Firstly, therefore, what evidence is there that such a battery existed at all? There turns out to be surprisingly little.

We have von Luck's testimony as to his actions on the morning of 18 July. His account appears to be the only existing source for this oft-told tale. That is to say, all records so far discovered of the actions of the Cagny battery can be traced directly to von Luck and no one else. Alfred Becker was active in the vicinity of Cagny throughout most of the morning of 18 July. In addition to receiving reports from his battery commanders, he kept in touch with von Luck, so must have been abreast of the most important developments of the day. Yet Becker makes no comment whatsoever in his memoirs of any Luftwaffe guns engaged in the area. Could this be due to an unwillingness to share the glory? Perhaps more surprisingly, the officer in command of all *Luftwaffe* 8.8cm guns in the area makes no mention in his memoirs of any Cagny detachment. Both Becker's and Pickert's testimonies are considered below.

There is a second piece of evidence. Around 11.00 hours on 18 July, the southbound advance of the surviving *Tiger I* of von Rosen's *3. Kompanie* was checked by antitank fire which cleanly penetrated the frontal armour of two of the heavy tanks. Assuming at the time that he had been engaged by some unknown Allied weapon, von Rosen concluded only several years later that the likely source of the fire was a unit of German guns.[1] Given the known position and facing of the *Tiger* at the time they were stopped, guns on the northern edge of Cagny are indicated. Since two *Tiger* were penetrated almost simultaneously, it is likely that the gun calibre was more than 7.5cm. At one thousand metres range a Pak 40 had some chance of penetrating the 100-110mm frontal armour of the *Tiger I*, but for a battery to achieve two such kills in quick succession would have been improbable. What is more, it is unlikely that any Pak 40 were positioned in front of the *Tiger* advance (i.e., in Cagny itself) at the time. Which leaves only three further possibilities: self-propelled Pak 40 of Becker's *Sturm-Panzer-Abteilung 200*; defensive fire by one or more British 17 pounder-armed 'Firefly' tanks; or von Luck's 8.8cm Flak. The first will be considered along with Becker's recollections; but in summary it seems improbable. British Fireflies remain a theoretical possibility though it is unlikely that any were in the right vicinity at the time, and no record has been found of any attributable British claims.

LOCATION: THE HUNT FOR THE GUNS

Von Luck's recorded story is imprecise as to the place in which he claims to have discovered the battery. In his published memoirs he writes that he spotted the battery 'as I was driving past the church of Cagny, which lay in the undamaged part of the village.' This is unhelpful, since the church was surrounded by devastation. He called a halt 'under a tree', then 'bailed out and ran to the battery', though whether he ran north or south we do not know.[2]

Expert analysis of aerial photographs of the area taken at midday on 18 July, using stereoscopic viewers, reveals no trace whatsoever of any 8,8cm Flak emplacements nor of any towing vehicles or their distinctive tracks. Of course, by 1944 the Germans were masters of camouflage against aerial observation, but this took time and large artillery pieces could not be hidden within a mere couple of hours of relocation.

If it is assumed that German 8.8cm guns were present somewhere near Cagny, the only feasible position would seem to be the walled orchard on the north side of the former Cagny chateau. This location allows superb vistas across the British line of advance (yet not too close to have been immediately obvious), and would permit frontal shots in the direction of von Rosen's oncoming *Tiger* tanks. The high walls (two metres) would have been ideal for screening an antiaircraft battery, yet at some time they have been loopholed, as would be necessary to permit outgoing fire against ground targets.

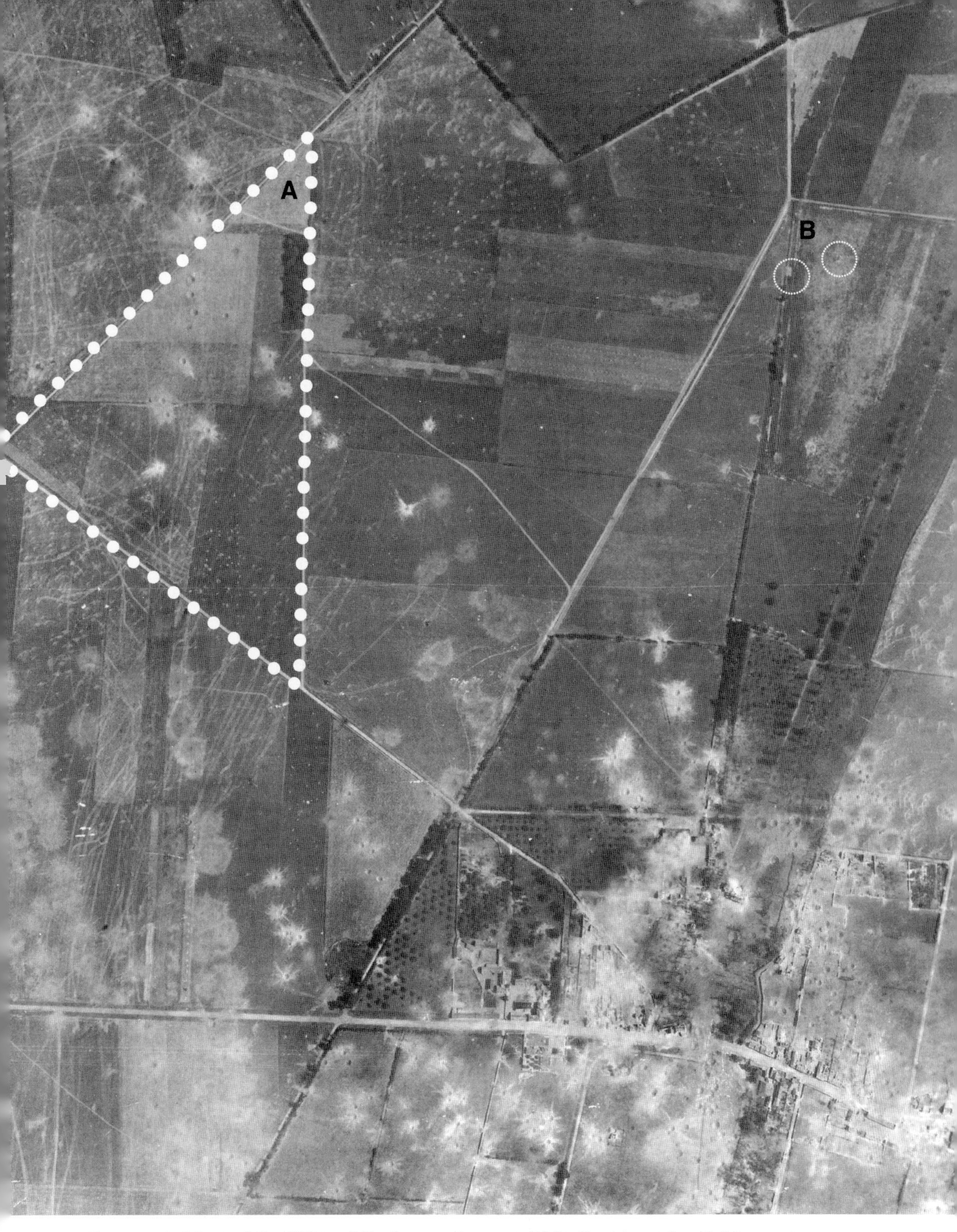

Cagny. A: Most of the Fife and Forfar wrecks are within the triangular field.
B: Two destroyed vehicles 1 km from central Cagny, 650 m, north of walled orchard. Westernmost is the size and shape of a Tiger I, facing south. The easterly wreck is shrouded in smoke.

VON LUCK'S STORY

Major Hans-Ulrich von Luck served with distinction throughout the war. His reputation survived unblemished by association with Nazism.[3] His long and successful service record spanned campaigns from the invasion of Poland to the last stand in Berlin. His exploits in Poland, France, Russia, and North Africa counted for more than his association from 1944 with the reconstituted *21. Panzerdivision*, whose reputation suffered, however unfairly, due to Feuchtinger's later disgrace.[4]

With GOODWOOD such an important feature of the Staff College annual tour, and the German defence an important study topic, von Luck was one of the obvious 'good Germans' to be invited to participate (as also was the then *Generalmajor der Bundeswehr*, Richard Freiherr von Rosen, a career soldier, and moreover a former *Tiger* commander happily untainted by SS membership). Von Luck clearly relished his role on the battlefield tours. He enjoyed lively debates with his sparring partner Pip Roberts, post-war friendship growing out of mutual respect which dated back to their armoured encounters on desert battlefields. And before groups of admiring students, von Rosen delivered his patter: a gently condescending story from which future British officers might learn from the 'mistakes' of their fathers and the example of energetic and decisive German leadership.

Indeed, so great was von Luck's self confidence that the tour organizers occasionally found 'We had to remind him that he had lost the war.' One standing joke between them and von Luck went, 'It's an odd-numbered year, so this year we win!' As the years went by, the 'regular' presenters inevitably picked up details of each others patter. As an example: von Luck quotes his 'good friend' Bill Close as saying, 'We had warned the Guards Armoured Division coming after us about Cagny... We were glad we had been able to turn off to the west and so escape the fire of your damned "eighty-eights".'[5] Whether or not these are the actual words of Bill Close, the account is misleading. Since Major Close was at the very front of the advance, he had no knowledge of Roberts' warning to Guards Armoured Division and first heard the story of this and of the '88s' long after the battle, though his comments as presented by von Luck might imply involvement with both events.

Von Luck's portrayal of the model officer came easily to him. The self belief that sustained his military career came through clearly in his lectures. Little wonder, therefore, that a generation of British Army officers came to regard von Luck's personal role as a major determining factor in the GOODWOOD battle. However, some who watched his performance year after year came eventually to doubt aspects of his story. And as more German accounts of the battle have come to light, some criticisms of von Luck's story have emerged. The picture of an individual single-handedly turning the course of the battle has been questioned.

Some of those critical of von Luck's story have wished their comments to remain 'off-the-record', insofar as they might be taken to impugn the integrity of a brother officer. These confidences are of course respected.

Central Cagny. A: area around church devastated (note craters).
B & C: some military debris but no guns.
D: Von Luck told Staff College Tours that guns were located here.
E: Orchard with loopholed walls, clear of bombing.

However, some published accounts shed light on the subject. As a former Staff College tour organizer, Brigadier Christopher Dunphie was well placed to write that, 'In fact the issue is not so clear cut as von Luck's story suggests.'[6] Dunphie suggests that on his return from Paris, von Luck encountered a chaotic situation in which not all events occurring on the battlefield could be known to him. Less sparing of von Luck's reputation was an American historian, accompanying the 1971 Battlefield Tour. In his dispassionate assessment, John Sweet concludes: 'Luck's full story was that he... came over the ridge just in time to see the bombers attack and did not even have time to change his uniform before single-handedly stopping the British. He most certainly played a major role in the battle, but he undoubtedly enjoys claiming an even larger role.'[7] This view appears to fit with the evidence.

From the first publication of the 'BAOR battlefield tour' book in 1947 to the Staff College 'film of the book' in 1978, von Luck's story of his ultimatum to the young *Luftwaffe* battery commander was recounted in full detail. However, nowhere in these publications was it explicitly stated that the *Luftwaffe* battery was responsible for the destruction of the Fife & Forfar. Similarly, some of the most authoritative German accounts of the action only credit the Luftwaffe battery with destroying German, and not British, tanks.[8]

BECKER'S GUNS

The story of Becker's batteries on 18 July has been told many times, with many variations. Where doubt exists, particularly with regard to the initial positions and subsequent movements of the five batteries of his *Abteilung*, this author gives preference to Becker's own memoirs[9], which fortunately are illustrated by highly detailed situation maps (*'Stellungs-Skizzen'*). Contrary to many accounts, when Becker's fourth and fifth batteries fell back before the British armoured tide, they did so respectively to the south of Four and to the west side of Frénouville (straddling the railway). Before retiring, *5. Batterie* fought a successful delaying action from the woods east of le Prieuré. Here they held up the advance of the 23rd Hussars, and screened the *Tiger* tanks of the *503. Abteilung* until at least some of their number were ready for combat). On its way to Frénouville, *5. Batterie* almost certainly moved through the cover of the orchards around Cagny. It is entirely possible that elements of this battery managed to find covered firing positions by the time that the Fifes' C Squadron came on the scene. From such positions and at point-blank range, even a single rearguard section of three Pak 40 could have achieved the destruction of the squadron, and might well have done so without the knowledge of a German officer passing briefly in his tank along the main road through Cagny.

PICKERT'S FLAKKORPS

A key element of von Luck's story is the fact that the gunners he found were *Luftwaffe* personnel and not in his direct chain of command. Of course, he might legitimately have demanded the obedience of any Luftwaffe gunners of the *16. Luftwaffenfelddivision*. But that division lacked any heavy Flak. (Its only antiaircraft component was found in the third company of its antitank battalion, which contained a dozen towed 2cm guns.)

Any Luftwaffe 8.8cm guns close to the battlefield would have belonged to *General der Flakartillerie* Wolfgang Pickert's *III. Flakkorps,* whose three heavy antiaircraft regiments were sited in a ring to the south and east of the battle area. In his memoirs, written in April, 1947, Pickert expressed pride in his *Luftwaffe Flakkorps'* effective cooperation with the army in Normandy[10]. However, he made perfectly clear the limits of that cooperation. His guns' primary role was to shoot down enemy aircraft; in this they were unquestionably successful. Their secondary role was to supplement the army's hard-pressed artillery (who suffered from shortages of equipment and ammunition, and increasingly from losses incurred by relentless counter-battery fire). Luftwaffe forward observers signalled target orders to antiaircraft batteries behind the lines whose 8.8cm Flak could rapidly switch from direct antiaircraft fire to the indirect artillery fire mode: 'The rapid swing of the 8.8cm guns made the transition from air targets to ground targets (and vice-versa) very simple and caused no loss of time.' There were limits to their assistance. For example, 'An undesirable restriction was that against ground targets, rounds with impact fuzes usually had to be fired, in

Could this be one of the Cagny '88s'?

order to preserve the valuable timed fuzes for use against air targets. That was unfortunate as the extraordinary effectiveness of airburst rounds against personnel targets could not be realised.'

As regards antitank fire, Pickert regarded his heavy guns as a last resort only. 'In the fight against hostile tanks these guns enjoyed less success than in the east [i.e., the Russian front], because in both areas of dense cover and also in the open areas the hostile tanks attacked much more carefully and with better fire discipline and thereby overpowered the firing 8.8 faster than had so far been experienced in the east.' Several times, Pickert stressed that the heavy Flak were only to be employed in an antitank role against 'deep penetrations'. He firmly resisted the dispersal of his regiments into forward positions where their primary role would be sacrificed and heavy losses incurred: 'The *Flakkampftruppen* were less successful when the heavy batteries were pulled forward into advanced positions, since then they were not then in sufficient numbers to employ their skilful defensive fire and attack methods against strong tank attacks. The dispersal of *Flakkampftruppen* was therefore rejected in principle, as the manpower and material losses bore no relationship to the expected success, and the undesirable dispersal of *Flakkampfgruppen* for antitank defence came about only later.'

Lastly, it has to be asked why an antiaircraft unit would have been positioned in Cagny at all. Some accounts follow von Luck's 1989 account, citing the young *Luftwaffe* officer in charge of the battery as claiming he was there to 'protect the factories and city of Caen against air raids.'[11] This is not convincing. The defence of the city of Caen (what was left of it) from air attack had ceased to be of interest to the *Luftwaffe* when the place fell into Allied hands. Local air defence of point targets such as the factories was the job of smaller-calibre, rapid-firing 2cm and 3.7cm guns, whose targets were the *jabos*, fighter-bombers descending to the killing zone below five thousand feet. The light Flak tactics that proved successful in Normandy, after some early and costly mistakes, involved protecting principal supply routes with highly mobile units armed with 2cm and 3.7cm automatic antiaircraft guns. These would typically lie in wait to 'ambush' low flying fighter-bombers with simultaneous fire from numerous concealed locations, after which they would move to new positions to retain the element of surprise.

The 8.8cm Flak were more concerned with the medium bombers, typically American B-25 Mitchells and B-26 Marauders, flying higher and in formation. Pickert recalled, 'The enemy air units intervening over the battlefield were mostly Marauder squadrons of from twenty to forty aircraft... and were suitable targets for the heavy Flak batteries.' Against such a target, whole regiments of 8.8cm guns would open fire simultaneously, and so 'They were often successfully engaged and forced to greater heights or to turn back. The numbers shot down were considerable.' These heavy Flak were not typically sited to engage low flying '*jabos*'.

In summary, if indeed a lone battery of four 8.8cm Flak was positioned in Cagny, far ahead of its parent regiment, the reason for its deployment there remains a mystery.

THE CHANCES

Given present knowledge, this author reaches the following tentative conclusions.

1. The destruction of C Squadron of the Fife & Forfar Yeomanry is not in itself evidence of the presence of a *Luftwaffe* battery in Cagny.

2. If a *Luftwaffe* battery was present, it probably did not change position at all, though it might have had to make adjustments in its emplacements to permit horizontal fire. A possible location would be the long, narrow, walled orchard north of the (former) Cagny chateau (Army map reference 112645).

3. 'Friendly fire' incidents were by no means uncommon amid the confusion of 18 July. It seems that a German antitank round penetrated *Königstiger 122* later that day. Early-arriving German antitank weapons unknown to von Luck might possibly have accounted for von Rosen's *Tiger* losses.

References

(1) 'The Combat History of Schwere Panzer-Abteilung 503', ed. A Rubbel, 2000, ISBN 0-921991-55-X, p 241.

(2) ' Panzer Commander, the Memoirs of Colonel Hans von Luck', 1989, ISBN 0-440-20802-5, p 193; also, Von Luck, interview at Staff College, Camberley, 1979. Note that von Luck's various versions of his story differ in details.

(3) As a serving officer, von Luck was throughout 1944 officially and repeatedly denied permission to marry his fiancée due to her ancestry. While remaining clear of politics, he continued trying to 'pull strings' through purely military channels. This was not hard, as he was known and respected by high-ranking soldiers, both Wehrmacht and SS.

(4) Generalmajor Feuchtinger became notorious both for his private life and his reluctance to obey orders he believed would lead to pointless losses. Such traits were not conducive to career development in the post-20 July German army. Feuchtinger was relieved on the night of 21-22 January, 1945, and sentenced to death by court martial. Reprieved in March, he was reduced to the ranks. He was fortunate to be captured by the British before his transfer to the eastern front was carried out.

(5) Von Luck, 'Panzer Commander', p 197

(6) 'The Pendulum of Battle', Christopher Dunphie, 2004, ISBN 1-84415-010-0, p 80

(7) 'Mounting the Threat, the Battle of Bourguebus Ridge', John J T Sweet, 1977, ISBN 0-89141-026-0, p 82

(8) Rubbel, p 241-242; 'Hitlerjugend: the History of 12. SS-Panzerdivision', Hubert Meyer, 1994, ISBN 0-921991-18-5, p 158

(9) Becker's unpublished 'Invasion' diary, particularly Section III 'Action at Orne from 18th to 20th VII. 1944'.

(10) Unpublished account, 'Das III. Flak Korps in der Normandie Schlacht', Allendorf, 20 April 1947.

(11) Von Luck, 'Panzer Commander', p 193

APPENDIX X

MIKE WETZ

On the morning of 18 July, 1944, at Northolt Aerodrome on the western outskirts of London, Flying Officer Mike Wetz of 16 Squadron was briefed on his mission for the day.

UNARMED AND ALONE

The men of 16 Squadron operated alone. Their missions were single aircraft, single pilot affairs. Their PR Mark XI Spitfires were either converted from Mark IXs or purpose-built photo reconnaissance models. Removing the guns made space for leading-edge wing tanks which extended endurance; reduced weight and retractable tail wheels allowed extra speed. The oxygen system was sufficient up to 30,000 feet; special pressure-breathing equipment enabled pilots in their unpressurized cockpits to remain conscious, for brief periods at least, at altitudes of 40,000 feet and more, on the very edge of the stratosphere. And they flew unarmed. Without guns or ammunition, with even some armour plating removed, the PR Spitfires relied on speed, altitude, and pilot skill to evade enemy ground fire and enemy aircraft.

This was a job for individuals. The pilot was briefed, flew the operation, and returned the exposed films for processing. He generally did not discuss the details of the op with his fellow pilots. Of course, pilots would report when a particular new threat had been discovered or some new tactic for evading the enemy's defences found. And the more experienced pilots had an unofficial policy of making themselves 'discreetly available' to offer advice to newly-joined squadron members. Mike Wetz recalled that some might have lasted longer if they had heeded the advice, but 'Most pilots were willing to learn and listen.'[1] The job was concerned with Intelligence. The pilot was given map co-ordinates and flew the mission. If he did not need to know the reason for the mission, then he preferred not to know. The less he knew the less he could tell if captured and interrogated. [2]

MISSIONS

16 Squadron had close links with the Army. A few of its pilots were former soldiers. Living in tents at Northolt, their aircraft exposed to rain, snow, mud and dust, they were somewhat looked down upon as 'brown jobs' by the RAF Photo Reconnaissance units at Benson. Legend has it that one pilot landing at Benson was requested to park his weather-beaten Spit out of sight of the immaculate home-based aircraft of the 'PRU' élite. At this time working directly for 21st Army Group, the job of 16 Squadron was mostly strategic, and commonly involved flying far into enemy territory. As a general rule, missions less than 150 miles behind the front line were conducted by the Tactical Reconnaissance squadrons, flying armed Mustangs

and (later) pink Spitfires. 16 Squadron normally operated further afield. Sometimes the mission was to photograph overlapping strips of ground from which the Army Geographical Section could piece together a mosaic of ground coverage for developing contour maps of the ground ahead of the advancing armies. At other times, pilots were sent to bring back photographic evidence of points of strategic interest. Later in the campaign these often included the bases of the new German jet and rocket-powered fighters, the ME 262 and ME 163 (which themselves were a serious threat to the fast PR Spitfires).

In theory, 16 Squadron pilots accepted missions in rotation: the next man on the roster took the next job on the list. Then his name went down to the bottom of the roster again. (In practice, Squadron Leader Tony Davis would sometimes pull rank and fly the more 'dicey' ops himself.) The mission Mike Wetz was allocated on the morning of 18 July was rather unusual. On this day, the co-ordinates of the area Wetz was to cover turned out to be very close indeed. He was to fly a mosaic pattern just beyond the front line of the Normandy battleground. So, not a particularly exciting or memorable assignment. Mike completed his briefing and walked out to his aircraft.

THE FLIGHT

Spitfire 654 was a PR Mark XI, painted light blue overall, with the single white identification letter 'F' abaft the fuselage RAF roundel and on the nose, directly under the spinner. Behind the pilot, between fuselage frames 13 and 15, were two K17, 20-inch focal length cameras. Mounted vertically, each of the 'split pair' of cameras was angled respectively to port and starboard, to achieve a lateral image overlap of 10 percent. The two cameras operated simultaneously, the pilot flying straight-and-level while adjusting the four to five second interval between exposures (allowing for airspeed and wind speed), aiming to produce the 60 percent fore-and-aft overlap needed for stereoscopic viewing of the images. It is a tribute to their skill that these Spitfire pilots, operating single-handed in hostile skies and with no direct view downwards over the subject area, consistently succeeded in achieving such fine precision.

Mike Wetz was airborne out of Northolt at 11.05 hours.[3] Climbing rapidly to cruising altitude, he was established at 25,000 feet well before crossing the coast at Selsey Bill, between Bognor Regis and Portsmouth. Crossing the enemy coast at Cabourg, he was just under five miles above ground and a similar horizontal distance behind the German front line, east of the dual waterways of the Caen Canal and Orne River. Here he descended rapidly to 15,000 feet QNH (the barometric scale on his altimeter set so as to display altitude above mean sea level; as opposed to 'QFE' which would give height above ground) to begin photography.

As part of his mission briefing, Mike Wetz would match the latitude and longitude he was given with visual cues on the ground identifying the point of at which his photo mosaic was to commence. It was important to spot the target in advance, since once established straight-and-level on a photography run there was no view directly downwards from the Spitfire cockpit; during a pass over the target, it was only by a rapid rolling manoeuvre in the few seconds between camera exposures that this could be confirmed. Wetz aligned with the conveniently prominent line feature of the dual-track Caen to Paris railway, possibly noting that the south-eastern extremity of his target area was marked by a distinctive wood with six roads radiating from its centre (today little trace remains of les Bois Drouet, but in 1944 it was just the sort of unique feature needed to confirm position).

About 11.40 hours, Mike Wetz began his first photography run, from east to west. Between that time and 12.25, he made eight further passes, each one a straight line over the target area. Altogether he captured 210 images on his port camera, 236 on his starboard. Job done, Wetz returned to Northolt via Cabourg and Selsey, landing at 12.50 hours. Apart from 'a number of a/c about 10,000 [feet] in area probably Allied light bombers', the mission had been unremarkable. Mike Wetz ended his report, 'No incidents'.[4]

THE MISSION

The light blue Spitfire at 15,000 feet had gone unnoticed on the ground, a blue speck in a blue sky above a heavy haze of dust and smoke. Nor was the pilot aware of the events his cameras were recording. In fact, the film canisters Mike Wetz brought back contained highly detailed images of a battle in progress. Pilots know that a layer of haze blocking visibility along the ground generally becomes easier to penetrate from on high: the higher the viewpoint, the nearer to the vertical becomes the line of sight, with correspondingly less mist getting in the way. 15,000 feet above the smoke and dust of battle, the cameras enjoyed a considerably clearer panorama than anyone on the ground.

No record has been found of the purpose of Wetz's mission. Nevertheless, it was almost certainly intended to assess the accuracy and effect of the aerial bombardment of the morning. The precise coordinates he was given (and was to photograph with great accuracy and thoroughness) contained an area which should, according to plan, by the time of the mission have been well behind the advancing front line. So there was little tactical interest. The fact that the photographs revealed a battle in progress was clearly unintended. There is a further clue in the timing. The last of the American bombers were to finish their bombing by 06.30 hours (army time). A photo reconnaissance mission five hours later might miss the action on the ground, but would be expected to reveal the effect of the bombing after the dust had settled. Ironically, whoever commissioned the sortie does not appear to have communicated its findings (assuming they were ever analysed at all) to the Number 2 Operations Research Section attached to 21st Army Group when its scientists set out to analyze the effectiveness of the GOODWOOD bombing.

Why was a long-range PR Spitfire allocated the task of a short-range mission in place of a Fighter Reconnaissance aircraft? Wetz delighted in being given the opportunity to take up one of these pink Spitfire FR IXs. Though their primary role was intended to be low-level photography, using cameras mounted obliquely, they were also armed. Wetz recalled, 'Around invasion time we were given rather shorter trips at low level and in addition were asked to count trains and say which way they were going. This was a nice change and in fact they gave us some Spits with two cannon and four machine guns. Provided we carried out our sorties, we were allowed to attack suitable targets... A train was most exciting.'[5] Whatever the mission, Wetz made it a point of honour to return with all ammunition, as well as all film, expended.

But a blue PR Spitfire XI, unarmed, with dual twenty-inch cameras did not normally photograph from as low as 15,000 feet. Again, the answer can be deduced with some confidence. The tactical photography intended to guide divisional operations and generate aerial photos to assist front-line officers had long since been conducted, and the prints distributed to the Army units' Air Photographic Interpretation Sections. The effectiveness of heavy bombers over the battlefield was still an unknown factor, a matter of strategic interest, at Army Group level and above. And 18 July was a busy day for 21st Army Group's dedicated PR specialists. 16 Squadron recorded '...an excellent day for flying. Seventeen high level photo recces were despatched over France during the day. Every sortie was a success. In fact it was a 100% performance.'[6] The exuberance of the normally staid Operations Record Book reveals an exceptional day: a day when the squadron was at full stretch and every operational aircraft and pilot was needed. Wetz and his aircraft simply took their turn.

THE OUTCOME

So, sixty years later, as memories fade and historians struggle to reconstruct a coherent picture from disparate viewpoints on the ground, aerial images enable us to see back in time. We are granted a grandstand seat for the GOODWOOD stakes, a view of the great tank charge of 18 July at its high water mark. We follow the tracks of 3rd RTR's Shermans they lead purposefully up the long open slope to Hubert-Folie; the foremost tanks billow smoke as they are halted; the survivors leave zigzag tracks as they frantically reverse downhill, left stick, right stick; and all too often the zigzag line ends with yet another smoking wreck. We witness the ruin of C Squadron of the Fife and Forfar Yeomanry, and the fate of A and B Squadrons in the cauldron of Four. We locate the outline of von Rosen's great Tiger tanks, stopped by a mystery weapon which years later turned out to have been German '88s'; and we follow the tracks of Oemler's King *Tigers* as they in turn drive to disaster.

References
(1) 'Spitfire in Blue', Hugh Smallwood, 1996, ISBN 1 85532 615 9, p 39.
(2) For these and other details, the author is deeply indebted to Flight Lieutenant H J S ('Jimmy') Taylor, whose remarkable memory so clearly recalls the deeds of the remarkable men of 16 Squadron.
(3) See Appendix 3 for further details of the flight timing.
(4) 16 Squadron Operations Record Book, Details of Sorties, 18 July, 1944
(5) Smallwood, p 40
(6) 16 Squadron Operations Record Book, Summary of Events 14 – 19 July, 1944

Flying Officer Mike Wetz (right) accompanied by Flying Officers Norman Godfrey (centre) and John Wendelker (left). Visible through the Spitfire's one-piece windscreen is the camera control unit.

INDEX